Legoland Windsor

Pilkington Sandomierz

Marks & Spencer Newcastle

Wellcome Trust Hinxton Hall

Hotel Intercontinental Paris

Waterloo International Terminal London

Waltham Forest London

Glyndebourne Opera House Lewes

Petronas Towers Kuala Lumpur

O'Hare International Chicago

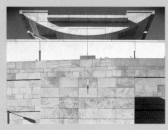

Museum of Scotland Edinburgh

New York

Building
Relationships

Building
Relationships

THE HISTORY OF
Bovis
1885–2000

PETER COOPER

CASSELL&CO

First published in the United Kingdom in 2000
by Cassell & Co

Text copyright © Peter Cooper, 2000
Design and layout copyright © Cassell, 2000

The picture acknowledgements on page 240
constitute an extension to this copyright page

A CIP catalogue record for this book is available
from the British Library

ISBN 0 297 82533 X

Art directed by David Rowley
Designed by Nigel Soper
Edited by Marilyn Inglis
Printed and bound in the UK by Butler & Tanner

Cassell & Co
Wellington House
125 Strand
London
WC2R 0BB

Contents

Diploma in Building

Awarded by

The Bovis School of Building

This is to Certify that

George Ernest Lewsey

has completed an Approved Course of Technical and Practical Instruction in Building, and has passed the examinations in the following subjects in the Final Stage of the Course, namely:

Building Construction
Quantity Surveying
Estimating
Book-keeping and Accountancy

E. Rothwell Vose
Principal of the Bovis School of Building

The Common Seal of Bovis Limited was hereunto affixed in the presence of

} Directors

Secretary

Dated this 23rd day of November 1938

Foreword

Quality, value and service are the three founding principles on which Marks & Spencer established its own business and they are the virtues it has always sought from its suppliers. It is no coincidence that Bovis has been one of the longest serving and most consistent of those suppliers. Good people, products and properties have also been cornerstone principles, which we have always pursued and shared as a common goal with Bovis.

The relationship began in the 1920s, borne out of Marks & Spencer's frustrations with the British building industry and its adversarial attitude towards its clients. Bovis responded with the pioneering Fee System, which delivered what Marks & Spencer wanted – a quick and reliable store-building service based on co-operation, not confrontation.

In the ensuing years Bovis has been by far our largest store development contractor, working on most of our British stores and almost all our overseas ones, either building, extending or refurbishing them. The tally now stands at well over 1000 projects, the most recent, and the biggest being our newly opened flagship store in Manchester.

As this history reveals, it was the ambition of Marks & Spencer to become a national enterprise that gave Bovis the initial impetus to expand as well. And, when Marks & Spencer looked to overseas markets for new opportunity, Bovis was so often there to assist us.

Today our government is urging the British construction industry to embrace the principles of partnering, to seek new alliances and put aside past practices with the dual aim of delivering a better service and earning better margins for its efforts. The enduring relationship between Bovis and ourselves would be an excellent benchmark.

The actual relationship has never been formalised. It is based on trust, mutual respect and the common goal of a better product at a more competitive price. The very fact that it has prospered for more than 70 years is the best possible testimony to the qualities of Bovis, the talents of its project managers, both past and present, and the consistent commitment to quality, value and service of its senior management.

SIR RICHARD GREENBURY
Chairman and Chief Executive of
MARKS & SPENCER PLC 1991–99

CHAPTER I

Charles William Bovis

It was in 1885 that Charles William Bovis decided to go into business on his own account. He was 35 years old, and had already worked in the building industry for almost a quarter of a century. Charles had probably tired of working for other people, and wanted to prove that he could run his own company. So he acquired an existing business in the prosperous London Borough of Marylebone from a man named Francis Sanders and changed its name to C. W. Bovis & Co. The Bovis building company was born. There are no records from the days of Francis Sanders. However, from material in the Bovis archive we know that Sanders had been in business for over 30 years, and that he sold the company on his retirement. This reputation must have been worth something, otherwise Charles Bovis might have started from scratch in 1885. Instead he chose to start with an established concern, very likely with some contracts up and running.

Yet Charles William Bovis would have needed the visionary powers of Nostradamus to have foreseen that 115 years later his small London building firm would have grown into a global giant with 77 offices in 35 countries, managing contracts worth more than $22 billion. Or that his company would have been responsible for construction of the world's tallest building in Malaysia. For Bovis would build a collection of the finest monuments to the affluence of the twentieth century, and make a unique contribution to the built environment. In 1885 C. W. Bovis & Co was just another minor London building firm, not even remotely close to being a national player – humble beginnings for such a glittering international future.

The group's founding father would also not have known the role Jewish émigrés were to play in its future. For around 1850, when Mr Sanders started the business that preceded C. W. Bovis & Co, the patriarch Joseph Gluckstein arrived in England. His descendants were destined to push the modest London firm into the major league of British construction companies in the first half of the next century, and establish the Bovis System as a part of the national building tradition. In the process they laid the foundations of the modern company that a much later émigré, Frank Lampl, transformed into the global construction giant we see today, and became Sir Frank in recognition of his services to the construction industry.

However, the beginning of the Bovis story belongs in a very different age, with a tale of rags to riches. Charles William Bovis was born at 3 Palmers Mews, Liverpool Road in the North London district of Holloway on 5 June, 1850. His father, Henry Bovis was then 35 years old, a bricklayer like his father John before him. Both Charles

1

1 *Charles William Bovis created the modern Bovis company in 1885 when he changed the name of an exisiting building business in the London Borough of Marylebone to C.W. Bovis & Co.*

Bovis' father and grandfather were master craftsmen. And under this system they would have been responsible for negotiating their own contracts and would have largely worked for themselves, rather as modern self-employed tradesmen.

The paternal Henry Bovis was born in the town of Battle in Sussex. The surname Bovis is actually of French origin, and is still fairly common in the English counties of East Sussex and Kent which are a short distance from France. In *A Dictionary of British Surnames* P. H. Reaney explains that Bovis is one of a number of modern derivatives from far older names that originated in the French region of Beauvais.

Henry Bovis married Mary Mathis while living in Battle in the 1830s. The couple had three children before moving to Holloway in North London in 1844. Over the next two years two further children were born, but both died in infancy. Childbirth was hazardous 150 years ago, and Mary Bovis also died. In 1849 Henry Bovis married his second wife, Sarah Moore. The founder of Bovis was their first child. Charles William Bovis' birthplace at Palmers Mews in Liverpool Road has long since

9

disappeared, and we can only assemble a general picture of what his family life must have been like in the mid-nineteenth century. The working classes in early Victorian London did not live well. London's population density of 66,000 per square mile was similar to a modern Chinese city, and living conditions were grim, as the novels of Charles Dickens so vividly portray.

The family home in Palmers Mews would probably have been an apartment rented from a private landlord. In 1850 there was no local authority housing, and owner occupation among the working classes was less than five per cent. The fact that the Bovis home was in a mews is significant. Mews usually contained residential developments known as 'courts'. Here three or four apartment blocks surrounded an open courtyard, sharing common sanitary and cooking facilities. A mews apartment would have been primitive to say the least. There would have been no lighting or heating inside the apartment. Running water and sanitation would have been found down in the courtyard. The term 'apartment' is slightly misleading in this context. Certainly the modern equivalent would not even be as large as a studio flat. This type of accommodation was often a single room of ten foot square. The rental was three to four shillings per week, and there were no Acts of Parliament laying down minimum housing standards. This was the true age of English slum dwelling, a legacy now bequeathed to the poor of the Third World.

As a bricklayer Henry Bovis would have been earning 30 shillings for a 60-hour week. This meant a rate of five shillings per day for the standard week, and overtime would be paid at just six pence per hour. It could have been worse; the pay for labourers was just 22 shillings a week. From this relative prosperity alone, it is reasonable to assume that the Bovis family took two rooms in Palmers Mews. All the same, bricklayers like Henry Bovis were hardly a privileged élite.

London's urban infrastructure lagged well behind its population growth, and the authorities were slow to implement legislation to clean up the city, even after incidents such as the 1831 cholera epidemic which caused 22,000 deaths. In 1835 local authorities were empowered to pave, light and cleanse the streets. Further legislation in 1846 encouraged local authorities to build public baths and washhouses, and in 1848 the Public Health Act required them to improve sanitation. However, the Government did not compel local authorities to act, and their powers were discretionary. All too often the interests of ratepayers took precedence over the public interest, and the local authorities did nothing. In 1850 London's water supply was still being drawn from the Thames downstream from the sewerage outfall, and there were 200,000 undrained cesspools in the city. Outbreaks of cholera continued, together with scarlet fever, whooping cough, diphtheria, typhus, dysentery and tuberculosis.

It was not that commentators failed to draw attention to the plight of the urban poor. Writers as diverse as Charles Dickens, William Cobbett, Friedrich Engels and even the Conservative Prime Minister Disraeli constantly made reference to a divided society. Disraeli described the rich and poor as 'Two nations between whom there is no intercourse and no sympathy; whom are as ignorant of each other's habits, thoughts and feelings, as if they were dwellers in different zones, or inhabitants of different planets.'

Education was one very big difference between the rich and poor 'planets'. There was no provision for state education in the boyhood of Charles Bovis, but we have written evidence that he attended Blackheath Park Church School. A note written by Charles Bovis to his parents at the age of thirteen has survived. Its elegant copperplate handwriting suggests that the founder of Bovis was a modestly literate man, with the benefit of an education somewhat better than the average tradesman, and seemingly better than that of his siblings. For over a decade earlier, the 1851 census lists his nine-year-old stepbrother and stepsister of seven as 'scholars', while his eleven-year-old stepsister is already employed as a 'flower maker'. Possibly by 1861 Charles' father was more prosperous, and could give him a better start in life.

Charles was also fortunate that his father was a skilled tradesman, and this gave him an advantage. It was very common in this period for a son to follow his father into a trade. These were also good times to be starting a career in the building industry. The third quarter of the nineteenth century was the era of the Great Victorian Boom, which represented an enormous upswing in construction activity. Historian C. G. Powell writes of the period: 'The growing national economy generated apace new buildings, suburbs and whole towns, on a scale never before seen in Britain. Expansion of manufacture, trade and social control meant investment in buildings'. Likewise Leone Levi describes: '...houses, churches, hospitals, gaols...exhibition buildings, and hotels springing up with wonderful speed, and in dimensions beyond precedent'. This was the great period of national self-confidence that followed the Great Exhibition of 1851. During this time Britain was acknowledged as 'the workshop of the world'.

This was a dynamic period, and perhaps contributed to a youthful rebellion, for the very young Charles Bovis chose not to be a bricklayer like his father. In an early demonstration of independent spirit, he decided to train as a carpenter, possibly because carpenters and joiners enjoyed a slightly higher status in the building world, or more likely because they earned more money. Nobody knows where and how Charles served his apprenticeship, but one candidate would have been John Glenn, a noted builder of the day, whose premises were in Liverpool Road near the Bovis family home. What would have his apprenticeship been like?

A contemporary account of such an apprenticeship is provided by J. W. Sawyer's reminiscences of his youth in a 1909 issue of *The Builder*:

According to my indentures I was to receive as wages four shillings weekly, and one and a half pence per hour for overtime, and so on until the fifth and last year when I was to be rewarded with the magnificent sum of twelve shillings per week and three and a half pence per hour for overtime. The hours of working at this time were 6am to 6pm for five days and 6am to 4pm on Saturdays. It was the rule for the joiners to come to work quite nicely dressed – many wearing frock coats and silk hats – as soon as the starting signal was given on went their aprons and stiffly starched linen caps and they were banging into it for all they were worth. These men worked very hard. A joiner was expected to take the stuff from the rough and turn it into an ordinary-sized pair of 12 light sashes and frame in a day of 10 hours. Or he must make a 2-inch door 3ft by 7ft and mould it both sides in the same time.

In those days an apprentice's life was not altogether a happy one. They were called upon to do, without grumbling, anything and everything: turning the grindstone, pushing trucks laden with materials; loading carts in the yard, and unloading timber trolleys, for sometimes a week at a stretch; prepare and thickness flooring boards and matchlining all by hand – this job generally given as a punishment for any trivial offence; to assist in the office, take tenders to the architects' office, and go to the various jobs and pay the men.

This was the sort of experience Charles Bovis must have gained between the ages of 14 and 19. After this apprenticeship he was a 'bang it all day' carpenter and joiner. Charles must have passed the grade, because in 1871 he was living in Fulham, employed as a carpenter. In the same year he married Elizabeth Lincoln Jarvis. Charles was 21 years old and Elizabeth was 18. We can only guess why he had moved from Holloway to Fulham. But as many housing developments were underway in this part of London in the 1870s, and given the rudimentary nature of public transport, Charles probably went where the work was. By 1873 the newly-weds had changed address again, to Adrian Terrace in Kensington, and it was here that their first child, Lilian Mary, was born. Three years later they were living at another address in Fulham, and produced a son, Henry William, named after Charles's father. Sadly the 21-month-old Henry died of meningitis.

Like his father, Charles Bovis also lost his first wife, who died in 1883. He was evidently still on good terms with her family, and two years later he married his late wife's cousin, May Lincoln Jarvis. Charles was 35 years old and his new wife was 26. The address given on their marriage certificate is Honeywell Road, Battersea, but significantly the document describes his occupation as 'surveyor' rather than 'carpenter'. This document dates from the same year that Charles formed C. W. Bovis & Co. So what had happened in the years between 1871 and 1885? How had a carpenter progressed to the position of surveyor? Where had the funds to finance C. W. Bovis & Co come from? At this distance of time exact answers are impossible, although intelligent guesswork can offer some reasonable explanations.

The death certificate of Charles' father, Henry, who died in 1896 at the then unusually old age of 81, provides one clue. This document lists Henry's occupation as 'master builder', a world away from the title 'bricklayer' that appeared on Charles' birth certificate in 1850. Upward mobility is the obvious conclusion. Maybe the Great Victorian Boom was kind to the paternal Henry. As a 'master builder' he could have carried out small works as a general contractor, or even have been a speculative house-builder in his own right. At the very minimum Henry would have been a model for his son to follow. And he could well have encouraged Charles to set up on his own, and even helped him find the necessary capital.

Of course in the nineteenth century anybody could call themselves 'surveyor' or 'master builder' to further their business interests, rather like a 'consultant' in the modern era. We know that Charles Bovis was not a member of the Institution of Chartered Surveyors. All the same, enhanced job descriptions still meant something. For Henry to be upgraded from 'bricklayer' to 'master builder' and Charles to jump from 'carpenter' to 'surveyor' could not have happened without some modest achievement in the building industry.

An article written in 1893 in the *Illustrated London* contains the only written account of the formation of C. W. Bovis & Co. It mentions: 'Mr Bovis. . .bringing with him the valuable experience he gained as the manager for a period of twenty years in some of the largest and most reputed firms of metropolitan builders'. There is some hearsay evidence handed down in the company that in those twenty years Charles worked for Watney's, the brewers. In those days a 'surveyor' would generally have been responsible for managing a building project for clients like Watney's. The title 'surveyor' actually survived in Bovis until the mid-twentieth century when it changed to 'contract manager'.

The *Illustrated London* article writes in such glowing terms that it is tempting to conclude that Charles Bovis wrote the piece himself – the first Bovis press release. It suggests, for example: '. . .the business has taken its stand permanently as one of the highest merit in North London, many handsome buildings and flats having been already constructed by the firm, and decorated throughout in the most modern and artistic style'. Such hyperbole was hardly the stuff of objective journalism, particularly given the array of larger contemporary London contractors. The article concludes: 'The business in all its branches is most capably and energetically conducted upon a thoroughly sound basis of honourable mercantile principle'. As an early example of good marketing, it is hard to fault.

This item is the sole surviving evidence of the company's formation in 1885. The opening lines are unambiguous: 'The history of this house dates back to the year 1855, when it was organised and developed with singular success by Mr F. Sanders, who, having realised a competency, retired in 1885, disposing of his business to Messrs C. W. Bovis and A. M. Atkinson, who trade under the name of C. W. Bovis & Co'. However, this appears to be another example of the truth being somewhat warped for marketing purposes.

For although Charles Bovis supposedly bought the business from Francis Sanders in 1885, it did not start operating under the name C. W. Bovis & Co until 1888 or 1889. Moreover, the annual Post Office London Directory does not list Charles as the occupier of Mr Sanders' premises in 1 New Street, Marylebone until 1890, and records show that he was not a ratepayer in Marylebone until that date. Strangely the name Richard S. Parker is given as the occupier in 1889 and ratepayer in 1887. The appearance of this Mr Parker in the records does seem to cast some doubt over whether Charles Bovis actually bought the business in 1885. Perhaps he bought it from Mr Parker at a later date, and was just looking to capitalise on Mr Sanders' earlier good reputation in the *Illustrated London* article.

The results of tenders published in *The Builder* also support the suggestion that C. W. Bovis & Co started life later than officially advertised. F. Sanders appears on a tender list in December 1887, R. S. Parker in May 1888, and twice in June 1888. Bovis appears in a tender list for the first time in January 1889, and its first successful tender in February 1889 was for 'sanitary and decorative repairs' at The Boltons in South Kensington. Reading between the lines it is fair to assume that one way or another, Charles Bovis was head of the company from 1885 onwards, even if he did not complete the purchase and change its name until 1889. He may have been on some kind of earn-out deal where the profits he generated helped to pay for the company. This would explain how he got the money to pay for it.

In any event we have no idea what role the Mr Atkinson mentioned in the 1893 article played or what happened to him. Was he another part of the earn-out arrangements? The true circumstances surrounding the foundation of the company are lost in the mists of time. What we can establish is that by November 1889, Charles Bovis and his second wife May were living above the business of C. W. Bovis & Co at 1 New Street in Marylebone, where their daughter Kate Margaret was born.

In contrast to the first two decades of Charles Bovis' career, the 1880s were not especially good for the building industry. The Great Victorian Boom of the third quarter of the nineteenth century had ended, and new foreign competitors were emerging to challenge British manufacturing. Other countries, notably Germany and America were industrialising and eroding Britain's share of world markets. In relative terms the decline of Britain as a manufacturing nation dates from this period. Investment slowed down, and inevitably that meant fewer building projects. Boom had turned to bust, and the Great Depression of 1873–96 began.

A statement from the Institute of Builders printed in *The Builder* in January 1886 headlined 'Depression in the building trades', caught the atmosphere of decline: 'Compared with the periods 1865–70, 1870–75 and 1875–80, profits are reduced from good to vanishing point. The number of men out of work has been increasing, and is larger than ever. The present time may certainly be described as depressed. It is impossible to see the future, which, however, looks very bad'. The explanation the Institute gives for such despair is a familiar tale to anybody with experience of the building industry, always a victim of boom-to-bust economic cycles. 'Too much outlay on speculative building, the existing system of ground-rents and building leases, the recent decision by which money lent by trustees on mortgages is limited, and want of confidence.' In his commentary C. G. Powell shows the stark reality of what the Great Depression meant to men on site. 'The worst off were the unskilled labourers, of whom there were perhaps a quarter of a million in the 1870s and 1880s, a large proportion of all labourers. Especially at their level, but also among skilled men, employment remained at best intermittent and vulnerable, with seldom a time when nobody was waiting to step into a job vacated because of sickness or unsuitability.' Jobs were very scarce. In March 1886 *The Builder* reported that an advertisement for the position of Assistant Surveyor to the Vestry of Fulham attracted 187 replies; and a Mr Pearce of Bedford Row said he received 120 letters in response to his advertisement for an assistant architect, and was 'unable to reply to all of them'.

2 *The Ladies Residential Chambers in York Street, Marylebone were completed in 1893, but only after the client wrote threatening to enforce a penalty. Won in open tender for £16,949, it represented one of the firm's first large projects.*

2

Yet there were glimmers of hope in this unrelenting gloom. The drop in private sector contracts was to some extent compensated by an upswing in public works, what modern economists would term Keynesian pump-priming. The passing of the Education Acts of 1870 and 1880 led to many school construction contracts. Similarly the formation of the London County Council, County Councils and County Borough Councils resulted in an enormous upsurge in contracts for various municipal buildings, hospitals, fire stations, magistrates' courts and police stations.

Even in the 1880s, the law required the public advertisement of these contracts. Tender lists of 25–40 names are another indicator of the work famine of the period, and significantly the names of contractors based a long way from the building sites began to appear. Out of the 36 tenders received for work on an infirmary in Peckham in 1888, there were contractors from as far afield as Bury St Edmunds, Grantham and even Sheffield.

On the other hand, the recently formed C.W. Bovis & Co seemed to thrive in this severe recession. Adding to its existing premises in New Street and Fulham, the company bought the freehold of a house and yard in 237 Kensal Road, Chelsea where it built a workshop and store.

One of the first large completed projects was the grandly titled Ladies Residential Chambers. This fine building is still standing in York Street, Marylebone, and the 1893 *Illustrated London* article mentions it. The successful Bovis tender was for £16,949, and the project started on site in late 1890. However, progress was not entirely smooth. Concern about delays to the project was expressed by the client in February 1892, it

3

being 'resolved that a letter be written to Messrs Balfour and Turner (the architects) saying that unless Messrs Bovis completed their contract by Easter, the directors would feel themselves justified in enforcing the penalty'. The archives have no further records, so it is reasonable to assume that the job proceeded to a satisfactory conclusion. Indeed, in March 1894 the minutes note that 'Messrs Bovis and Co's estimate for papering and painting the York Street Chambers was accepted', and further minor works were carried out in 1895.

Another incident in the early days of C.W. Bovis & Co was a fire in 1890 at its joinery works known as the West London Sawmills. The *Fulham Chronicle*'s contemporary report says 'the building was of two floors, 80 feet by 60 feet' and notes that 'the upper floor and contents were burnt out'. The fire also did serious damage to the rest of the building and its contents. But the company reinstated the building, and used the premises until at least 1895.

The caretaker at the West London Sawmills was a man named Arthur John Henderson. He was probably related to a Bob Henderson who joined C.W. Bovis & Co as a carpenter in 1896, and did not retire until 1934. Bob Henderson's recollections of Charles Bovis are the only eye-witness account to survive: 'That man had real style. He must have been one of the few builders who went to work in a carriage, wore a top hat but would spend time picking up stray screws and nails when he found them on site.' He also describes Charles Bovis as an expert who liked to have his own way. 'If a client did not like his methods, they could find another builder – that was his attitude. Inevitably some clients did, but those who employed Bovis found they got a first class job'.

3 *The opulent Windsor Hotel was finished in 1899 for the Hazama Corporation.*

This rather cavalier approach to handling clients does not square with the extremely competitive business environment of the 1890s, and should probably be taken with a pinch of salt. C.W. Bovis & Co was still just a minor building company, and did not feature on the tender lists for larger jobs, so Charles Bovis could hardly have wandered about London dictating his terms of business. As it was, the company was doing very nicely by this time, and must have been assiduous in cultivating its clients. There were probably at least two further reasons for this success.

4 *C. W. Bovis & Co's premises at 1 New Street in Marylebone photographed in 1904. The signage 'Builders, Decorators, Surveyors & Valuers' suggests that Charles Bovis may have also acted as an estate agent at that time.*

The first is that C. W. Bovis & Co almost certainly engaged in some speculative building. Most Victorian builders mixed contract and speculative work, and used the cash flow from contracting to finance house building. This practice also allowed a firm to move men from contract to speculative jobs, according to the flow of work. The Bovis-owned West London Sawmills was also probably handy for both activities. In addition as mentioned previously, Charles Bovis' father Henry, 'the master builder', could well have acted as his guide and mentor in speculative building.

A second explanation for the relative prosperity of C. W. Bovis & Co must have been the firm's geographic location in the heart of the capital. Gordon Mackenzie writes that at the end of the nineteenth century Marylebone was 'London's newest, richest and most fashionable quarter – an area large, opulent, modern and architecturally distinguished; and so filled with people of birth, wealth and talent, and with the artists, craftsmen and tradesmen who administered such a community, that Macaulay and others could dub the place a city'.

The sweeping Regency terraces of Marylebone represented an excellent hunting ground for a building firm, with plenty of work to bag amongst the 'people of birth, wealth and talent'. That must have been Francis Sanders' original reason for starting a building business there in 1855, and a major attraction to Charles Bovis as the buyer of this firm 30 years later. His New Street premises stretched from the south-east corner of Dorset Square to Upper Baker Street, a distance of some 150 metres. The street is still in existence, but its name changed to Melcombe Street in 1931. The C. W. Bovis & Co base at number one was on the south side at the junction with Upper Baker Street, and the site is now occupied by a theatre ticket agency and a patisserie.

In 1896, and again in 1904, photographs were taken of every building in New Street, and copies deposited in the Marylebone public library. They comprise a fascinating record of a complete streetscape. The photographs show the C. W. Bovis & Co premises as part of a concentration of shops and tradesmen, including a linen draper, butcher, greengrocer, oilman, baker, decorator, plumber, chimney sweep, the Hope public house and two orphanages.

By the middle of the 1890s the Great Depression vanished. New markets overseas compensated for the ground ceded to Germany and the United States. An imperialist foreign policy increased trade with India, the Far East, Australia and Africa and there were also emerging markets in Japan, China and South America. Nevertheless, exports were different. British plant and machinery, railway rolling stock and coal were now in demand rather than British manufactured goods. Wages went up, while the cost of living remained static. The middle class became more numerous and wealthy, and the nature of trade and commerce was changing, with new inventions such as the motor car and electricity. Department stores were starting to multiply. But it was not just the middle class which was thriving; even the poor were getting a better deal.

As the Victorian age drew to a close, legislation passed in the previous 20 years was involving the state in much-needed social reform. Education, health, reforms of national and local government, housing, trade unionism and the beginning of social security entered the statute book. Such legislation had a direct impact on activity in the construction industry, particularly the provision of public buildings and housing. In an attempt to ensure good building practice on its sites, the London County Council drew up a list of approved contractors. Naturally the list included C. W. Bovis, and the company features on many public tender lists at this time.

For Charles Bovis, however, private tragedy once more marred his public success. By 1891 the Bovis family home was at Broderick Road. It was here that Charles' second wife May died in July. But C. W. Bovis & Co was doing better than ever. By 1896 its ever-mobile owner was living in a mansion called Hearne House at Hayes, Middlesex, rented from the Minet family, and the business of C. W. Bovis & Co was conducted from addresses in New Street, Linhope Street, Kensal Road and James Mews as well as the sawmills and joinery shop in Fulham. We also have a copy of his passport from relatives, who report that he was an annual visitor to Baden-Baden during this period.

Charles lived in his Hayes mansion until 1901 and married his third wife, Elizabeth Agnes Phillips, in 1899. At just 25 years old, she was almost half his age, and on the marriage certificate he upgraded his occupation once again, describing himself simply as 'builder'. Four years later, the couple moved to Addison Mansions in Hammersmith where their son John Henry was born, named no doubt after his great-grandfather and grandfather.

The photograph of 1 New Street taken in 1904 provides some evidence that C. W. Bovis & Co had expanded the scope of its business. The words 'surveyors, valuers and estate agents' appear in the window. This new business activity was probably linked to speculative house building by the company. Photographs of the owner himself show that Charles had become a rather portly, well-built man, and according to Bob Henderson's testimony he was suffering from increasingly bad health. Bob Henderson also said that the business went into steep decline in the last few years before its sale in 1908 for £750. 'The business had fallen so badly that the office staff ran down to two men and a secretary. In addition, there was a plumber called Tingley and a yard man called Roberts.' Later Morrison Halcrow recalled how the new owners used to say that they bought a 'horse and cart, a ladder and a telephonist'. If that was really true, they paid too much.

Failing health seems to have persuaded Charles Bovis to sell C. W. Bovis & Co. He then retired to yet another house, in Putney, where he lived for a further five years. At 62 Charles suffered a heart attack and died in March 1913. However, the birth of his last child, Joan Dorothea, in 1912 indicates a reasonably active retirement. His will left an estate valued at £1209 – almost a case of rags-to-riches – and certainly a far cry from the poverty of his birthplace in Palmers Mews and his early apprenticeship as a carpenter.

5

5 *In 1899 Charles Bovis married Elizabeth Agnes Phillips. He was 61 years old at the birth of his last child in 1912 and died the following year leaving an estate valued at £1209.*

6 *Charles Bovis became a rather portly, well-built man and suffered increasingly from bad health towards the end of his life.*

6

CHAPTER 2

Under new ownership

7 *In July 1912 Bovis handed over the Walpole Hall cinema in Ealing to the Clozenberg brothers. The young Samuel Joseph and Sidney Gluckstein were quick to realise the commercial opportunities presented by the picture palaces.*

Sidney Gluckstein almost certainly bought C.W. Bovis & Co in November 1908. But, as in the supposed purchase of the company by Charles William Bovis in 1885, the exact circumstances of the sale are not at all clear and require a certain amount of interpretation, bordering on licence. The young Sidney Gluckstein was 20 years old in 1908, and in background and education a completely different man from Charles William Bovis. However, new ownership meant a new beginning for this young London building company, which had lost its way during the long illness of its founder. The Glucksteins and their relations, the Josephs, were destined to become the driving forces behind the development of Bovis for more than half a century.

The new owner was born in South Africa on 2 April, 1888, the middle son of Henry and Emma Gluckstein. Sidney Gluckstein's grandfather Joseph, had come to London from Prussia in 1848, and formed the tea shop chain J. Lyons & Co with members of the Joseph and Salmon families. His father Henry Gluckstein was reluctant to enter the family firm, and spent several years living in Pretoria, South Africa. 'Such independence from the family caucus almost certainly influenced my father in his lifelong determination to remain independent,' commented Dr John Glyn, Sidney's second son.

In the 1890s the Glucksteins returned to London, and the family home was established in Addison Gardens, Kensington. Sidney went to St Paul's School in Hammersmith. The future proprietor of Bovis was not a brilliant pupil, judging from his final report in 1903. It states: 'Latin and Greek – fair, makes steady progress, untidy; French – good; Maths – good, might be neater; General – has done good work in French and Maths particularly. Should be neater.' On leaving school, Sidney was expected to enter the family firm J. Lyons & Co. At first he rebelled against this idea and wanted to enter the medical profession. An eye complaint frustrated this ambition, so he joined the family business after all, and went to work for the building department at Cadby Hall, Hammersmith. This was Sidney's initiation into the builder's world. He also studied for a Board of Education Certificate in Building Construction from 1906–8 at the Regent Street Polytechnic where his cousin and future business partner Samuel Joseph was a fellow student.

Barely out of college, Sidney Gluckstein set about buying C.W. Bovis & Co in late 1908. But a mystery surrounds Sidney Gluckstein's acquisition of Bovis, which parallels Charles William Bovis's purchase of the business from Francis Sanders. Once more the observer has to interpret certain facts, and there is another unknown third

7

8

8 *The 1908 sale agreement between Charles William Bovis and Alfred Grace. Mysteriously the name of Sidney Gluckstein does not appear on the document, although he was definitely present at the first board meeting of the newly acquired C.W. Bovis & Co.*

party, a character called Alfred Grace. What we do know for certain is that Charles Bovis signed an agreement with Alfred Grace to sell C. W. Bovis & Co and various leases for £750 on 4 November 1908. The agreement does not mention Sidney Gluckstein. Records exist of the first board meeting of the newly acquired company and both Sidney Gluckstein and Alfred Grace were present at this meeting, as was a Mr Holt, representing the company's solicitors Bartlett and Gluckstein. Alfred Grace was in the chair, and the board assembled at Bartlett and Gluckstein's Piccadilly offices. In the sale agreement, the leases referred to were: the shop and offices in New Street; the yard and stores in Linhope Street; the house, yard and workshops at 237 Kensal Road; and the stables in nearby James Mews. Charles Bovis remained the freeholder of Kensal Road and he rented the premises out for £100 per annum. The minutes of the first board meeting note the incorporation of C.W. Bovis & Co Ltd, with registered offices at 1 New Street, Dorset Square. Also minuted is the allocation of shares: Mrs Sarah Ann Grace 125, Alfred Grace 25, H. Gluckstein 75, Sidney Gluckstein 75, and they confirm London and County Banking Co as the company's bankers. It is clear enough from the records that 'H. Gluckstein' is Sidney's father Henry, assisting his young son's first business venture. But who is Alfred Grace? Why did his wife have a larger share allocation than he did? How did Sidney Gluckstein and Alfred Grace meet? And what made them decide to go into business together?

Little information exists about Alfred Grace. Only one piece of paper in the company archives mentions him. It establishes that he was owner of H.&E. Lea, a contractor of similar size to Bovis. The name H.&E. Lea appears on London tender lists between 1890 and 1920. Clearly Alfred Grace was an experienced builder and useful counsel for the young Sidney Gluckstein, yet there are other connections that may explain Alfred Grace's presence on the share register. The offices of H.&E. Lea were in Warwick Street, just off Regent Street, and not far from the Regent Street Polytechnic where Sidney Gluckstein was studying just before the acquisition. It is also possible that H.&E. Lea carried out work for J. Lyons & Co, and that is how the two men came into contact.

Family legend has it that Sidney paid £500 for C.W. Bovis & Co, but the purchase agreement states £750 to be paid in instalments at the rate of £20 per month. The explanation for this discrepancy is the stipulation that 'surety is to be reasonably approved by the vendor'. Doubtless Henry Gluckstein acted as 'surety', but perhaps for just £500, hence the family legend. The precise role of Alfred Grace is still unresolved. Roger Dawe, later for many years a director and company secretary, believed that Alfred Grace's actions were a part of a prearranged plan. Dawe reckoned that Grace purchased the business from Charles Bovis on the understanding that he would later resign and sell his shares to the Glucksteins. We can only speculate on why the Glucksteins could not have acted more openly. It could be that Grace knew Charles Bovis, and therefore got a better deal. Or perhaps Charles Bovis would never have sold to the Glucksteins. However, in that case why did Grace take the chair at the first board meeting? It could have been in deference to his age and experience. As for his wife's larger shareholding, that could have been a simple expedient to save tax.

The year 1908 was not the best time to buy a building company. The upsurge in public expenditure that characterised the close of the century had ended. When Sidney Gluckstein bought C. W. Bovis & Co, investment overseas was rising. The amount of lending abroad grew from £37.9 million in 1900 to £154.7 million in 1908, while domestic capital formation fell from £188.4 million to £32.4 million in the same period. Less investment meant less building. C. P. Powell comments 'What had once been purely local building investment decisions became more and more bound up with national, and later international, events. Seen in this light, the choice facing a potential sponsor might lie between new houses in the London district of Hoxton or a railway in Argentina'.

Each successive month in 1908 *The Builder* reported a lower workload than in the comparable month of 1907. Competition was fierce. In January 1908 no less than 51 tenders were received for the new Westminster County Court, and there was a startling gap between the highest figure of £11,096 and lowest at £8429. It became normal for tender lists to contain 25–40 names, reminiscent of the Great Depression years of the 1880s. A new secondary school for girls in Bromley attracted 39 tenders in October 1908, and there were 33 for a county council school in Letchworth Garden City that November. Employment opportunities were also squeezed by the downturn. There were 120 applications for the post of city architect in Bradford, and 119 for the position of surveyor to the Council of Deptford.

Once again C. W. Bovis & Co managed to make good progress in a poor market. The directors' first report to shareholders in March 1910 posted a profit of £674 three shillings and eight pence. Considering that the same shareholders had paid just £750 for the company less than eighteen months earlier, this result was a cause for celebration. The first Annual General Meeting took place in the Trocadero, Piccadilly, at 3pm on Saturday, 2 April 1910. Sidney and Alfred were the only people present for what must have been a very good lunch. There was plenty to celebrate, an excellent financial result and Sidney's twenty-second birthday.

Amazingly, the balance sheets and trading accounts for the last two months of 1908 and the whole of 1909 have survived. They support Bob Henderson's testimony that the business had been slipping before the takeover. The company completed work valued at just £267 in November and December 1908, while the £7708 noted for the whole of 1909 represents a five-fold increase in volume. It looks as though the new management was extremely good at winning new contracts. Perhaps some large jobs were already in the bag at the time of the takeover, although in view of the building slump that seems unlikely. Or it could be that

9 *Balance sheets and trading accounts for the first two months of 1908 have survived and support Bob Henderson's testimony that the business had been in decline before the takeover.*

9

work from J. Lyons & Co was boosting the workload. But the brief history of Bovis written much later by Sidney Gluckstein's nephew Harry Vincent claims: 'through the years Bovis has done little work for Lyons'. Of course, other family friends and contacts could have helped considerably in filling the order book.

An alternative view is that Sidney and Alfred were simply cashing in on the good name Bovis had established in nearly 20 years of trading in central London. Charles Bovis had done much the same when he bought Francis Sanders' business, and £750 was not an inconsiderable sum to pay for a business that was faltering due to the ill health of its proprietor. The price must have reflected the potential to revive the former glory of the Bovis name. Yet the new owner's energy and enthusiasm in winning new contracts must have been the key factor behind its success.

There were no plans to change the company name from 'Bovis' to 'Gluckstein'. In the year 1888, when Sidney Gluckstein was born, a wave of anti-Jewish sentiment swept across Eastern Europe, in the form of pogroms. A wave of Jewish refugees came to Britain, settling in London, Glasgow and Birmingham; these new immigrants caused a certain amount of anti-Semitic feeling. It was not a serious social problem; nevertheless, Jewish boys like Sidney would have grown up with a defensive attitude about their background, and to have called a building company 'Gluckstein' would not have been good for business.

The minutes of the first AGM also note the first-ever acquisition by Bovis: 'the company has acquired the business of the late G. W. Wiles of 43 Upper Berkeley Street'. The Post Office Directory for 1910 shows that Wiles ran a building company at this address, and shared its premises with the National Telephone Company. It may be that Bovis bought G. W. Wiles to acquire its bigger premises in Upper Berkeley Street, or as a way of acquiring some good contracts. Not long after the euphoria of the first AGM, Alfred Grace resigned from the company. The minutes of a director's meeting in July 1910 reproduce Sidney's letter of acceptance. The letter is quite formal, although warm in tone. It gives no reason for the resignation, another reason to surmise that this was part of a prearranged plan. At the same meeting Sidney nominated his cousin, Samuel George Joseph, to the Board and the Grace's shares were transferred to him.

Samuel Joseph was 22, the same age as Sidney. The two men had studied together at the Regent Street Polytechnic from 1906–8, and it is almost certain that Samuel was part of a family plot to gain control of Bovis. Perhaps the two students mapped out their future business as a joint venture from the start, and decided that Samuel should first gain some experience as a quantity surveyor and join Bovis later. The new partner had been well groomed for the position. After leaving the City of London School at the age of 15, he worked for James Smith and Sons of Norwood, and later J. Lyons & Co at Cadby Hall, with a particular interest in joinery and carpentry. A model timber staircase complete with balustrading, handrail and panelling made by Samuel is still displayed in the Harrow offices of Bovis Construction. He also studied quantity surveying and spent two years with the firm Selby and Sanders which gave him a valuable insight into handling building contracts.

The day Samuel Joseph arrived in the office was a historic moment for C. W. Bovis & Co. It marked the beginning of a powerful business relationship between two remarkably compatible partners who shared a common vision and commitment. The two men took turns in spending nine months on-site and nine months in the office. They made a policy decision to employ only the best men available and to keep them.

10

10 *Samuel Joseph's model staircase complete with balustrading, handrail and panelling is still on display in the Harrow offices. He joined his cousin Sidney Gluckstein in the business in 1910, forming a partnership that lasted until his death in 1944.*

One early recruit was Daniel 'Darny' Graham, who joined as a general foreman on a £500 contract. When he died in 1962 at the grand old age of 94, Darny was still involved with one aspect of Bovis's business. His son followed him into the company, and then his grandson. This was another Bovis tradition that was duplicated by many fathers and sons. Another Bovis veteran who joined at that time was Tommy Boyce, a ganger, who was also followed by his son, Tommy. There was general foreman Harry Barrow, whose son Ron also worked for Bovis. Keeping good staff was one of the secrets behind the subsequent success of the dynamic young Edwardians Sidney and Samuel. They were particularly quick to appreciate the true value of foremen. If we refer again to the address given by J. W. Sawyer in 1909 to the Builders' Foremens Association, he remarks:

> Must he not be acquainted with the by-laws of the district in which his job is located? Is he not badgered from morning to night with sometimes half a dozen specialists? He must know something of electricity and heating, and must he not be an expert diplomatist so as to keep on anything but fighting terms with the drain and other inspectors, the ground landlord, the adjoining property owners, and last but very much not least, the architect and the building owner?

Sawyer was stating an established fact of building life. The foreman was the linch-pin to the financial success of a contract. His efficiency, drive and building knowledge were of paramount importance. Yet the industry still hired so many foremen on a job-by-job basis, part of the endemic casual labour system. The young Sidney Gluckstein and Samuel Joseph realised this was a big mistake. If foremen were vital to the profitability of a contract, the company should encourage them to stay as permanent staff. It was not altruism, just good business.

In the period before the First World War, a number of staff joined the company who would spend their entire working lives with Bovis. Leonard Smith began his career in 1911, and later became chief negotiator, known across the company as L. A. Smith. Other new recruits became veritable Bovis stalwarts: Jim Cameron and Reg

Jefferys (1911), Charlie Harrison, Sid Herbert and Sid Rayment (1912), Monty Lewis (1913), Charlie Allday, Fred Mumford, Betty Neale (Mrs Fitch) and Jim Waters (1914).

The company convened its second Annual General Meeting under new ownership at New Street in May 1911. It confirmed Samuel Joseph as a director with a remuneration of £100. The next recorded meeting of the board was in April 1912, at the newly registered offices of the company at 43 Upper Berkeley Street, which G. W. Wiles had occupied before the Bovis takeover. Minutes of this meeting give an indication of the sort of contracts Bovis was carrying out before the First World War. They mention the cinema at Ealing, Walpole Hall, which Bovis was building for the Clozenberg brothers. The silver screen was just beginning to flicker in the suburbs, and the young men behind Bovis were quick to grab the construction limelight, realising the extraordinary demand that lay ahead for new cinema buildings. While the Ealing cinema was under construction, Bovis was also building the Majestic Picture-drome in Tottenham Court Road. Many more cinema projects followed.

In June 1912 the capital base of the company was increased to £2000, and an Extraordinary General Meeting was held to agree to change the name of C. W. Bovis & Co into Bovis Ltd. The records show that Sidney and Samuel earned £1000 each, so things were obviously going very well for the young entrepreneurs. It was not all

11 *In 1910 Bovis acquired the business of the late G. W. Wiles at 43 Upper Berkeley Street, its first-ever acquisition, and promptly moved to these spacious premises.*

11

12 *Inside the Walpole Hall cinema in Ealing in 1912. Silent movies were a very popular innovation, even if the seating looks rather basic by modern standards.*

plain sailing, however. In 1913 Bovis ended up in court over a client's failure to pay for works on the Rendezvous Restaurant in Dean Street, Soho. Out of a total bill for £5000, the balance of £2100 remained unpaid. According to an article in *The Builder* in January 1914, the client, a Mr Gallina, claimed 'a tender of £1500 before action', and alleged his quantity surveyors had misled Bovis. While the case was in progress the two parties settled their dispute. Bovis Ltd agreed to accept payment of the full balance, less £27 and Mr Gallina's costs. An additional problem followed the erection of a new joiner's shop at Kensal Road in 1913. There were complaints from the owners of adjacent houses, culminating in the payment of compensation by Bovis.

These were fairly minor difficulties for the two partners, who were doing exceptionally well in a harsh economic climate. The depression in the British building industry lasted until the year before the First World War. In January 1913 the noted builder and director of the Imperial Property Investment Company, J. J. Jarvis, summed the situation up in the annual trade review of the *Chamber of Commerce Journal*: 'A study of international conditions lends colour to the belief that throughout the world there are evidences of a "boom". There is, however, no boom in the building trade, nor is there likely to be for some little time to come…but an all-round improvement in the trade can be predicted with some reasonable degree of certainty.'

In the same item, Jarvis also accurately predicted that the rising prosperity of the building industry would lead to labour disputes 'since the cost of living in recent years has risen disproportionately to wages'. Although the various trades involved in the building industry were not organised on either a national or a local basis, this was a militant period; labour disputes featured prominently in *The Builder* throughout 1913 and up to the outbreak of war in 1914. For example, one issue of *The Builder* in June 1913 reported nationwide militancy; a strike by building labourers in Cardiff had just ended and 200 labourers were on strike in Dewsbury where some plasterers were also on strike. The dispute in Letchworth Garden City 'which began on May 1st, and affected about 400 carpenters, joiners, bricklayers and labourers' was resolved. A

demonstration took place in Trafalgar Square by the London Building Industries Federation to support striking plasterers in London. Some 350 men downed tools on the new London County Hall project and a walk-out by men in Pitlochry was 'practically concluded'. In September and October 1913 there were reports of industrial action in Londonderry, Oxford, Rotherham, Thirsk, Ipswich and Wakefield. The owners were slow to respond. But the 16 January 1914 issue of *The Builder* notes:

> The London Master Builders' Association has given notice to five of the operative unions, viz. bricklayers, carpenters and joiners, plasterers, masons and labourers, that the working rule agreements signed during 1912 and 1913 are no longer in force. This action has been taken as the result of numerous lightning strikes which have taken place in recent months against the employment of non-union men.

Industrial action to impose a 'closed shop' and exclude non-union men, and secondary actions such as the London Building Industries Federation's demonstration in Trafalgar Square in June 1913, were evidence of the growing influence of the syndicalist movement. Its aim was to merge the different building trades into one union and force companies to hire its members alone. The Federation was not a recognised body, and was actually unpopular with many trade union officials. The employers hated it. Indeed, they feared the Federation's influence and began to fight back. The London Master Builders' Association declared that its members should not discriminate between union and non-union workers, and instructed firms to get employees to sign a written undertaking that they would work alongside non-union men. Bovis had joined the Association in 1912 and duly asked all staff to sign such an undertaking. Apparently unionists generally refused to sign, and the dispute rumbled on until the declaration of war in August 1914.

It seems likely that Bovis decided to join the LMBA in 1912 as a reaction to the growing tide of union militancy. From 1910 to 1913 trade union membership mushroomed from 2.4 to 4 million, and employers' associations grew just as fast in response. Membership of the LMBA also added to the respectability and status of Bovis, and made it easier to get on the tender lists for the more prestigious projects. Clients were no doubt happier with LMBA membership, if only as a perceived line of defence against trade union extremists. Sidney and Samuel attended the LMBA dinner at the Hotel Metropole at Charing Cross Station in January 1913. It sounds a rather sober occasion. Henry Riley from the *Quantity Surveyor* made a speech on the preparation of a standard method of measuring building works. Also present were the building industry's top brass: Mr F. Higgs (F.&H. Higgs), Mr F. G. Minter (F. G. Minter Ltd), two Mr Hollidays and two Mr Greenwoods (Holliday and Greenwood), Mr F. Shingleton (Leslie and Co), Mr E. C. Holloway (Holloway Brothers) and two Mr Hills from Higgs and Hill.

Labour disputes do not seem to have prevented an impressive range of completions by Bovis Ltd. In addition to the new cinemas at Ealing and Tottenham Court Road, Bovis handed over the D. H. Evans marble-faced building in Oxford Street. There was also a new frontage to Baker Street Station, offices in Argyll and Princes streets and a bus garage in Vauxhall Bridge Road. On the eve of the First World War, Bovis Ltd was already a success story, albeit as a small London contractor rather than a national builder. The two young men, Sidney Gluckstein and Samuel Joseph, who had revived

13 *Paris House in London's Regent Street was completed in 1912. The Bovis logo is clearly visible on the horse and cart in front of the building.*

14

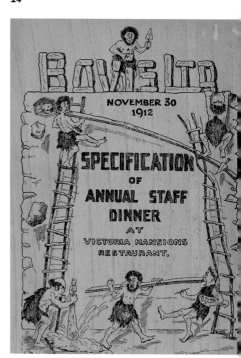

14 *The amusing menu for the Bovis Ltd annual staff dinner in 1912, an early forerunner of the Guvnors' Club which did not start until 1929.*

the company's fortunes, pushed its workload and reputation forward. Nevertheless, the war left these 26-year-olds with a dilemma. Should they go to war, or man the home front? Samuel Joseph enlisted in early 1915. According to Morrison Halcrow: 'He had gone off to war on the spin of a coin. He and his partner agreed that one of them ought to stay and mind the shop while the other joined up. They tossed for it, and Samuel won – or lost, as the case might be'. The minutes of the board meeting of 13 February 1915 adopt a more sombre and realistic tone. In accepting his commission, Samuel Joseph automatically resigned from the company. 'It was further resolved that Abraham Joseph should retire from the board, but that he should automatically resume that position in the event of the death of Samuel G. Joseph'. The minutes also record the death of Sidney's father Henry Gluckstein, and confirm the appointment to the board of Sidney's brother Samuel H. Gluckstein, and Samuel's brother Bertie Joseph.

However, Samuel Joseph had actually applied for and received his commission before the declaration of war, and at the Sixth Annual General Meeting held in June 1914 the shareholders approved his 'acceptance of a commission in HM Forces'. Sidney Gluckstein's son John recollected that Sidney also wanted to join up, but was talked out of it by his father. Instead, he became a special constable, and 'got so bored parading the streets during the occasional Zeppelin raids that he told me it was one of the worst experiences of his life'.

Ironically, the start of hostilities abroad brought peace to the building industry at home. Industrial strife was about to reach a crescendo, with a planned nationwide lock-out by the employers in support of the London Master Builders. *The Builder* comments: 'We are glad to announce that the protracted labour dispute which has disorganised the building industry in London is at an end. . .The present should prove a good time for building enterprise, as in spite of the fact that money is dear. . .the uncertainty of trouble in the labour world is now removed.' With the benefit of hindsight, it is difficult to comprehend such optimism. But in the autumn of 1914 nobody was predicting a four-year conflict with the highest number of casualties suffered in any war fought by Britain. The general mood caught by *The Builder* was a feeling that business and commerce could go on as usual, and that war would be no more than a localised disturbance in a far-away place. This had certainly been the British experience during the Boer and Crimean Wars.

The First World War was completely different. The Government was quick to take action and declared a general moratorium on trade, resulting in the complete paralysis of building operations. All new works stopped, although the later lifting of the ban allowed the completion of projects that had already started. Two Bovis projects to enter cold-storage were Bush House in the Strand and Liberty's premises in Regent Street, as well as a substantial building on the site of the old London General Post Office. In fact a survey of planned building activity in early 1914 listed dozens of current and planned projects in Central London.

The First World War proved to be far longer lasting and more onerous than the Government could possibly have imagined, and it increasingly managed the country as a single economic entity. Almost no industry remained unaffected by the overriding need to direct all the means of production to the war effort. Except for the mineworkers, the unions agreed to a 'no strike' policy, and legislation made it compulsory to settle trade disputes by arbitration. In practice the Government virtually took over the building industry. The Government sponsored most building work, directed manpower and materials, and imposed a £500 limit for expenditure on private building works. As a matter of expediency, the authorities discontinued lump-sum fixed price and replaced them with 'cost plus'.

Bovis seems to have survived these dramatically altered circumstances very well. It could not have been easy with Samuel Joseph away at the front, and shortages of manpower and materials. Most of the work executed in these years was in support of the war effort. And some of it was well away from the company's London base, with contracts for digging defence trenches completed at Ongar, Essex and Lydd in Kent. Bovis also built the American Soldiers' Hospital near Dartford on a site so inaccessible that it took two hours to reach by foot. Further construction work included large fuel tanks and gas storage for balloons. The joinery plant made huts for military use, ammunition boxes and even wooden bases for gas masks.

However, the biggest Bovis wartime project was the transformation of the White City Stadium in West London into temporary housing for Lord Kitchener's army. The Bovis archives also reveal an intriguing project 'to supply very large amounts of bulky war material, involving the use of thousands of tons of steel and timber; and to build and equip a special factory for its manufacture. The whole of this work was accomplished and delivery of the material commenced within two months from the time of order'. The site was at Peckham in South London, and sounds like a factory to produce tanks, or something similar. All the same, Bovis Ltd was still a comparatively small building concern, and its contribution to the war effort was proportionate in scale.

The ninth Annual General Meeting coincided with the end of the war, and was held at Upper Berkeley Street in June 1918. It resolved that Sidney and Samuel should resume their positions as joint managing directors at a remuneration of £1750 each, plus £250 in directors' fees. Samuel was not present at the AGM, but he soon returned from the 56th (1st London) Divisional Royal Engineers with a distinguished war record, having been mentioned twice in dispatches. The 30-year-old partners were back in business.

In August 1918 the two managing directors appointed their wives, Mrs Clara Gluckstein and Mrs Edna Joseph as directors. That year the board also decided to establish the Peckham factory as the company's joinery works, and to terminate the lease on the Dorset Works in Kensal Road, thereby severing the last link between the company and the Bovis family. There is a reference to Mrs Bovis as the landlord in one of the letters that survived from the period.

When an Extraordinary General Meeting took place in April 1919 Samuel Joseph was back from the war and took the chair. The EGM enlarged the issued share capital from £2000 to £51,000 by the creation of 48,000 £1 preference shares and 1000 £1 ordinary shares. If nothing else, this action demonstrated what outstanding progress Bovis had made under its new owners, despite the burden of the war.

Another scion of the Gluckstein family joined Bovis. After demobilisation from the balloon section of the Royal Flying Corps in early 1919, Sidney's younger brother Vincent entered the firm. He had attended St Paul's School like his older brother, and was also an alumnus of the Regent Street Polytechnic's building construction course. Before the war Vincent had worked for J. Lyons & Co as a clerk of works on the building of the Regent Palace Hotel. The arrival of 25-year-old Vincent Gluckstein completed the triumvirate that would, over the next twenty years, lay the foundations of modern Bovis. Bovis Ltd was about to hit the big time.

CHAPTER 3

Going public

In the decade that followed the First World War Bovis moved into the major league of London builders with a succession of high-profile commercial building contracts, and completed an almost unheard-of public flotation in 1928. In the Roaring Twenties Bovis built large sections of Regent Street, many City offices and dozens of cinemas and theatres. This would prove to be a golden age for the British building industry.

Britain greeted the end of the First World War with a mixture of great relief and euphoria. The human cost was terrible. With 745,000 dead and 1.7 million wounded and 1.2 million on disability pensions, the conflict had decimated a whole generation. The first total war of the modern era had touched almost every member of the population, and marked a turning point in social and economic history.

Victory brought new hope, and rising expectations. *The Builder's* leader writer gave an optimistic assessment of the outlook. 'The pent-up dam of war's restrictions in architecture is about to burst. At first, no doubt, the stream will merely trickle, but the torrent will come.' Yet the immediate prospect was not good, because the war had severely weakened the British economy. This was not true for rival nations, such as the United States and Japan, which had used the war to build up their industrial bases. In contrast, Britain had almost entirely geared its industrial output to the monumental war effort. It was like the sudden completion of a massive project, and nobody was really quite sure what to do next, although everyone agreed that returning to the pre-war status quo was quite impossible.

The cost of living was also much higher. Import prices had rocketed in wartime and, although wages were better too, trade unionists were itching to press long-delayed wage claims and return to their pre-war militancy. This desire was particularly strong in the building industry where workers had not forgotten the bitter disputes of 1914 that were ended by the outbreak of war. In anticipation of victory, the building employers gave consideration to 'the problems of reconstruction' in the early months of 1918. President of the Institute of Builders, Walter Lawrence, warned what this might mean: 'It seems likely to involve government control of building operations and materials for a considerable period after the war. This, I hope, will be resisted to the utmost by the building trade'.

At first glance the immediate prospects for the building industry seldom looked rosier. No civilian work of any consequence had been carried out in four years. Nowhere was the impact more obvious than in house building. A Government

15 *Offices for* The Glasgow Herald *in Fleet Street in Art Deco style.*

committee estimated that the 'working classes' needed 500,000 new houses, and Prime Minister David Lloyd George made his celebrated commitment to build 'homes fit for heroes' as a national priority. It was undoubtedly a policy designed to win popular support for the Government, and show a commitment to the working classes, a more pressing concern in view of the Russian Revolution of the previous year. The government machine set about its task with a spirit of great earnestness, albeit with little understanding of what it was doing.

Its first step was to pass legislation compelling local authorities to take responsibility for the provision of housing, and so the first-ever council house-building programme started. The Government also kept many of its wartime powers over the economy in place and, as Walter Lawrence had predicted, the control of building materials continued into the post-war era. Despite good intentions, the post-war public house-building programme was a complete shambles. This was partly the fault of the local authorities which possessed little knowledge about house-building, and did not have sufficient staff of the right calibre.

Immediately after the war an Industrial Council for the Building Industry was formed and charged with reporting on how the building trade should be organised to produce such a huge number of houses. Its first report, not issued until August 1919, suggested the need for a 'team spirit' between staff and employers, creating 'the whole industry into one great self-governing democracy of organised public service'. To achieve this objective, it proposed 'a central committee, with regional and local committees under it, all over the country, composed of employers, operatives and an architect'. *The Builder* thought the 'central committee' plan revolutionary, and five out of the eight employers on the Council refused to sign. It was a time when nationalisation of the building industry was first being considered and many employers saw these proposals as an extension of public control. Nonetheless, the war-time consensus had produced some benefits for the industry, and the wartime creation of a National Conciliation Board to resolve labour disputes did much to pacify industrial relations in the post-war era.

Wages were up by around fifty per cent since 1914, and further increases in 1919 and 1920 pushed the rates for craftsmen up to two shillings and four pence per hour, and for labourers to two shillings and a penny. A Bovis board meeting in June 1920 recorded various wage rises for foremen, and also mentioned 'clerical staff receiving less than £6.10.0 per week'. Isolated strikes did occur, however. There is an unauthenticated story in Bovis that a strike took place in the Peckham joinery works in 1919, and that Sidney Gluckstein went down to address the men. Apparently a heckler called him 'Kaiser'. This had the reverse of the intended effect and the men rallied behind Sidney and threw the heckler out.

Private house-building was in disarray. There was much discussion in the industry about the role private house builders should play in the public housing programme. They were the traditional suppliers of homes for the working classes, but building-for-rent was now in abeyance. Legislation had imposed a tax on land development, rents were restricted and controlled, land prices were high, labour and material supplies were uncertain, and funding was in short supply. In brief, private sector building-for-rent was almost impossible.

That left the state to muddle on with its ill-considered housing programme. Schemes for payment-by-results were condemned by the trade unions as a threat to employment. And when local authorities employed architects to speed up the process, the profession saw this as a threat to its independence. Everybody joined in with wacky ideas, and the columns of *The Times* and *The Economist* were full of suggestions. One person even wrote to *The Builder* in January 1921 proposing a National Lottery to raise funds for public housing. Government control of the building industry proved a hopeless failure. By the end of March 1922 the industry had completed just 100,000 homes out of the target of 500,000. Four years after the war, there were still a lot of heroes without homes. Perhaps it was just as well that Bovis made little headway in winning public sector housing contracts.

The re-united Bovis managing directors Sidney Gluckstein and Samuel Joseph threw themselves into tendering activity, but work was thin on the ground. *The Builder* published the results of several unsuccessful tenders, which were almost exclusively for public sector contracts. In October 1919 Bovis bid unsuccessfully for the erection of 35 cottages for Yeovil District Council at Sherbourne for £44,457, the furthest distance from London it had operated to date. Another unsuccessful distant tender was for 100 cottages at St Neots for the Rural District Council in 1920 for £100,000, the first six-figure bid by Bovis. Success in bidding for public housing contracts finally came when Bovis won a contract to build 86 houses for Lewisham Borough Council in September 1920.

Some worries over the flow of work are noted in the minutes of a board meeting held in January 1921 when it was decided to form a company 'B.V. Ltd' to 'carry out cheaper work than Bovis Ltd would like to handle' with Samuel Joseph and Francis Walter as directors. Yet one week later, minutes recorded 'the formation of this company has been abandoned owing to pressure of work'. However, the idea of forming a building division for cheaper work soon surfaced again and the company formed Nox Ltd in 1923. This curious title apparently derived from the second syllable of the word 'obnoxious', reflecting the directors' general distaste for this sort of work even if it was an economic necessity.

One spur to commercial and industrial building in the 1920s was the falling cost of wages, which reduced building costs significantly. New legislation in 1921 from the Ministry of Labour tied wage increases to a cost of living index. When worldwide deflation pushed down the cost of living, so wages automatically fell. Between January 1921 and May 1922, craftsmen saw their wages drop from two shillings and fourpence to one shilling and tenpence per hour. The stimulus that this reduction in costs provided to new building activity was very considerable indeed.

An article in the *National Builder* of December 1921 contains an insight into the Bovis order book of this time. It lists 'Examples of the work of Bovis Ltd, which include: the London School of Economics in Houghton Street, a factory for Cadillac Cars, Africa House in Kingsway and a warehouse for the Navy, Army and Air Force Canteen Board in Kennington.' Also highlighted in the same *National Builder* article were 'extensive work carried out at Broome Hall for Lord Kitchener, structural alterations and decorative work for the Rt. Hon Winston Churchill and Lord Leconfield, and internal and decorative work and

16 *A new seaside pavilion constructed for the Brighton Corporation. Leisure amenities were a booming market in the 1920s.*

16

structural alterations to the London Opera House for Sir Oswald Stoll'.

For some builders the falling wage levels were not enough, however, and the London Master Builders' Association took an aggressive stance in March 1923 when negotiations with operatives broke down. It told members to post notices on sites informing operatives of a reduction in wages and increase in hours. The news was not welcome at Bovis. The company was extremely busy and eager to avoid labour disputes. Minutes of the board meeting held in April 1923 shows a great reluctance to follow the London Master Builders' Association's led, although the directors agreed to do so 'with the sole objective of obviating any advantage which might accrue to us if we carry on our work during a general strike or lock-out'. At the same time, the Bovis board took the dramatic step of 'resignation from the Association in support of our very strong feeling in this matter'.

The resignation from the Association lead to a celebrated libel action in which Bovis sued the executive council members of the LMBA. The latter had put Bovis Ltd on a list of 'wage-rate default' companies' that it sent to everybody associated with the London building trade, including public sector clients. In the witness box Sidney Gluckstein admitted that Bovis had paid over the standard wage rate in one instance, but after resigning from the LMBA the company was not bound by its rules. This admission resulted in Bovis losing its action. But Bovis appealed and the Court of Appeal ordered a new trial.

The evidence from the trial gives an interesting insight into the scale of the Bovis operations in 1923. Sidney Gluckstein repeated his admission 'that for a month he exceeded the standard rate of pay to half-a-dozen bricklayers out of some thousand employees'. It was a special job, and he wanted an increased output. Samuel Joseph said that contracts in the year before the circular was issued amounted to £445,000, but had fallen to £283,000 the following year. He noted that since the libel action had rallied public support, the figure was now £555,000. In the event the jury found that the letter was defamatory, but for technical reasons there was no libel, nor was malice intended. The jury awarded Bovis Ltd £25 in damages. Neither Bovis nor the LMBA were happy with the outcome. Bovis did not rejoin the LMBA for over twenty years and became known as something of a loner, spoken of as 'that Jewish firm' by its detractors at the LMBA.

It is tempting to argue that the LMBA executive was trying to put the newcomer Bovis out of business. There must have been considerable jealousy in the building trade at the success of the young upstarts running the company. On the other hand, it is easy to imagine the consternation which must have been felt within Bovis with its future threatened by the establishment of the building industry. The trial certainly took its toll on Sidney Gluckstein. His son John recalled the day it finished: 'I remember that my father took my mother out that evening. He fainted in a restaurant and had to be brought home.'

But Bovis still found ways of avoiding the reduction of wages in line with deflation which was the general pattern in the 1920s. The company introduced a staff bonus scheme to compensate for falling wages and salaries, and guaranteed 'at least an equivalent amount to the reduction, and as much more as you may earn under the scheme'. It paid the money from net profits and was generous considering that jobs were in short supply. Again the directors chose to motivate and retain employees rather than secure a short-term advantage.

Whatever its legal problems, Bovis Ltd soon needed more space because of its

17 *Winning the £300,000 contract for Africa House in Kingsway in 1920 marked a breakthrough into large projects for the firm.*

18 *The cornerstone of Africa House records Bovis Ltd as its builder.*

TREHEARNE & NORMAN

ARCHITECTS

BOVIS LTD.

BUILDERS

burgeoning workload and decided to replace the Peckham joinery works. It concluded the acquisition of a suitable site in Princess Street, north of Marylebone Road, in June 1920 for £5500. The architect Mr Joseph, who was probably a relative, was appointed to prepare a plan, and the directors negotiated a £40,000 loan to cover the building costs. Bovis quickly extended these premises to take over land extending into Hatton Street, and by 1923 needed another £30,000 mortgage from the Halifax Building Society to pay for the Hatton Street works.

Charlie Austin, who joined the company in 1924, remembered the expansion very well. He had lived in Princess Street, and reminisced: 'Bovis bought whole blocks of houses in North Street, Carlisle Street, Princess Street and Hatton Street. They started knocking down the houses to build a factory'. Austin's parents thought that they would have to leave until the factory building stopped at their garden wall. At this time Charlie Austin played for a boys football team in nearby Regent's Park on a pitch without goal posts or sponsorship. An appeal to Bovis produced both, with goal posts from the joinery shop and shirts with a red 'B' on the front and back. The grateful team became the Bovis Juniors.

The breakthrough into large projects actually came in early 1920 when Bovis won the contract to build Africa House in Kingsway. The minutes of a board meeting in February 1920 do not record the value of the project, and rather laconically note: 'It was resolved to accept the contract for the erection of this building on the basis of our tender'. This gives no hint of the excitement that must have accompanied the winning of a contract worth in excess of £300,000 (this is equivalent to over £30 million today). When Africa House was nearing completion in 1922, an anonymous contributor to *The Builder* commented on the quick progress of the job 'showing how very rapidly the modern contractor achieves his aims'. It was the first of many accolades for speed and efficiency that this scrupulously independent journal would bestow on Bovis over the years.

In December 1919 the Bovis triumvirate split the running of the company between them. Samuel ran the decorating department, which specialised in high-class jobbing work in the affluent areas of Marylebone, and was highly profitable. Vincent became works manager at Peckham, and Sidney looked after the contracts department, particularly larger contracts that required competitive tendering. However, in 1921 there was a characteristic rotation of roles, with Sidney now looking after internal management, Vincent running the sites and Samuel devoted to securing new contracts. Later observers agree that the great strength of Bovis Ltd was the close personal affinity between these three men and their sense of corporate responsibility. Yet the three men were very different characters. Sidney was taciturn and introspective; Samuel was the opposite, charismatic and extrovert, while Vincent was innovative and questioning. Staff members later recalled their innate intelligence in financial and commercial matters, sound knowledge of building and once you got to know them, their kindness.

Every year the company paid for a Christmas treat for its tenants around Hatton Street. As Charlie Austin remembered: 'They used to clear out the joiners shop and have a fine big Christmas tree and a Father Christmas and about a hundred kids. Mrs Sidney used to give the children a gift off the tree and they used to take the children to a pantomime'. There are many instances of charitable gifts. Bob Henderson was put on half pay during his illness in 1921; Thompson, a manual labourer, was sent 'to the seaside' when he became sick and later given lighter work; the widow of a workman named Cashen received £1 per week in recognition of his 'excellent service'; and the company paid for W. Beckley's treatment at the London Jewish Hospital when he became seriously ill in 1923 and sent £100 to his widow when he died.

Viscount Bury joined the board in 1923 to 'use his best endeavours to promote the business of the company'. One more Bovis character of this time was Charles 'Digger' Dee, the company secretary, a chain-smoker whose waistcoat was usually covered in ash. Charles Collett joined as assistant secretary in 1923, becoming company secretary in 1928 in the same year that William Charles Ide and George Mott joined the board.

The board meetings for 1920–28 contain a seemingly ever-increasing list of contracts won. Sadly no comprehensive records have survived. Samuel Joseph actually wrote an instruction in 1924 to stop the collection of such records because they were becoming 'excessively tedious'. Nonetheless, many interesting insights into the jobs the company was undertaking have survived, often with regard to late payments. A list

19 & **20** *In the Roaring Twenties cinemas spread across Britain and Bovis built many 'picture palaces' in London such as the 3000-seat Forum cinema.*

19   **20**

21 *The Fortune Theatre almost bankrupted Bovis in the early 1920s, and the company took a financial charge on the building until it finally passed to new owners in 1927.*

21

of bad debts for the end of 1923 shows 98 unpaid accounts, ranging from one shilling and three pence to £2250, and feature famous names such as the Hon. Mrs Asquith, Viscountess Watislaw, Hon. C. W. Forester, Hon. Fitzgerald and and institutions such as the Potters Bar Golf Club.

In 1921 Bovis concluded some work at Lords Cricket Ground prompting the board to agree the contents of a letter from Sidney Gluckstein to 'Mr F. E. Lacey, secretary of the MMC re account'. Bovis constructed a pavilion for the National Rifle Association at Bisley in 1923, and contracts to build many private homes are recorded in the minutes, mostly in London but also in Kent, Surrey and Hertfordshire. Another important landmark contract took the company into the entertainment and leisure market in 1922. This contract was for alterations and additions to the Grand Theatre, Blackpool for the Blackpool Tower Company. It was also the company's first major contract away from London. The minutes often explain Vincent Gluckstein's absence from board meetings during these years as 'in Blackpool', and the Blackpool contract was the first of many theatre and cinema jobs undertaken in the 1920s.

Cinemas spread across Britain in the Roaring Twenties. Television was still to be invented and the public flocked to this new mass entertainment. Bovis built 'picture palaces' in London at Palmers Green, Harringay, New Gallery in Regent Street, Ealing, Old Kent Road, Lewisham, Leytonstone, Clapham, West Ham, Villiers Street and the London Cinema de Paris. The collection of theatre projects was equally impressive. In London there was the Shepherd's Bush Empire, the Empress Theatre in Brixton and the Fortune Theatre in Drury Lane, as well as the Vaudeville and Dominion theatres in Tottenham Court Road. Outside the capital Bovis built the Pavilion Theatre, Ilfracombe and carried out work on the Birmingham Hippodrome.

The building of the Fortune Theatre, originally named the Crown Theatre, nearly brought the curtains down on Bovis. Samuel Joseph's son and famous Conservative cabinet minister, Lord Joseph later recalled that this project ran into serious financial difficulty and a delay in payments almost bankrupted Bovis. Indeed, the change of name may well have been suggested by the Bovis board as a wry comment on this

22 *Nos 84–88 Regent Street, London. From 1922 to 1925 Bovis built many of the major developments in Regent Street, creating a new up-market shopping district in the heart of London.*

23 *No. 174 Regent Street, London. The stockmarket boom of the 1920s sparked an upturn in commercial building. Regent Street survived the Blitz, unlike the early Bovis office projects in the City of London.*

24 *Chesham House provided the largest Bovis contract in Regent Street. Bovis bought 20,000 £1 preference shares in Chesham House Ltd.*

22

23

episode, which cost Bovis a fortune. Bovis completed the project in 1924, and had to take a financial charge on the building. The charge remained until the theatre passed to new owners in 1927.

The commercial building market slowly regained confidence after the war, and the rebuilding of Regent Street started in earnest. This massive redevelopment was the first large-scale commercial project undertaken by Bovis and a further milestone in the history of the firm. Between 1922 and 1925 Bovis was responsible for many major projects in Regent Street, including the rebuilding of numbers 84-88, 127–31, 174, 175, 199, 201, 302, 304, 306 and 308, and equally large works in Mortimer and Margaret streets. Future Bovis director Fred Cosford recalled: 'When I joined Bovis in 1923, the rebuilding of Regent Street had just begun. All the basements were dug out by hand. I can remember seeing hundreds of men, like ants, all using clay-spades and Wimpey and Mowlem with their horses and two-wheel carts coming up the ramps'.

The largest Bovis contract in Regent Street was the office development Chesham House for Liberty & Co and Chesham House Ltd. There is a note in the archives recording that Bovis bought 20,000 £1 preference shares in Chesham House Ltd. Many other London commercial construction contracts were won by Bovis in the 1920s, especially in the City.

In the years before the 1929 stockmarket crash, the City was growing rapidly as a financial centre, and Bovis was a leading contractor in the Square Mile. It was the same story much later in the 1980s at the time of the 'Big Bang' building boom. Sixty years earlier, the Bovis nameboard was a common sight to City gentlemen in bowler hats as they went about their business. There were new offices for the Union Insur-

25

25 *The Bovis nameboard dates from the early 1920s. George Roberts received £3 for his suggestion of 'Bovis' in red cast-iron letters and 'London W1' in the bottom right-hand corner.*

ance Society of Canton at 78–80 Cornhill, and projects in the Minories, Bush Lane, Cork Street, the Corn Exchange, Cheapside, America Square, Worship Street, New Bridge Street, City Road, Finsbury Square, St Swithins Lane and Tokenhouse Yard. Another was in Addle Street, where the company again ended up taking a financial charge on the building. The Bovis reputation for building in the City of London therefore dates from the Roaring Twenties, even if Broadgate and Bishopsgate in the 1980s was the firm's greatest hour.

The Bovis nameboard was an innovation of this time. Most builders' boards contained a bewildering array of information and rather obscured the corporate identity of the firm. Vincent Gluckstein saw that this was a missed opportunity, and his answer was a white board with the name 'Bovis' in red cast-iron letters in the centre and 'London W1' in the bottom right-hand corner. Credit for the cast-iron letters goes to George Roberts, the longest surviving employee at the time, who received £3 as a reward for his idea. Vincent issued a standing order that site managers were to get the boards cleaned every day. The *National Builder* commented: 'We congratulate Messrs Bovis on initiating a sign worthy of the building trade by reason of its dignity, distinctiveness and character'.

This was one of several marketing initiatives in the 1920s. The company also commissioned a series of cartoonists and writers to produce a humorous publication of 'Bovisms', and it sent 5000 copies to clients, architects and surveyors. That year Vincent commissioned a jig-saw puzzle from H. Bateman, an eminent cartoonist, and 10,000 copies of 'The man who did not know' were produced. Bovis also gave tickets for Wimbledon and Christmas presents to architects and surveyors, with varying degrees of success. Fred Cosford remembered delivering golf balls one Christmas, and when one surveyor saw the name 'Bovis' on the balls, he gave them back.

STRUCTURAL ALTERATIONS
REMOVING A HOUSE IN THE DEAD OF NIGHT
FROM THE NEIGHBOURHOOD OF A DUSTBIN

Drawn by W. HEATH ROBINSON.

26

PLUMBING

New Assistant (to Old Hand): "I'll tell you *my* opinion, 'Erbert—
it's the 'ole in the pipe wot's causin' the trouble!"

Drawn by PETER FRASER.

27

26 & **27** *Celebrated cartoonist
W. Heath Robinson (left) and a
number of other cartoonists were
commissioned to draw a series of
amusing cartoons called 'Bovisms' as
an early marketing ploy to entertain
existing and prospective clients.*

28 *The London School of Economics in Houghton Street, a landmark contract for the company as its reputation grew in the 1920s. Bovis returned in the 1990s to install a new library.*

29

30

31

29 *The Liberal Jewish Synagogue in St John's Wood Road, was handed over in 1925 – another prestige project for the dynamic young Bovis company.*

30 *Bush House in Aldwych, which was completed in the early 1920s, had been delayed by the outbreak of the First World War.*

31 *Workmen responsible for erecting a steel frame in Charlton in 1927. Sid Capon is the suitably attired foreman-carpenter at the back.*

There were also highly prestigious projects outside the City, such as further phases of the London School of Economics and the west wing of Bush House in nearby Aldwych. Bovis also built the Liberal Jewish Synagogue in St John's Wood Road and carried out unspecified work at the Houses of Parliament in 1925. Lesser projects undertaken by Bovis subsidiary Nox Ltd included an extension to the Strand Palace Hotel for J. Lyons & Co, and the Howard Hotel, where financial problems resulted in shares being taken in lieu of payment. Then there was a string of hospitals, nursing homes, blocks of flats for private developers, public houses, club buildings, restaurants, bank premises and many private homes.

Bovis also got into the retail sector in the 1920s as the fledgling consumer society began to emerge. Most important retail clients were Home and Colonial Stores, Haymarket Stores, Selfridges, Steinways and Cellular Clothing. Bovis built Warwick House in Birmingham for C&A Modes, and extensively redeveloped a site on the corner of Oxford Street and Tottenham Court Road for Horne Brothers. However, the company's most celebrated new client of the era was Marks & Spencer. Bovis won its first job for M&S in 1926 in Wood Green, North London. It would mark the beginning of a long and fruitful association that lasts to this day and forms the subject of the next chapter.

A final element of the Bovis order book in the 1920s was a series of factories and warehouses at Poplar, the Borough, Bermondsey, Edgware, Tottenham, Willesden, Bourne End and Canning Town. There was an industrial project for the dangerous sounding Berkel & Parnels Slicing Machine Manufacturing Company at Enfield, as well as more humdrum electricity sub-stations, signal boxes and pumping stations all around London.

It was perhaps predictable that the new Hatton Street premises would quickly become inadequate, and in 1926 land was acquired in Cricklewood at Oxgate Farm. The new joinery works opened at what became universally known as Oxgate in 1928. Charlie Austin remembers that the workers from the now closed Peckham factory were willing to travel the extra distance: 'They were already getting themselves up from Peckham to Victoria, and then catching a No. 16 bus up to Hatton Street. It meant they stayed on the bus until it got to Cricklewood'.

The main reason for opening the Oxgate joinery works was the phenomenal success of the Compactom wardrobe, a piece of furniture believed to have been invented by Samuel Joseph. The Compactom wardrobe represented a forerunner of modern furniture. It is a purpose-made gentleman's wardrobe with drawers, shelves, tie and shoe racks, and special fittings to hang twelve suits. Making the wardrobes began as a useful sideline to keep the joinery works occupied throughout the year, and then became a significant profit centre in its own right. Lord Joseph told the story: 'My father, Samuel Joseph, designed the first Compactom wardrobe in answer to my mother's complaint that she thought there must be something better in which to hang clothes than a bare cupboard'.

As early as January 1924, a board meeting records: 'The output of Compactom cabinets is very considerably in excess of the joinery for Bovis Ltd, and consequently the greater portion of Hatton Street Works, and the whole of Kilburn Works are devoted to Compactom work'. Compactom was a hit with the public. But the Compactom wardrobe was not mentioned at board meetings until December 1919. By then manufacturing was in progress and the price fixed at 79 guineas. Bovis secured the services of an Edward Pinto, a designer who assumed responsibility for the Compactom product. Eventually Bovis took out patents and concluded manufacturing agreements for New Zealand, Australia, India, South Africa and Kenya. Samuel Joseph also visited Paris and Berlin to market Compactom, and opened bank accounts in both cities, although there is no evidence of any European trading. The directors ignored a letter from a Dutch company in 1921 asking about Compactom, as they felt the Dutch just wanted to copy it.

The directors flirted briefly with the idea of selling Compactom as a going concern, and the subsidiary was incorporated in 1921. They appointed Francis Walter to the board in that year to take over 'private proprietorship of Compactom at a valuation to be agreed'. The business was to be 'severed from that of Bovis Ltd'. Walter was unable to agree terms for the sale, and his resignation was accepted 'with regret' at a later board meeting. Compactom then added other pieces of furniture to its range: a lady's wardrobe, a dressing trolley valet and bedside trolley. And Bovis formed another company, Fitrobe Ltd, to manufacture and market a cheaper line of furniture. It patented these items in many different countries. There was even a Compactom boiler to capitalise on the new fashion for central heating.

Marketing the Compactom products was easy-going by the standards of today. Compactom took a stand at the Olympia Ideal Homes Exhibition in 1920, 1922 and

32

32 *Compactom wardrobes for gentlemen were a phenomenal success and began as an initiative to keep the joinery works busy in the winter months. The wardrobe features drawers, shelves, tie and shoe racks and special fittings to hang twelve suits.*

1927, and was widely advertised in journals. The board also discussed setting up a showroom for Compactom in 1922, but it was not until 1924 that Compactom took temporary premises in Regent Street, finally signing a lease for 143 Regent Street in November 1925.

A later senior Bovis director Pat O'Brien remembered an anecdote about the marketing of Compactom. 'Sammy Bond used to tell a story from the twenties. One day Sam Joseph told Sammy he wanted him to go down to Brighton and sell a Compactom wardrobe, and not come back until he did. He toured the furniture shops of Brighton without success until one shopkeeper said to him "Why should I buy one of these wardrobes?" Sammy poured out the whole story, and told the chap that if he didn't sell one he'd lose his job. The shopkeeper took pity on him and bought one. When Sammy got back to London, Sam Joseph called the Compactom salesmen together, and told them "You see, if a teenager like Bond can do it, why can't you?"'

Company cars appeared for the first time after the First World War. A board meeting in December 1919 resolved 'that Sidney Gluckstein has the use of the Wolseley car with the right of purchasing the same from the company for £400; that S. G. Joseph has the use of the Chevrollet (sic) car with the right of purchasing the same for £400; that Vincent Gluckstein has the use of the A. V. Mono car with the right of purchasing same for £75'. The company cars caused a rare frisson of tension between the directors. Sidney Gluckstein did not want to use a car, and the minutes rather seriously proposed the re-election of Bertie Joseph as a director to 'vote on this matter, the two directors present not being able to arrive at an agreement'. The board did not discuss the matter again, so it must have been sorted out. Subsequently both Sidney and Samuel employed chauffeurs, and this was probably the compromise.

It was very unusual for the directors to fall out. Perhaps they were normally just too busy to argue; the post-war period was one of outstanding progress for Bovis Ltd. The company carved a niche for itself as one of London's leading commercial builders. Its problems – such as the Fortune Theatre debacle and the libel action against the London Master Builders – were the problems of success. The crowning achievement was to obtain a listing on the London Stock Exchange in 1928. This was the year before the great stockmarket crash of 1929 that heralded the depression of the 1930s. Unfortunately no record of the many discussions that must have taken place about the public flotation of Bovis have survived. Possibly the board would not allow minuting of such a confidential matter. Indeed, there were few other publicly quoted builders in 1928.

A board meeting of 13 June 1928 contains the resolution 'with a view to the sale of its undertaking to another company this company be wound up'. The new owner was Bovis (1928) Ltd. A prospectus shows audited profits averaging £40,206 per annum in the previous three years, and net assets worth £167,252. It says Bovis 'can fairly claim to be in the forefront of the building world', and mentions the 'well-known Compactom clothing cabinets which are in great demand'. The flotation was a success. On 11 July 1928 the first board meeting of Bovis (1928) Ltd was held at 199 Piccadilly. It was the first day of the new era for Bovis.

34

BOVIS (1928) LIMITED

CAPITAL - - - £300,000

33 *The new Oxgate joinery works opened in 1928 supplying both Bovis projects and the demand for Compactom wardrobes. Note the bold company logo, much like the site signs, on the side of the lorry.*

34 *In 1928 Bovis made its Stock Exchange debut. The group delisted after the P&O takeover in 1974.*

CHAPTER 4

The Bovis System

As a stockmarket-quoted building company Bovis considerably enhanced its public reputation through a novel contractual arrangement called the Bovis System, which the company had devised at the end of the 1920s. The Bovis System played a vital role in winning the firm a constant stream of new clients in the 1930s, and brought the company to national prominence. It was prompted by the needs of national retailers such as Marks & Spencer which required a new approach to contracting in order to construct shops for the inter-war consumer boom.

The Bovis System is a building contract that brings the client and contractor together in a unity of interest, in sharp contrast to the adversarial relationship established in the traditional lump-sum contract that often leads to disputes. In practice, the Bovis System pays the builder the prime cost of the work plus an agreed fee to cover overheads and profit. The client receives any savings made during construction instead of the contractor. In its day, this was a revolutionary innovation.

The company adopted the Bovis System in 1928, although unhappiness with the traditional lump-sum contracts was nothing new. In 1913 *The Builder* criticised the standard form of contract, and concluded: 'It does seem as if there is an appalling waste of money and effort in the tendering system. . .and it would be to the benefit of the building owners if this waste could be curtailed'. And the same article went on to argue: 'The competitive system of tendering. . .divorces the interests of the contractor from that of the building owner. If some system could be devised whereby the contractor was paid in a way which would make him. . .stand in the shoes of the building owner, it would confer on the latter many of the advantages of doing the work himself'.

The outbreak of war in 1914 put concerns about such matters on hold. To speed up work even competitive tendering was abandoned in the war years. Instead the Government let contracts on the basis of paying prime cost, plus an agreed percentage for overheads and profit, a system which became known as 'cost-plus'. The contract debate resumed in peacetime. In June 1919 the RIBA held a conference to consider 'what form of contract will best meet the drastically altered conditions in the building trade'. *The Builder* reported: 'That the competitive system was not considered satisfactory in many respects was evidently the consensus of opinion of the meeting, but as to what was to replace it was left undecided'. The writer of the same article argues that a 'cost plus a fixed-fee' system used by an American contractor Frank B. Gilbreth was 'well worth considering'.

35

35 *Workmen unload a highly polished lorry resplendent in the new Bovis livery.*

36 *By mid-1935 Bovis had completed over 200 contracts for Marks & Spencer. This store in Croydon was handed over in the following year.*

Official recognition of this system came in Lord Colwyn's report of 1919 on the public housing building programme. It also incorporated another Gilbreth idea, the contractor's bonus, which would be an agreed proportion of the saving between the estimated and final cost. But Lord Colwyn's committee saw this as a temporary measure during the 'present difficulties' and not a permanent replacement for traditional lump-sum contracts.

Lewisham Borough Council was one of the first post-war clients to experiment with a prime cost plus fixed-fee contract. When lump-sum bids for 92 homes at Lewisham Park came in too high, the Council invited twelve firms to tender on the basis of the newfangled cost plus fixed-fee contract, and Bovis won the job. The Bovis board minutes recorded the signing of the contract in September 1920. Nobody at the time seems to have had the slightest idea that they were discussing the forerunner to the revolutionary Bovis System; it was just another addition to the order book. In fact, the Lewisham contract was a financial failure. The Lewisham Housing

37

Jno Luther Green
28 OCT 1927

Articles of Agreement

made the   day of   One
thousand nine hundred and   B E T W E E N
Messrs. MARKS & SPENCER, Limited, of No. 21 Chiswell
Street, London, E.C.2. (hereinafter called "the Employer")
of the one part and Messrs. BOVIS, Limited, of 47 Upper
Berkeley Street, London, W.1. (hereinafter called "the
Contractor") of the other part WHEREAS the Employer
is desirous of

and has caused Drawings and a Specification describing
the work to be done to be prepared by
                AND WHEREAS the said Drawings numbered
            and the Specification and the Bills of
Quantities have been signed by or on behalf of the parties
hereto AND WHEREAS the Contractor has agreed to execute
upon and subject to the conditions set forth and the
Schedules attached hereto the work shewn upon the said
Drawings and described in the said Specification and
included in the said Bills of Quantities for a Fee to be
paid to him and the refund of the prime cost thereof as
defined in the Schedules "A", "B" and "C" hereto.
        NOW IT IS HEREBY AGREED AS FOLLOWS :-
1.   IN consideration of the Fee above referred to and
of the refund of the prime cost of the works to be paid
at the times and in the manner set forth in the said
Conditions the Contractor will upon and subject to the
said Conditions execute and complete the work shewn upon
the said Drawings and described in the said Specification
and Bills of Quantities.
2.   THE Employer will pay the Contractor the said Fee
and refund the prime cost or such other sum as shall become
payable hereunder at the times and in the manner specified

- 1 -

37 *The original fee-based contract with Marks & Spencer, the basis of the Bovis System.*

Committee report of March 1923 notes: 'The contractors' final account proved very difficult...the actual cost being £96,846 10s 2d, plus minimum profit remuneration of £1720 (£20 per house)'. The guaranteed minimum of £20 per house compared with a guaranteed maximum of £40, and could not be judged a success for the contractor.

A further cost plus fixed-fee job was awarded in 1921 by the Navy, Army and Air Force Institutes (NAAFI) for its premises in Kennington. And the Majestic picture palace in Palmers Green built between 1920 and 1921 also seems to have been a prime cost contract, as the directors refer to a 'bonus claimed of £150'. However, there was nothing to indicate that the Bovis board recognised that cost plus fixed-fee contracts were a marketable concept. The directors probably thought such fee-based contracting would prove a short-lived expediency.

Company legend dates the first contract award under the Bovis System to 7 June 1926, the day that Marks & Spencer signed its first-ever contract with Bovis for a new store in Wood Green, London. The general assumption is that prime cost contracting began on the Wood Green store, but the diaries of the project's architect, William Arthur Lewis, suggest otherwise. He notes that M&S let all its work by competitive tender at this time, and Lewis says the Wood Green store went to Bovis, 'with the lowest tender of £2550, and after adjustments for additional work a final contract price of £2813 10s was agreed'.

So, although Wood Green was the first project for a very important future client, this was not the birth of the Bovis System. Neither was a second M&S contract won in July 1927 for a store in Gravesend. The real reason for the introduction of the Bovis System arose from the company's failure to win a third M&S project in open tender. The lost tender was for the prestigious M&S head office contract at 35 Chiswell Street. Lewis notes in his diary that the Chiswell Street contract went out to tender, and that Ashby and Horner made the lowest bid of £21,587. Shortly afterwards Lewis held a meeting with Mr Marks, Mr Isaacs and Mr Shrewsbury of M&S, and recorded: 'I am to accept Bovis at £21,600, six month contract, but I am to see Bovis and explain they will only get the £600, or part, as a bonus if they work satisfactorily'.

A fair interpretation of events is that Bovis impressed Marks & Spencer on its first two contracts, and that M&S was keen to move away from the pitfalls of traditional lump-sum tendering such as spiralling costs and missed completion dates. So when Bovis failed to win the Chiswell Street headquarters in open tender, Vincent Gluckstein went to see the M&S board to suggest an alternative based on a different form of contract. Thus the vitally important Bovis System was probably introduced as an opportunist expedient to win a single contract.

Bovis certainly needed the work, as Lord Joseph recalled: 'My father used to say that when work was scarce in the late 1920s, he could leave home early and visit all the Bovis sites and still get home for a late breakfast. He was particularly keen to see that the Bovis nameboards were cleaned'. In the course of negotiations with M&S the

38   **39**

40

idea of forging a long-term relationship between the client and contractor may well have proved decisive. It was how M&S liked to deal with its clothing suppliers. Nevertheless, it is clear from Bovis board minutes that the directors were not idealists pedalling a revolutionary contract, just businessmen after a job. They were as surprised as anybody else by the future success of the Bovis System.

The draft form of contract still exists in the M&S archive, and is dated 28 October 1927. It is a 'prime cost plus fixed-fee contract' with the provision of a bonus to Bovis 'if the actual cost is lower than the estimated cost'. This represented the first true Bovis System contract, and was probably modelled on the experience of the Lewisham and NAAFI contracts. Bovis also won a contract for a store in Brighton at the same time, presumably on similar terms.

The marriage between client and contractor proved outstandingly successful. In June 1928 M&S awarded six contracts to Bovis covering a wide geographic area from Little Pulteney Street and Catford in London to Chatham, Watford, Hereford and Blackpool. A letter from the quantity surveyor Gleeds confirms that the Blackpool project used the prime cost system of contract. It shows a prime cost of £4636 and a fee of £595. Indeed, the patronage of Marks & Spencer is a watershed in the history of Bovis. At the end of 1928 nine more M&S projects were awarded, including

41

41 *United Dairies awarded its first Bovis System contract in June 1930, for this shop in Kingsbury, North London. Many other retailers also decided to copy Marks & Spencer in using the non-adversarial Bovis System.*

Sheffield, Liverpool, Birkenhead, Maidstone, Manchester and Bristol. And in 1929 there were twenty-two more, one as far afield as Glasgow. It is, therefore, no exaggeration to say that the Bovis System transformed the company, and was pivotal in the development of its special relationship with Marks & Spencer.

There is good reason to believe that M&S was partly responsible for the public flotation of Bovis in 1928. M&S floated on the stockmarket in 1926 to finance its ambitious expansion plans, and may well have encouraged Bovis to do the same. In his book, *Marks & Spencer 1884–1984*, Asa Briggs explains the benefit having a single contractor could offer: 'Thereafter M&S could maintain an experienced workforce and secure advantages of bulk purchase and continuity of operation'. Bovis formed a separate division for M&S work under the control of Gerry Munn, the surveyor responsible for the first M&S contract at Wood Green. Frank Holland became his chief assistant.

As so often happened, Marks & Spencer set a trend. The concept of having a single contractor attracted a number of expanding retailers, notably United Dairies. It awarded its first Bovis System contract in June 1930 for a shop at Kingsbury. Twelve more contracts followed that year and a further twenty-three in 1931. Timothy Whites and Taylors, the household goods chain, was another convert. It opted for the Bovis System on a Taunton project in October 1934 and within the next twelve months awarded eight more stores across the country. Times Furnishing also became a big Bovis System client from 1935 onwards.

In his speech to the Annual General Meeting of May 1935, Sidney Gluckstein could boast: 'The rationalised system of building known as the Bovis System has proved very attractive to architects, surveyors and all others interested in the development of property. In the result we have opened important new accounts, and it will be evident to you that the satisfaction of all parties with the working of this system is evinced by this steady growth'. Not all Bovis System contracts were for retail clients. In May 1933 Messrs Jacobs, the biscuit manufacturer, appointed Bovis to build a new factory at Aintree, Liverpool. Then in October 1934 there is a reference to a contract to build the terminal building at Liverpool airport, where 'Bovis would not take any share of the savings effected'. It is actually impossible to determine from the company records which contracts employed the Bovis System, as no differentiation is made between them.

The company was still active in the tender market. Bovis appears regularly on tender lists of the early 1930s. One unsuccessful tender was a £692,627 bid for a further phase of County Hall, by far its biggest ever tender. Contracts won in open competition included a department store for Marshall Roberts in Camden, Holborn sub-station, Walsingham House, the John Roan School for Boys, an extension to Regent Street Polytechnic, Forum Cinema in Fulham Road, Marshall Street Swimming Baths, Ontario House in the Strand and the London Oratory Central School in Wandsworth. A much publicised contract was a £200,000 extension to Claridges Hotel, and also the New Theatre in Charing Cross Road for Sidney Bernstein. In May 1930 the *Financial Times* commented on the tremendous amount of building work going on in London, and noted: 'among the boards

42 *In the early 1930s Bovis completed the Oratory Central School in Wandsworth, South London.*

43 *Bovis also won the John Roan School for Boys in Greenwich in open tender in the early 1930s.*

42

43

frequently to be seen on buildings is the conspicuous one adopted by Bovis'.

The board of directors was slow to realise the importance of the Bovis System and continued to see it simply as a pragmatic tool to win contracts rather than a serious innovation. Despite enjoying commercial success with Marks & Spencer from 1928, there is no mention of the Bovis System in the minutes of board meetings until 1933. Then it was 'resolved that a new private company to be called Bovis Ltd be incorporated immediately. . .and that the business of Bovis Ltd be restricted to building carried out under. . .the Bovis System'. Confusingly Bovis (1928) Ltd reverted to the title Bovis Ltd in March 1931, and the old company was to become the chief promoter of the new Bovis System. From now on all tender work would be executed by Nox Ltd and in 1937 Bovis formed Yeomans and Partners to undertake smaller works.

In his report to the board in 1933 Vincent Gluckstein commented that 'Bovis Ltd was practically off the tender system'. This was an astonishing testament to the success of the Bovis System. In addition to the list of clients already mentioned, there was: the Brighton Corporation, the London Electric Railway Company, the London School of Economics, Barclays Bank, Fisher Foils, Hotel Rembrandt, Liptons and the London Hippodrome. All of these clients must have been using the Bovis System, and by Sidney Gluckstein's speech to the AGM in 1935, the list had grown to include: the Gas Light and Coke Company, Lloyd's Bank, Westminster Bank, National Bank, Credit Lyonnais and the Royal Court Hotel.

Meanwhile, the relationship with Marks & Spencer blossomed to such an extent that Bovis had completed over 200 contracts by mid-1935, and the original shop at Wood Green had been extended twice. Perhaps the most significant contract for M&S was the fitting-out of the Oxford Street store in 1932. The *Daily Telegraph* commented on the speed of construction, three weeks rather than the usual four months. It quotes 'an official of Messrs Bovis' who says, 'It is an entirely new speeding up idea. . .the work is split into zones. Each zone has a squad of skilled workmen, and work proceeds on the whole building the whole time'. For those in the company who think Bovis invented 'fast-track' construction in the 1980s, it may come as something of a shock to realise that their forefathers were doing exactly the same thing in the 1930s. Building quickly is not a new idea, nor is the imperative of not sacrificing quality to speed, a common failing among building companies. Bovis never fell into this trap.

One sure method of ensuring such quality is a commitment to staff training, and Bovis directors were quick to appreciate the necessity of proper training. Paul Gilbert, who became chairman of Bovis Holdings in 1960, was the first trainee in the early 1920s, and the later head of housing, Fred Cosford, was among the many in-house trainees. Later the training schemes became more formal, particularly as the Bovis System became so important to the company. Vincent Gluckstein gave constant lectures on the Bovis System to all the young men who joined Bovis in the 1930s. One of the messages drummed into them was the importance of putting the client first. 'You look after the client, and I'll look after Bovis,' was Vincent Gluckstein's favourite saying.

When the company moved to Great Stanhope Street in 1936, the directors decided to open a special school, the Bovis School of Building. It was a great innovation for its day, and the school took a lease on premises at 77 South Audley Street with Eric R. Vose appointed education officer. The school took one hundred trade apprentices and management trainees, and was affiliated to the Hammersmith

44

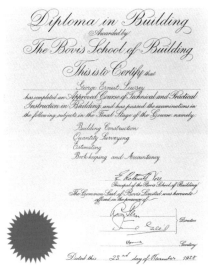

44 *The Bovis School of Building opened in 1936 with Eric R. Vose appointed as education officer.*

School of Building. Naturally the non-adversarial Bovis System was at the core of the curriculum. At the end of a three-year course the management trainees sat an examination for a diploma, and also spent periods on secondment to various Bovis departments.

The opening of the school attracted favourable press comment. H. W. Mole, principal of the Hammersmith School of Building commented: 'I know of no other firm which has gone to such an expense in providing their own school, or who maintained so much interest in the education and welfare of their employees'. And a later managing director of Bovis Construction, Bernard Heaphy, explained: 'To do something like this in those times of poverty and deprivation was very courageous. They were putting the cost of an investment in the future up front when the future looked very bleak.'

This commitment to education and training could be fairly extreme. In 1938 Sidney Gluckstein told the Annual General Meeting: 'Personnel should possess the highest degree of technical and practical ability, and should be imbued with enthusiasm, amounting almost to fanaticism, to make it certain that those who used the System would receive all the advantages which it provided'. He added that this 'could only be achieved by recruiting specially selected young men with no preconceived notion of the industry, and giving them special training in the company's works, on their jobs, and later in their own school'.

Former trainee George Lewsey later recalled that the Bovis School of Building covered the equivalent of the five-year Higher National Certificate in just three years, and entitled students to sit the Institute of Builders examination that cost thirty shillings. This was two weeks' wages, and Lewsey decided to leave the IOB exam because of the cost. Sidney Gluckstein told him off for not sitting the exam, and gave him thirty shillings, saying 'What's your excuse for not doing the exam now?'

The Bovis directors found themselves increasingly drawn into the establishment, as the former whizz-kids became highly successful businessmen. Samuel Joseph received a knighthood in 1934 for his services to local government. He was a councillor in Marylebone for many years, and mayor of the Borough from 1928 to 1930. In his comments to the Annual General Meeting in 1937 Sir Samuel highlights the importance of the Bovis System. 'The Bovis System was started ten years ago and after seven years' satisfactory experience the company has turned the whole of its operations to this system. It is my pleasure. . .to repeat that with this system the company has never had a dissatisfied building owner.'

However, the Bovis System had its critics. For example, in a paper for the RIBA in 1938 Oliver W. Roskill says 'I believe the origin of the Bovis System lay with the requirements of a building owner carrying out a succession of similar jobs in which the need for speed and experience in the particular type of work concerned pointed strongly in the direction of choosing one builder and sticking to him'. Roskill goes on in the paper to claim 'it does introduce a new feature of salesmanship into contracting and, if carried to excess, the personality and entertainments allocation of the managing director may tend to become more important than the figure put forward with the tender'.

It is true that the Bovis System required a greater marketing effort than traditional lump-sum tendering. The concept had to be explained, or sold to clients. And in 1933

45

45 *In the early 1930s the British economy improved and Bovis completed many luxury houses in London, but shunned volume housing developments.*

the directors resolved: 'never to attempt to explain the Bovis System in writing, but to confine explanations to personal interviews'. Roskill's concern was that marketing would triumph over more objective considerations in the awarding of contracts, which probably underestimated the commercial acumen of clients. But the Bovis System certainly took some explaining. By the late 1930s the form of contract was fundamentally different from the M&S version of 1928. The bonus clause was dropped, as was the principle of Bovis sharing the saving on estimated cost with the client. The client got the full amount, but paid a fee scaled according to the saving achieved. It was the reverse of the lump-sum system where a bigger final cost benefited the contractor.

To some extent the success of the Bovis System took the company away from the more conventional business strategies adopted by rival builders in the late 1920s and 1930s. This was an age that saw the re-emergence of the private house builder and the building of vast suburban housing estates in London. Interest rates plunged after the 1929 stockmarket crash, making mortgages cheap, and builders and building societies worked together to find ways to make home ownership more affordable. Contractors found house building a useful source of work when conventional contracts became scarce in the depression years.

Not only did the Bovis System keep order books full at Bovis, it seems to have deflected the company away from house building. Instead Bovis decided to take advantage of the need for shop units to serve the new housing estates, which often included a parade of shops as a focal point of the community. This was more in line with its retailing speciality, and of course contracts were let under the Bovis System.

Following the public flotation in 1928, a series of land acquisitions was made for retail development, and in most cases Bovis approached potential tenants before the purchase. For example, Boots Pure Drug Company, W. H. Smith and Home and Colonial Stores were joint developers on several sites. In 1928 land was acquired at Waddon, Beckenham and Bromley, and over the next two years Bovis bought land and property for redevelopment in Central London, Harrow, Wembley, Greenford, Southend, Cheam, Hillingdon and Rayners Lane. Such development work gathered pace in the 1930s. But Bovis kept capital investment and risk low. In some cases Bovis would fund the speculative building of retail schemes, although generally the firm operated as a co-developer. The directors also bought units speculatively on their own account, but only after discussing the matter among themselves. Surprisingly this activity does not appear to have caused any bad feeling between directors whose speculative rewards must have been rather uneven.

Between 1932 and 1935 retail developments were carried out on land purchased in Kingsbury, Neasden, Orpington, Hayes in Kent, Eastcote, Welling, Tolworth and Cockfosters. However, the creation of a property committee in March 1936 formalised this rather haphazard handling of property interests, and the committee was incorporated as Audley Properties Ltd in October 1936. The minutes suggest that the auditors were unhappy with the mixture of the directors' private interests and the public company's property development. There is no indication of improper action by the directors, although the resolution forming Audley Properties Ltd notes that 'building operations. . .carried out for directors. . .should attract the same profit and percentage addition as for other joint adventurers'.

As the British economy began to improve in 1933, Bovis looked again at house building. Rather than engage in suburban estate development, the company searched for a niche where it had a competitive advantage, and settled on upmarket apartments and luxury houses in London. This resulted in a spate of prestige residential projects in the capital, and before the Second World War Bovis built such developments in Hampstead, Marylebone, Paddington, St John's Wood and Hyde Park.

The redevelopment of its own premises in this period also reflected the considerable success of the company. At the time of the flotation in 1928 it was already obvious that the Upper Berkeley Street offices were too small. Later that year negotiations started in order to acquire a site on the High Street in Marylebone for the construction of new offices. By early 1931 these premises were the venue for a board meeting. High on the agenda was the weighty matter of the purchase of a new boardroom table. Staff welcomed the relocation to Marylebone High Street. Upper Berkeley Street was a converted house, whereas Marylebone was purpose-built. There was a staff restaurant on the top floor and a social club, something of an innovation in those days. The restaurant had a small stage and Fred Cosford recalled how he joined a small trio with saxophone, piano and himself on drums. Meanwhile, the works at Hatton Street and the Oxgate joinery factory were both extended.

Yet the Marylebone office was almost too good for a builder. In 1935 the Bovis board opened discussions for its sale to the BBC, and agreed the sale in June 1936 for

46

46 *Bovis constructed this building in Marylebone High Street in 1931 as its new headquarters, but sold the premises to the BBC in 1935 for £100,000.*

47

47 *The first meeting of the Guvnors' Club in 1929, the ever-popular annual get-together for site foremen. On the top table (left to right): Viscount Bury, Vincent Gluckstein and club chairman Paul Gilbert. Tea-cans are raised for the toast.*

£100,000. The offer was too good to refuse. Bovis made a nice profit by moving to 1 Great Stanhope Street, where it bought the freehold for the lesser figure of £31,000. The directors told staff that the new premises were a 'temporary' measure. In the event, Bovis stayed for 25 years.

As the Bovis System won contracts the length of Britain, Bovis directors became increasingly concerned about maintaining contact with their general foremen. When projects were in London, it was not a problem, but Bovis was now asking general foremen to leave home and work on their own in far-flung corners of the United Kingdom. Vincent Gluckstein came up with a solution; the company would form a club for every member of staff referred to as 'Guvnor' on site – the all-important general foremen – and bring them together on regular occasions. The aim of the Guvnors' Club was 'to promote and further the social interests of its members...with a view to fostering friendship, co-operation and service to each other'. Vincent Gluckstein was the first president of the club and Paul Gilbert its first chairman. The club restricted membership to general foremen, and the company provided the financial support.

An inaugural dinner was held on 7 October 1929 at Olympia. Guvnors could bring one guest. It attracted widespread press comment. The *Daily Telegraph* described the event in some detail:

> When the Guvnors arrived they were announced by a man in navvy's garb, and were ushered into a dining hall that represented a scene such as one sees in any thoroughfare where building is in progress. The floor was a staging of rough planks on scaffold poles, and as each guest entered he clocked in.
> Cocktails were shaken in a miniature concrete mixer, and the fare, having been brought up a hoist, was sent to the centre of the room in a conveyor. No glass was on the table, for everyone drank beer out of cans. The rolls were in little packets that looked like bags of cement, and when the chairman wanted salt, an engineer brought it on a tiny travelling crane. The ice cream was brought in on mortarboards and served with trowels. Upon the menu the courses were described as 'grout', 'underpinning', 'brickwork', 'joinery' and 'finishings'.

It certainly was not the sort of society event normally reported by the *Daily Telegraph*. All the same, its commentator conceded that it was 'a very delightful and novel evening'. A well-known comedian of the day, Billy Bennett, provided entertainment, and humorously 'dropped a few bricks' according to another press report.

On the night Vincent Gluckstein was quoted as saying that he hoped the club would also be open to foremen from other companies. This never happened. Membership was confined to Bovis employees only, and became so popular that the initial 50 members had doubled by 1939. The novelties of the first dinner became a tradition: the waiters' dress; the whistle blowing; the beer cans; the tradition of an eminent guest. Guvnors' Club speakers of the 1930s were: Sidney Bernstein, Shaw Desmond, Maurice Webb, Grey Warnum, Carre de Behague and Howard Robertson.

Vincent Gluckstein's second big idea in the 1930s was the Building Centre in London. The idea came from his visit to the Architects' Samples Bureau in New York in 1929. It was a showroom 'in which were assembled samples of the materials and

48 *Menus for the Guvnors' Club always feature a construction theme. The first menu in 1929 is one of the simplest.*

49 *Ransomes and Rapier gave the first Guvnors' Club this immaculate silver 'cocktail shaker' which is placed on the top table to this day.*

48

49

50 *The Building Centre in Store Street was Vincent Gluckstein's idea. He visited the Architects' Samples Bureau in New York in 1929 and thought London needed a similar institution. It remains a thriving organisation.*

50

equipment an architect would use in a particular building, and to which he could bring the client'. Like the Guvnors' Club, the Building Centre is still a thriving institution today. On his return from New York, Vincent invited a number of leading architects to a lunch at the Carlton Hotel and explained his plan. Vincent reckoned that manufacturers would be happy to pay for a permanent display, and that it would be self-financing. The concept was greeted with much enthusiasm. Architects were tired of being bombarded with product literature and samples, and welcomed an alternative method of keeping up with new products. Many more informal meetings took place over the next two years, and the Architectural Bureau held its first board meeting in December 1931. Vincent and Sidney Gluckstein both became directors, so too were Bovis men C. Collett and H. Wolff. Bovis also provided the start-up capital of £11,000. The records show that Sidney attended 45 meetings in the first twelve months of operation and Vincent attended 41.

The board adopted the snappier title of Building Centre Ltd in February 1932, and agreed to lease premises at 158 New Bond Street, and carry out the necessary alterations. Ironically for the showcase of London building, this work was late and overbudget, and Bovis 'lent' a foreman and estimator to sort things out. The Building Centre opened on 7 September 1932 with Frank Yerbury as managing director and Vincent's brother-in-law, Leonard Fischer, as business manager. Financial problems dogged its early years, and the records show that the Glucksteins gave unstinting support. In his book *Forty Years On – The Success Story of the Building Centre 1932–71*, Ian M. Leslie pays tribute to their public-spirited attitude and acknowledges that the Building Centre would not have succeeded without them. It is possible that Vincent Gluckstein initially intended the Building Centre to become a Bovis subsidiary, yet whether he did or not, his support and enthusiasm for success of the Building Centre remained undiminished.

A less praise-worthy initiative was Bovis's first, and disastrous, foray into a foreign market. During late 1934 or early 1935, Vincent Gluckstein visited Palestine, now part of modern Israel, at the invitation of Victor Konn, a Haifa resident. The three Bovis board directors then formed a 'small limited company', Eastern Holdings, with Victor Konn as a shareholder and instructed him to buy a piece of land in Haifa for £17,000.

In July 1935 the board resolved to pursue work in Palestine due 'to the immense opportunities which the development of Palestine offers to builders at the present time'. The directors saw Palestine as a 'stepping stone' to work in the Middle East, and formed a subsidiary called Haifa Holdings, which actually bought the Haifa site. Bovis gave Konn power of attorney in Palestine, and sent out Roderick McLeod to take control of development work, which initially comprised one small office block.

Things began to go wrong almost immediately. By June 1936 Sidney Gluckstein had visited Palestine again. Subsequent board discussions highlighted 'insufficient experience of working in Palestine' and 'the extreme pressure of business in England' as good reasons for leaving. However, Bovis started two further projects on the Haifa site, as well as contracts for the English Girls' School in Haifa and St George's School in Jerusalem. Perhaps Bovis should have left.

The next mention of Palestine in the archives is in June 1938. This records the appointment of Alexander Blumenfeld to institute proceedings 'in the matter of a claim by Bovis Ltd of London against Mr Victor Konn of Bath-Galim, Haifa, in the amount of £153,580'. This litigation dragged on, and was last mentioned at a board meeting in June 1944. Konn was a con-man and Roger Dawe reckons the loss was

51

51 *In 1939 Bovis built an air-raid shelter in Derby for its valued client Prudential Assurance, whose Bovis-built premises are illustrated above.*

eventually written off. As an introduction to the perils of contracting abroad it was a salutary lesson.

Events nearer to home were a more pressing concern in the late 1930s, as the preparation for war moved to the top of the national agenda. The rebuilding of the German military machine caused considerable disquiet, even if most people believed that war was unlikely. As early as 1936 men from the Territorial Army were mustered, and plans made for civilian evacuation and air-raid precautions. Yet in general it was business as usual right up until the declaration of war. From a modern perspective this failure to face reality is shameful. Harold Macmillan's memoirs point out that decisive British military action after Hitler marched into the Rhineland in 1936 would have prevented the Second World War. However, in the prevailing atmosphere of appeasement and pacifism Hitler was allowed to get away with more and more.

Business was booming for Bovis in this pre-war period, as the relationship with Marks & Spencer flourished. Bovis was awarded over 40 M&S contracts in 1936 alone, and this intensity of work continued right up to the outbreak of the Second World War. In fact from the first contract in Wood Green through to September 1939, M&S had placed an astonishing total of 370 contracts with Bovis.

Regular clients like United Dairies, Timothy Whites and Times Furnishings also continued to operate on the Bovis System, and there were new clients such as Pyrene and W&R Jacobs. Bovis built eleven more Granada cinemas for Bernstein Theatres between 1936 and 1939, and other retail clients included Woolworths, Freeman Hardy and Willis and Prices Tailors. In Coventry Bovis erected a large department store for Owen Owen, and in Birmingham constructed the city's tallest building, the nine-storey Times Furnishing store. At the same time, Bovis built factories in London and Liverpool, and a foundry in Leeds. There were public houses in London, Cheltenham and Gloucester, as well as the Hackney Synagogue. In 1938 Bovis opened a branch office in Manchester under Fred Cosford, and one of its first projects was the Manchester Dental Hospital.

Reminders of the storm gathering across the Channel were never far away. From April 1938 there were many board-level discussions about air-raid precautions and evacuation plans. Two Manchester papers reported a strike on a site where Bovis was building a militia camp at Moore, near Warrington in early 1939, although strangely this project does not appear in the company records. Bovis also won a contract to build 39 air-raid shelters for W&R Jacobs at Aintree, and a garage and air-raid shelter for Prudential Assurance at Derby. Naturally Bovis also built its own air-raid shelters at Oxgate and Stanhope Gate, and took the precaution of joining the Property Owners' War Risks Mutual Society. The company formed a committee to make grants 'in cases of hardship arising from members of the staff being called up for service'. And Sidney Gluckstein issued a memorandum to younger staff announcing paid leave of absence to attend camp if they joined the Territorials.

Remarkably the Bovis Social club organised a trip to Paris over Easter weekend in 1939, just four months before the declaration of war. John Gillham recalled it cost £5 each for the train fares and two nights bed and breakfast. It was a light-hearted break. A fellow reveller remembered how one man left his wife behind in the hotel and went out with his friends for a drink. When the party returned to the hotel, they tied the chap to his bed with a bra borrowed from an obliging female colleague. The next day they teased him about a woman that he had insisted on taking to bed. He looked white, and said 'does my wife know?' They never told him the real story.

52

52 *The Gaumont Cinema in Holloway Road, London, completed in 1938.*

53 *Bovis' popular Compactom furniture range expanded to include this tea trolley, marketed from 1937.*

Bovis was 30 years old in 1938, and the directors realised that the company should give some sort of reward for long service. At the Annual General Meeting in 1939 the company began the presentation of silver salvers to employees with 25 years' service. It was a further illustration of 'business as usual' right up to the declaration of war. A special cloud hung over the Glucksteins. This was not a good time to be Jewish and news of the Nazi persecution of the Jews was highly alarming. The widespread destruction of Jewish property in Germany and Austria on Kristalnacht on 9 November 1938 made a particular impact. A flood of refugees began to appear in Britain. Openly racist political parties were in the ascendant all over Europe; Britain had the likes of Oswald Mosley and his fascists. In this climate of fear, one practical solution was to try to hide racial origin by a change of name.

For once the Bovis directors could not agree a common policy, although this was obviously a very personal matter. Vincent Gluckstein was always known as 'Mr Vincent', so he decided to become Vincent E. Vincent in 1937. Sidney Gluckstein opted for the surname 'Glyn', partly because his poor handwriting already made his signature look like 'Glyn'. To complicate matters further, their brother Samuel Gluckstein decided against a change of name, but both his sons took a new surname. Thus Harry, who joined the company in 1931, and Neville Gluckstein became Harry and Neville Vincent respectively. It was an effective, if confusing, disguise and from now on this book will refer to Sidney Glyn, V. E. Vincent, Harry Vincent and Neville Vincent. The Josephs would not consider a change of name.

When the storm clouds broke on 3 September 1939, Bovis faced its first serious crisis for a decade. The golden age of the Bovis System was history; retail and commercial building contracts dropped off the edge of a cliff, and for Bovis directors the future could not have looked more bleak.

53

CHAPTER 5

Wartime and reconstruction

On 3 September 1939 Prime Minister Neville Chamberlain announced 'this country is now at war with Germany' in a radio broadcast. It came as no surprise to anybody. Conflict had become inevitable as Hitler's war machine rolled across Europe and the invasion of Poland proved the final straw. A period of controlled panic followed in the phoney war of the first six months, when very little actually happened, and the population occupied itself with preparations for air-raids.

As in the First World War, key Bovis men were drafted into the war effort. V. E. Vincent was called up as a member of the Royal Air Force Voluntary Reserve. George Lewsey, John Gillham, Roger Dawe and Harry Vincent also marched off to war, and managing director Paul Gilbert was later seconded to the Ministry of Works for a period as Director of Building Programmes. At Bovis board meetings air-raid precautions were high on the agenda. The board decided to evacuate staff to the Oxgate premises in an emergency, otherwise business would continue at Stanhope Gate. However, work on the Stanhope Gate air-raid shelter was not finished by September 1939, so as a temporary measure Sidney Glyn 'secured permission from Trollope & Colls to take possession of a shop in Leconfield House'. The directors gave Paul Gilbert the task of equipping it as a temporary shelter and sandbagging the walls.

Fred Cosford was in charge of the Manchester office and spoke of 'the panic about war'. In particular, he recalled a car journey from London to Manchester with 'a bloke going past me towing a caravan and driving like a madman. The caravan was in the air most of the time'. Future Bovis managing director Herbert Cruickshank remembered the outbreak of war for a different reason. He got married the day before war broke out and had to cancel his honeymoon due to Paul Gilbert's concern that 'We might get called by a client to build more air-raid shelters or something. . .My wife was marvellous about it'. Paul Gilbert was right. Bovis was asked to construct air-raid shelters for Marks & Spencer, Prudential Insurance, Marylebone Borough Council and the Portman Estate. Bovis also built a shelter as far away as Plymouth for J. Hepworth and Sons. Herbert Cruickshank thought it was 'childish stuff' in retrospect, and remembered the company being involved in digging trenches in Hyde Park, the purpose of which was not entirely clear.

There was an element of farce to the phoney war. Another example was the Manchester office's contract to build a gun site. For security reasons the only information provided was a piece of Ordinance Survey map six inches square. It showed part of the Manchester Ship Canal and a railway bridge running over it; as a

54

54 *Preparation for air-raids proved an immediate pre-occupation in the six months of phoney war. Bovis installed many air-raid shelters for its clients.*

55 *The declaration of war on 3 September 1939 signalled a change of direction for Bovis in support of the nation's war effort.*

56

56 *Workmen remove the railings in Hyde Park, opposite the Bovis headquarters in Stanhope Gate. Trenches were also dug in the park.*

result Fred Cosford had to buy a bigger map to work out the 'secret' location. He then went to a contractors' meeting in Chester and was addressed by 'a major left over from the last war, with an old uniform which did not meet in the middle'. The major said a clerk of works would show the contractors the site. They soon became lost and Fred Cosford led the way. He recalled: 'We got to a spot where there was a field full of corn and people cutting it with sickles, so my clerk of works went up to them and said: "Is this where they're going to build a gun site?" and they said "yes". Despite all the security, it was apparently common knowledge'.

The National Federation of Building Trades Employers warned as far back as June 1936 that the release of an immense number of government contracts would have 'an inflationary effect on costs in an industry already becoming overheated'. Its observations went unheeded. The war effort soon caused manpower shortages and wage inflation in the building trade. Press advertisements appeared offering £7–8 per week, more than double the basic wage for craftsmen at that time.

For Bovis the 'childish stuff' of the phoney war came to an early and abrupt end in October 1939 with the award of the contract to build the Swynnerton munitions factory in Staffordshire. This was the largest job in the company's history, and was part of the Government's strategy to relocate munitions production to the countryside. There were to be eight new factories on a number of greenfield sites hidden from enemy air-raids. Sir Samuel Joseph is generally credited with winning the giant Swynnerton contract. His City and Government connections were strong and senior people from many industries were in constant discussions with the Government on how to harness industry to the war effort. In this climate of panic, the newly formed Ministry of Supply called in a number of large companies and quickly handed out contracts and told them to get on with the work. The authorities thought air-raids were imminent and that the existing Woolwich Arsenal was an obvious target. The estimated cost of the Swynnerton munitions factory was £5 million, and the Ministry of Supply decided to split the project. Bovis won the contract to do the building work and John Mowlem & Sons was responsible for the civil engineering package.

Plant and labour manager Herbert Cruickshank was the first on site: 'Three weeks after war was declared, I was called to Gilbert's office. He said "Cruickshank, we're going to do the biggest job Bovis has ever done. I want you to go to a place called Swynnerton, it's near Stafford, and meet a civil engineer called Ash of Sir Alexander Gibb and Partners. You've got to decide with him where to put your plant and labour departments on the site". I went up by car and met Ash, and remember looking over a five-barred gate into a field and him saying, "Well, Mr Cruickshank, this is the boundary on this side and we've got 1000 acres over there to build on. I suggest we put a main road here and I suggest you put your plant department and site offices here" and that is what we did'.

Paul Gilbert was in overall charge, although he returned to London every Friday, ready to report to the board on Monday. Cruickshank took up residence on site, and the accounts department set up in nearby Eccleshall under George Mott. Freddie Miles and Sidney Proops stayed at the Ash Hall Hotel near Hanley during the erection of accommodation on site. Sidney was the husband of Marjorie Proops, who later became a famous newspaper columnist.

At its peak the Swynnerton project employed 11,500 people on site, including 50

57 *The Government made construction of munitions factories a priority, and Bovis built a huge munitions complex at Swynnerton in Staffordshire and a smaller factory at Featherstone near Wolverhampton.*

57

58

58 *Managing director Paul Gilbert, seconded to the Ministry of Works as director of building programmes.*

59

59 *Wilfrid Ash worked with Bovis on the Swynnerton munitions factory. After the war Bovis formed a lump-sum contract division called Gilbert-Ash.*

Bovis general foremen. Freddie Downing recalled that there were over a hundred architects and draftsmen to 'translate the original pencil sketches into proper drawings'. Some Bovis staff brought their wives. Joyce Miles worked for the quantity surveyor's office and Herbert Cruickshank's wife worked for Bovis. Freddie Downing was single, but fell in love with the catering supervisor, Pat Seymour of J. Lyons, and returned to London a married man.

The supply of labour was at a premium. As Herbert Cruickshank remembered: 'Site labour was recruited from outlying towns as far south as Wolverhampton, Stoke and the Potteries. Special trains and coaches ran daily. Men recruited from London were housed in camps constructed on site – a really massive housing operation'. Labour supply was still a problem. One day Sir Samuel Joseph called Cruickshank back to London and told him: 'I want you to teach women how to lay bricks and after that I want you to teach women carpentry and painting.' Bovis established a training school for female employees and Cruickshank recruited 'some pretty hefty women who worked as labourers in the brick and tile factories in the Potteries'. Harry Wheeler, one of the best foremen, was their instructor. The scheme was regarded as a great success.

Cost control was rather less successful at Swynnerton. A report to parliament in 1941 contained a revised figure of £7.6 million. Later, in 1941, the Auditor-General Sir Gilbert Charles Upcott commented that 'costs would be more than 40 per cent higher than the original estimate' and would total £15 million. His report did not pinpoint the reason for the cost over-run. Herbert Cruickshank remembered 'not only design and redesign as the work progressed, but the very considerable programme of new hostels for the munitions workers'. Sir Gilbert's estimate in fact proved too pessimistic. The final cost of the huge Swynnerton munitions complex was £13.6 million.

The Swynnerton project did not initially involve the Manchester office. Fred Cosford in Manchester was kept busy finishing contracts started before the war, notably the Manchester Dental Hospital, work for Owen Owen in Liverpool and a factory for Reynolds Chains in Manchester. Of course, there was also the 'secret' gun site on the Manchester Ship Canal. On completing these projects in 1940, Fred Cosford recalled Paul Gilbert telling him to 'come back to London and take over what we've left down here and then come up to Swynnerton when you've finished'. He found the Bovis headquarters in Stanhope Gate almost deserted since 80 per cent of the staff were either in the forces or working at Swynnerton, and the balance had been evacuated to Cheltenham.

In May 1940 the board took a three-year lease on Hillcrest, a house in Battledown, Cheltenham, and two other properties nearby. It had abandoned an earlier plan to evacuate to Newbury for some reason, and the accounts and insurance departments moved into Hillcrest almost immediately. 'Hillcrest was a lovely house with a big garden,' according to Margaret Henderson who worked in the insurance department. 'Our accommodation was in two houses which had been joined together and within walking distance of the office. We had a housekeeper, Mrs Adshead, who had worked for the Joseph family. It was through the family that we got her. She ran the place with two foreign girls. We didn't have to pay for anything. We were allowed a weekend leave every fortnight. I used to travel up by coach and sleep in the air-raid shelter at Stanhope Gate.'

The Bovis School of Building was an early casualty of the war. The principal Eric

60 *As part of the war effort, Bovis established a training school for women bricklayers, carpenters and painters. Herbert Cruickshank recruited 'some pretty hefty women who worked as labourers in the brick and tile factories in the Potteries'.*

61 *Evacuation of children from London. Bovis took a three-year lease on a house in Battledown, Cheltenham, and evacuated staff and families from the accounts and insurance departments.*

60

61

62 Vose went to join a ministry in Newcastle, and at the last graduation ceremony diplomas were presented to Leonard Thompson, Ronald Stotter, Bryan Cooper, Michael Holme, Anthony Knapp, Joseph Cousins, David Rolfe and Henry Malycon. Sadly, Anthony Knapp was later killed in action while serving with the Royal Air Force. The Bovis board voted to pay staff called up for military service the difference between their services pay and Bovis salary at the outbreak of war. This practice later changed, so that only men with dependants received an allowance. In addition, the company paid life insurance premiums for everyone, and gave remaining staff a special war bonus in 1940.

In February 1940 Lady Joseph also started a Bovis and Subsidiaries Comforts Club to send clothing and other items to staff in the forces. This club sent a record 180 parcels in 1944. The reactions of recipients varied. John Gillham said: 'They were absolutely fantastic. Knitted balaclavas, gloves and practical things like toilet paper and soap'. George Lewsey felt differently, 'Woollen socks and gloves were not much use to me – I spent five years in the western desert'.

The Government soon imposed a £500 limit on non-essential building work, as in the First World War, and the limit fell to £100 in 1941. However, food processors still had licences to build, and in 1940 United Dairies awarded Bovis contracts at Herne Hill in London, Highbridge in Somerset and Whitland in Carmarthenshire. United Dairies also asked Bovis to 'set up a twenty-four hours a day, seven days a week emergency service in case of bomb damage to their London bottling plants'. Fred Cosford recruited a gang of men for this purpose, put a toilet in the air-raid shelter at the Oxgate factory and the men slept in the shelter with the lorry outside. He recalled: 'I told them if they got a call from United Dairies about bomb damage they must phone me straight away. . .and every time the blighters went out I had to go with them. I'd drive over from Northwood in the pitch dark wondering when I was going to fall into a crater.'

Daytime gangs were also in demand from clients such as Marks & Spencer, although as Fred Cosford remarked: 'In a lot of cases we couldn't do much except cut off services, salvage what we could and clear up. The buildings were past hope.' The first recorded contract for 'the reinstatement of premises damaged by a bomb' was in November 1940 when a bomb hit the retailer Whiteleys of Queensway. During this period bombs rained down on London causing terrible damage and loss of life throughout the city.

In late 1940 a bomb fell on the Hatton Street joinery works, and as a result Compactom transferred to Oxgate. May Ball remembered: 'I heard the explosion and then someone came running in and told me to get out. We found out afterwards that two workmen were killed. . .we couldn't continue to work at Hatton Street anymore, and we went to Oxgate, where we continued to make ammunition boxes, army huts and things like that'. A bomb narrowly missed the Bovis headquarters at 1 Stanhope Gate in April 1941. Fred Cosford went to investigate: 'We couldn't see Sam Joseph's Daimler, but we could see the top of Sidney's Wolseley – it had a steel girder going right through it. I remember Sidney coming in the next morning and saying 'They don't like us Cosford, do they?'.

Reinstatement of premises razed by the Luftwaffe became a considerable source of new building orders. Fred Cosford recalled how Bovis repaired the damage in the Coventry branch of Owen Owen in late 1940, but the very day they finished working the store was bombed absolutely flat: 'I remember our foreman ran miles through the

62 *St Paul's Cathedral from Fleet Street on the morning after a heavy bombing raid. The Ludgate bridge survived the Blitz, but was removed by Bovis as part of the Ludgate redevelopment project in the early 1990s.*

63

63 *Bombs rained down on London. Bovis formed daytime gangs for clients such as Marks & Spencer to help clear up bomb damage and cut off services.*

64 *A single bomb devastated Bank underground station outside the Bank of England. The City office buildings constructed by Bovis in the 1920s and 1930s were largely destroyed.*

64

65

city to where his wife and family was sheltering. The shelter had been hit, but they were all right'.

In Birmingham during 1941 repairs and reconstruction were carried out for Fisher and Ludlow, Tangyes Ltd, Bakelite Ltd, William Newman and Son, and Smith and Davies. However, wartime mobilisation meant that the Government was still responsible for letting the majority of contracts. When the Oxgate joinery factory became short of work in 1940, the board approached the Ministry of Supply for alternative production. The result was that Oxgate was commissioned to make 5.5 inch howitzer shells, and the board announced the appointment of a Mr Bessell as manager. Sidney Glyn voiced his disquiet at the lack of progress at the board meeting of 18 March 1941. The minutes note: 'Mr Glyn again mentioned that he was extremely apprehensive of Mr Bessell's capacity to get the shell factory into production, or keep it working at maximum efficiency'.

Whatever the outcome of the shell factory, Bovis was successful in winning the contract for another munitions factory in late 1940. This smaller £2-million project was located at Featherstone near Wolverhampton, and Herbert Cruickshank was again the first man on the site. Bovis also had a Government contract to build pre-cast concrete huts in various parts of Oxfordshire and Hertfordshire in 1941.

In mid-1941 Government policy shifted away from prime-cost contracting, and towards lump-sum awards. Bovis responded by forming Bovis (Public Works) Ltd in order to pursue lump-sum contracts. In fact, there was usually no time for the tendering process, and the authorities appointed a contractor on the basis of an agreed schedule of rates. The final lump sum did not generally emerge until the completion of the project. Bovis (Public Works) Ltd won contracts for two residential estates for factory workers in April 1941: one for 114 houses and 36 flats at Newport, and a second for 100 houses and 100 flats at Blackpole, Worcester. An article in *Architectural Review* in September 1942 mentions the finished estate in Worcester, although it kept the exact location secret. And in early 1942, Bovis won its third contract to build a munitions factory, this time at Padiham in Lancashire.

During 1942, in the depths of the war, Sir Samuel Joseph was elected Lord Mayor of London. He was 54 years old at the time. Press reaction to his appointment was very favourable, and the newspapers made much of his impressive record in the First World War and of his Jewish origins. At a time when the current chairman of Bovis, Sir Frank Lampl, found himself incarcerated in a concentration camp in Poland, London was rallying to the Jewish cause. As the newspapers pointed out, the runner-up for the Lord Mayor's post, Sir Frank Pollitzer, was also Jewish.

Sir Samuel Joseph was unstinting in his duties. Londoners were heartened by the symbols of tradition amid the privations of wartime, and the Lord Mayor stood alongside the monarchy and Prime Minister Winston Churchill as symbols of the bulldog spirit which refused to bow before Nazi ideology. Sir Samuel received a baronetcy in November 1943 in recognition of his wartime contribution, yet most of Sir Samuel's wartime duties were part of his role as Lord Mayor of London and had little to do with the Bovis story. The exception to this rule was a dinner he gave to mark his appreciation of the Bovis staff in July 1943. 'I have never forgotten it. We had a decent meal for a change,' said Louise Tolmie. 'There was entertainment with Vera Lynn, Jewel and Warris and Tommy Trinder,' added Eileen Gertsch. And Herbert Cruickshank commented, 'I can confirm the excitement and pleasure of attending Sir Samuel's dinner at the Mansion House – especially my wife's'.

65 *Bovis repaired bomb damage to the Coventry branch of Owen Owen in late 1940, but on the day of completion the store was bombed flat.*

66

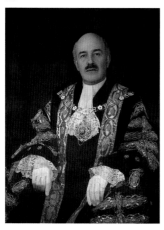

66 *Sir Samuel Joseph became Lord Mayor of London in 1942 and gave himself unstintingly to his duties. One of the two cousins who bought C.W. Bovis & Co, Sir Samuel received a baronetcy in 1943 in recognition of his contribution to the war effort.*

67 *On 3 July 1943 Sir Samuel Joseph invited Bovis staff to dinner at the Mansion House. For many it proved a welcome change from the austerity of rationing.*

68 *The invitation to the Mansion House dinner.*

Sir Samuel did not attend any board meetings while he was Lord Mayor of London. However, he kept in regular contact with the company. As Tony Braddon, who joined in 1942 as a school leaver, recalled: 'My first months in Bovis were spent scuttling back and forth between Stanhope Gate and the City taking company papers to Sir Samuel Joseph.' Nonetheless, Sir Samuel's elevation does appear to have had one notable impact on company history. It seems to have prompted the London Master Builders' Association to invite Bovis to rejoin, after a breach of some twenty years. The LMBA executive which Bovis had sued in 1926 had long gone, and the industry had widely recognised the leadership which Sidney and Vincent Gluckstein demonstrated in forming the Building Centre. The building establishment embraced the former renegade Bovis and the firm was re-elected to the LMBA in November 1942. In October 1943 the Association gave a lunch at the Savoy in honour of Sir Samuel.

The rechristened Ministry of Works and Planning kept Bovis busy in 1943 with new contracts for three airfields in Lincolnshire, Essex and Norfolk, and the building of a new emergency hospital at Sudbury in Suffolk. In January 1944 *Contractors Record* reported that Bovis had won another Ministry of Works contract. Security considerations concealed its identity, but it was probably the commando camp at Bursledon in Hampshire. Fred Cosford said: 'The site was in a thickly wooded area, and to camouflage it as much as possible, we were instructed to fell trees only where the huts were sited. The result was that some unfelled trees were so close to the huts you could not open the windows.'

Staff were returning to London from the giant Swynnerton and Featherstone projects, and found plenty of repair work in the capital. Around this time Bovis became involved in the preparations for the D-Day invasion of Europe and the construction of the vast Mulberry harbours to be towed across the Channel to service the invasion fleet. In size and scope the Mulberry harbours were equivalent to the challenge of constructing the Channel tunnel, and they were built in nine months.

The project had an inauspicious beginning. In September 1943, 50 or 60 representatives from the country's top building and civil engineering firms assembled in Portsmouth Dockyard, among them, Paul Gilbert and Herbert Cruickshank from Bovis. Herbert Cruickshank learned of the meeting the day before:

I got a telephone call from Gilbert. "Cruickshank, I want you to meet me in Portsmouth Dockyard tomorrow." Nobody knew why we were there except that we had got to do some building work in the dockyard. Suddenly an adjutant in full dress came in and said: "Please stand for the admiral." Gilbert didn't like being told what to do by a junior, but we all stood.
In came the admiral looking magnificent in his hat, braid and full regalia. Even Gilbert was impressed. The admiral told us we could sit down. He remained standing. He said: "Gentlemen, I understand you have been deputed to do some work in my dockyard. I must tell you that I don't like it one bit. It is important work but I don't know what it is. I want you to obey navy discipline and secrecy and I want you to behave in a responsible manner. Thank you gentlemen." and he walked out. Gilbert turned to me and said, "magnificent".

The authorities told the assembled contractors that they were to build huge concrete caissons called 'Boom Defence Units', code named 'Phoenix'. Their impression was that these units would be for repairs to British harbours in the event of damage by

67

68

enemy action. The contractors were not told that the massive caissons were sections of a unique floating harbour to be towed across the Channel for the invasion of Europe. A month earlier in Quebec, the Allies had agreed the strategy, 'Operation Overlord'. Military chiefs realised that attempting to capture the heavily defended Channel ports would be difficult, and would lack the element of surprise. An alternative strategy was to land on the beaches of Normandy, and establish a bridgehead for the invasion. But that meant installing new portable harbours to allow rapid offloading of the invasion force and the maintenance of supply lines.

Code-named 'Mulberry', a number of different elements formed the harbour, with concrete caissons joined end-to-end to form the harbour wall and pontoon-supported roadways. The authorities stressed the need for teamwork between contractors. Portsmouth only had two dry docks, and needed one of these for the repair and servicing of warships. So Bovis and Laing had to share the second bomb-damaged dry dock, and built six units each. On the toss of a coin Laing was landed with the bomb-damaged end of the dock. The Phoenix caissons were watertight

69

69 & **70** *Thirty concrete caissons were constructed by Bovis for the temporary Mulberry harbours which played a vital part in the D-Day invasion. Bovis foreman Dudley Wheeler received the British Empire medal for his role in saving the caissons.*

structures with 18 compartments each, 200 feet long and 60 feet high. Portsmouth dry dock was large enough to build four caissons at the same time, and work went on around the clock. Caissons reached a height of 25 feet in the dry dock and were then towed to a wet dockside for completion.

Freddie Downing has distinct memories of the time. The first thing he noticed was that both Bovis and Laing had set up their concrete batching plants at the bottom of the dry dock. When the dock was filled with water, the engines were removed. The concrete mixers, barrows and scaffold then remained under water until the dock emptied again, and work could resume.

When the caissons floated out the contractors took great care to balance the concrete structures in the water. Freddie Downing recalled that the authorities did not allow the use of concrete pumps because: 'We would often get a blockage in the pipe with the result that the unit was in danger of tilting over and you could not get the pipes across to another section quickly enough. We decided that the old way was best – an army of barrow runners.' The Oxgate joinery works also became involved in the construction of the Mulberry harbours. Charlie Austin remembered: 'We used to make all the shuttering for the concrete units – three-quarter inch plywood in huge sheets which had to be cut into different shapes, and hundreds of ladders 12 feet long, all pine and reinforced with wire down the sides'.

Pauling & Co were building nine more caissons in Southampton nearby, and Bovis was called in to help when Pauling fell badly behind schedule. Freddie Downing was sent over with a gang: 'At Southampton you get two tides of 17 feet. The units were going up and down like yo-yos. Anyway, Ernie Page, one of the foremen made the mistake of taking the concrete too far on one side, the unit tilted and water started pouring in through some scaffold holes low down.' Bovis foreman Dudley Wheeler quickly went down inside the unit and opened some valves on the other side. He later received the British Empire medal for this prompt action which had the effect of balancing the caisson, but nothing could prevent the unit sinking to the bottom. 'When it hit the mud' recalled Downing, 'it started sliding and ended up in the middle of Southampton water. A team of divers went out to raise the caisson. It took them a week to get it back in the dock.'

But this incident proved to be a blessing in disguise. The War Office had planned to sink the caissons and then refloat them for D-Day, but thanks to this experience it realised the problems involved in refloating the units and subsequently allowed enough time to do so successfully. By D-Day on 6 June 1944 Bovis had finished 15 caissons and was working on another 15 at Barking Creek and Merseyside. In all the 24 contractors had made a total of 147 caissons. Despite severe weather conditions the two Mulberry harbours were successfully installed by July, providing a vital supply line to the invasion force. More than 50 years later the remains of 30 Phoenix caissons survive, a lasting reminder of the contractors' contribution to the D-Day landing.

Sir Samuel was in the chair for the board meeting of 23 August 1944 to congratulate Bovis on this achievement. But on 26 September *The Times* reported that 'Sir Samuel Joseph is indisposed and, on medical advice, is taking a complete rest for some weeks'. In his absence, Sidney Glyn chaired the next board meeting on

70

4 October, and the minutes record that the directors had commissioned a miniature painting of Lady Joseph to commemorate Sir Samuel's year as Lord Mayor. Unfortunately Sir Samuel never saw the miniature, as he died on the day of the board meeting. At their next assembly the directors recorded: 'Their profound grief at losing not only a wise counsellor and esteemed colleague, but one who was held by them all in the highest affection.' In 34 years Sir Samuel had led the transformation of Bovis from a small London builder into one of the great names of British construction. It was a sad loss as the war drew to a close.

Victory in Europe in May 1945 was greeted with relief and euphoria, tempered only by the continuing war against Japan. Demobilised Bovis staff began to trickle back to Stanhope Gate. Two men were decorated for gallantry: Major John Gillham of the Royal Artillery received the Military Cross; and warrant officer Ron Leonard was awarded the Distinguished Flying Medal.

There was a great deal of discussion at board meetings about the right strategy in the post-war era. It was not easy to see the way forward. Air-raids meant that office closing time was 5.30pm during the war and it was symptomatic of the shortage of contracts that the board extended this practice in May 1945 'while present conditions last'. Bovis System work was minimal, and was confined to projects at Cardiff and Crewe for United Dairies. War damage repairs were obviously a diminishing market. Competition for public works was fierce, as demonstrated by a list of 50 contractors tendering for public works in Guildford in 1944. Joinery manufacturing activity was low and no Compactom wardrobes had been made since before the war. But gradually a new business strategy emerged.

In January 1946 Paul Gilbert was promoted from an employee to ordinary director of Bovis Ltd. The same board meeting resolved to change the name of Bovis (Public Works) Ltd to Gilbert-Ash Ltd, and that this company 'shall carry out building and civil engineering contracts for public and private bodies, whether secured by tender or private negotiation'. The idea was to ensure that Bovis was only associated with work carried out under the Bovis System. The name Gilbert-Ash came from a combination of Paul Gilbert's surname, and that of Wilfrid Ash, the civil engineer involved with Swynnerton.

Gilbert-Ash Ltd was incorporated in February 1946, and Paul Gilbert set about recruiting staff. One person approached was Herbert Cruickshank, also of Swynnerton fame, who joined after an assurance that he was still an employee of the Bovis Group. Another recruit was Sir Keith Joseph, the son of the late Sir Samuel, who had inherited the baronetcy. In November 1946 he was appointed to a committee formed to study the organisation and expenditure of the plant department.

Lord Joseph remembered: 'My first job was the British Plaster Board factory at East Leake. One day I was helping to dig a drain trench, and being young and keen, really put my back into it. And one of the labourers said to me: 'Steady on Guv'nor, all of us are in this for life.' It was a muddy debut for a man destined to become mentor to the future Prime Minister Margaret Thatcher and a senior cabinet minister in the 1980s. Sir Keith's Bovis career was equally meteoric. He was a main board director from 1951, but relinquished his executive responsibilities on becoming a Member of Parliament in 1956. Sir Keith resigned from the board on his appointment as a junior minister in 1959, although he returned in 1964 when Labour won the General Election. After relinquishing his seat in Mrs Thatcher's cabinet, he came back to Bovis for a third time as a non-executive director in the late 1980s.

The Bovis School of Building reopened in response to the chronic shortage of skilled men in the late 1940s, and many demobilised servicemen were offered training for a new career in civilian life. The company reconstituted the Bovis Social Club and appointed a company welfare officer, W. R. Bateman. It introduced new job titles such as contract manager, and a standardised system of expenses and allowances. Bovis also decided to restart the manufacture of Compactom furniture. The ever-ingenious Edward Pinto designed a new trolley table during the war, and in 1945 he was instructed to patent it in America and Canada. The board recorded in 1948 that 'Compactom is to operate independently out of Oxgate', yet Compactom was always something of a shadow of its pre-war glory.

Fortunately the Bovis System fared rather better with Sidney Glyn and V. E. Vincent in charge. In December 1945 Bovis landed two new contracts, one for Times Furnishing at Holborn, and the other for industrial premises at Hackney. Contracts for British Plaster Ltd factories at Nottingham and Newark followed in January 1946. But the modernisation of the old silent film studios at Shepperton for British Lion Studios was the biggest contract won in 1946. As always the Bovis System relied on personal contacts and salesmanship to explain its unique features, and its post-war revival was thus largely down to hard work by Sidney and Vincent. Things were looking up by 1947 when three Bovis System pre-war clients – Marks & Spencer, United Dairies and Owen Owen – awarded a clutch of contracts to Bovis Ltd. By 1948 eleven more M&S contracts had assured the future of the Bovis System, thoroughly vindicating the decision to separate Bovis Ltd and Gilbert-Ash.

In contrast to Bovis Ltd, the newly formed Gilbert-Ash division achieved rapid success in winning new contracts in open tender under the control of Paul Gilbert, who received an OBE for services to the building industry in the 1947 New Year's Honours List. Gilbert-Ash won a reservoir at Meriden near Coventry, schools at Stevenage and Chigwell, the Royal Marine barracks at Deal, government offices in Whitehall Place, Hatfield Technical College (now Hertfordshire University) and the celebrated Brabazon building at Filton for the Bristol Aeroplane Company. Gilbert-Ash quickly became the main revenue earner in the Bovis stable. In 1947 Herbert Cruickshank was sent to the United States to 'search out new plant' for its civil engineering operations, which had found the acquisition of new plant hampered by post-war restrictions. This trip also signalled a new interest by the board in overseas markets, and Gilbert-Ash had already secured its first overseas appointment, building a barracks in Gibraltar.

The Government had practically taken over the construction sector by the cessation of hostilities, and private building activity had ground to a halt. But as victory became assured the massive programme of military construction projects wound down, and the priority became the repair of 3.5 million bomb-damaged houses. For the building industry this was more than a repeat of the 'Homes fit for Heroes' policy of 1918. Not only had there been no house building in six years of war but over 200,000 dwellings had been destroyed by German bombing. There was a massive shortage of housing. Fortunately the Government machine had learnt some lessons from its earlier failures in housing policy. It set a national target of 100,000 new homes in the first year after the war, 200,000 the next year and a target of three to four million homes in the next decade. There was also a national commitment to a school building programme from the 1944 Education Act.

Planners saw prefabrication as the best way of speeding up construction, and a rash

71

71 *Bristol Aeroplane Company's aluminium hangar for the Comet, an early passenger jet aircraft, showing the doors erected and work started on the annex. This contract followed Bovis subsidiary Gilbert-Ash's success with prefabricated aluminium schools.*

of rather crude timber and asbestos bungalows was the result. Bovis built one of the first prefabricated housing estates at Hemel Hempstead in 1945. *Contract Journal* reported in March 'work is proceeding rapidly' and 'it is believed this is one of the most advanced schemes of temporary bungalows in the country'. This was the era of post-war austerity, and nobody pretended the 'prefabs' provided much more than a roof over your head. But they were better than not having a roof over your head at all. The pre-fab policy led to a somewhat frantic search for new building materials and techniques. Bovis became involved in several such initiatives.

Gilbert-Ash reached an agreement with the Bristol Aeroplane Company for the prefabrication of houses and school buildings using aluminium. The Bristol Aeroplane Company had suffered a catastrophic reduction in workload with the end of hostilities, and was keen to employ its design and manufacturing capacity to produce something else. Contracts for prefabricated houses in Easington and Hanley in 1948–9 followed the BAC agreement. But the real breakthrough in aluminium construction came with a contract to build a school in Coventry, and Gilbert-Ash built 20 more schools with BAC, including its own apprentice school at Filton. As late as 1956 Gilbert-Ash and BAC won a hospital contract at Benghazi in Libya using this system of prefabrication.

The Government encouraged British companies to seek out new opportunities abroad to help supply the raw materials and food desperately needed in post-war Britain. Harry Vincent visited South Africa in early 1947, and in August the directors confirmed his appointment to the board. Paul Gilbert followed in January 1948, and identified a small building company as a possible acquisition. The board sent Herbert Cruickshank and Frank Nott to Johannesburg to examine the firm and by July 1948 Gilbert-Ash South Africa Ltd was incorporated, underpinned by a £50,000 guarantee from Bovis Ltd to the Bank of South Africa. Still the company's trouble-shooter, Herbert Cruickshank spent eight months in South Africa, and witnessed the National Party's rise to power. The racist policies of the apartheid era began to emerge at this time. Bovis had an early warning to leave South Africa from an ex-Bovis surveyor called Gaiger who visited Herbert and Frank Nott in their hotel one evening. He told them to pull out. Herbert Cruickshank recalled: 'We reported this but, understandably, no action was taken.' Sidney Glyn visited South Africa in December that year.

After Herbert Cruickshank's return to the United Kingdom in late 1948, Gilbert-Ash secured a contract with the Overseas Development Corporation for 110 miles of road and bridges in Nyasaland, then a British Protectorate. The directors sent Herbert back to look after the job until a new engineer was appointed. Unfortunately the engineer resigned when he got there, and Herbert stayed for another six years. The venture was another foreign fiasco. Herbert Cruickshank told the story: 'Needless to say, for a major road contract, estimated in England, and working in a country of biblical environment, Gilbert-Ash was on to a loser from the outset. We just survived by taking on profitable building work from Shell and Unilever, and a final claim of some £80,000'. Gilbert-Ash also won the building of a brewery in Bulawayo in Southern Rhodesia, but in general its African adventure was regarded as a failure.

Closer to home, in 1948 negotiations started to buy Leslie and Company, a reputable London builder founded in 1885 by a Major Shingleton and most famous for replacing the façade of Buckingham Palace in just 13 weeks back in 1913. By the end of 1948 Bovis agreed to purchase the company for £21,475, plus a further £5000 for the right to use the name Leslie. This was a quality company and employed some interesting characters. Tom Morris tells the story of Leslie's old ganger Jimmy Golding: 'He had a shovel which he kept highly polished. I've seen him fry up his breakfast of bacon, sausages and tomatoes, holding his shovel over an open fire.'

Bovis merged its small works division, Nox Ltd, into Leslie and Company. To capitalise on the reputation of the new acquisition, the board decided to call the combined operations Leslie and Co Ltd. Directors of the new subsidiary were William Ide, Harry Vincent, H. W. Francis and R. C. Andrew, and Bovis staff moved to Leslie's more spacious premises in Kensington Square. There were many signs that life was returning to normal after the massive upheaval of wartime. Presentations for long service returned in December 1948, and the first post-war event for staff with more than 25 years' service attracted a record 71 people. The Guvnors' Club also restarted in 1948, with author and playwright J. B. Priestley as the guest of honour.

This was also to be a time of company restructuring. Before he left for South Africa in December 1948, Sidney Glyn told the directors that the Board of Trade had given provisional permission to alter the title of Bovis Ltd to Bovis Holdings Ltd. He explained: 'After the change of name became effective, it is proposed to form a subsidiary company called Bovis Ltd for the purpose of operating the Bovis System. The structure of the group would then consist of a holding company holding the shares of all the subsidiary companies, each of which would be an operating company.' Bovis Holdings Ltd was formed in March 1949. Its first board meeting was held on 12 April 1949 with Paul Gilbert in the chair. Sidney Glyn was back from South Africa, but unwell. V. E. Vincent was also absent, although he was shortly to be appointed managing director of Bovis Ltd to concentrate on the Bovis System.

Never again would Bovis go to war and face the challenges of national mobilisation. The new peace was built on solid foundations in a new world order and, ten years after the outbreak of World War Two, the restructured Bovis Holdings Ltd was in good shape to tackle the opportunities of the post-war boom. Bovis was about to find that it had never had it so good.

72

72 Bovis subsidiary Gilbert-Ash built this brewery in Bulawayo, Southern Rhodesia, but such contracts in southern Africa were not particularly successful. Bovis would return in the 1990s.

CHAPTER 6

Austerity to the sixties

73

73 *Vincent E. Vincent, founder of the Bovis System. As Vincent Gluckstein, he joined Bovis in 1919 and retired in 1952 at the comparatively young age of 58, frustrated by the slow recovery of the Bovis System after the Second World War.*

74 *Bovis chairman Sidney Glyn, formerly Sidney Gluckstein, the man who bought C.W. Bovis & Co for £750 in 1908. He was Vincent E. Vincent's older brother. In this photograph taken in 1953, Sidney Glyn was 65 years old and had spent 45 years running Bovis.*

uilding licences disappeared in the bonfire of controls of 1953, and it became much easier for private businesses to extend their premises and rebuild war damaged property. The austerity of the post-war era was lifting, but the legacy of a greatly expanded public sector remained and would continue to exert a heavy influence on the workload of the building industry for the next three decades.

In the 1950s Bovis adopted a strategy of expansion on several fronts. Firstly, the group aimed to boost its contracting business in open tender and by marketing the Bovis System. Secondly, there was also to be a renewed search for construction contracts abroad, notwithstanding the previous unhappy experiences in Palestine and Southern Africa. And finally Bovis intended to carry on investing in manufacturing ventures for the prefabrication of buildings and new materials. The chairman's report to shareholders in 1950 refers to 'the company's policy of being in the forefront of all technical developments in the building and civil engineering fields, both at home and abroad'. And he highlights the fact that the group started 1951 with 'the prospect of a record volume of work'. On the other hand, Sidney Glyn also said that subsidiaries formed to market new materials 'have again sustained losses'.

It was at this time that V. E. Vincent announced his intention to retire at the comparatively young age of 58. There was some speculation that Vincent was dismayed by the group's reliance on competitive tendering, and the slow recovery of the Bovis System. In any event, he did not sever his links with Bovis entirely; he became a consultant and concentrated his efforts on selling the Bovis System. With Sir Samuel deceased and Vincent taking a back seat, there was a vacuum at the top. However, a successor was waiting in the wings; Sidney Glyn had recruited 25-year-old Peter Trench (later Sir Peter Trench) in 1945. He finished the war as a lieutenant colonel on General Montgomery's staff and was awarded an OBE in 1945. An economist by training, his introduction to Bovis was rather unusual. Sir Peter explained:

It was my wife's birthday and I said "let's go to the Dorchester for a last lunch on a colonel's pay." There was a big party going on the other side of the grill room, and just as we were having coffee a young chap came across from the party. It was John Glyn with whom I had been at Cambridge before the war. He invited us over to meet the family and I was introduced to Sidney Glyn, who invited us down for the weekend to the family home at Newbury. At the

74

75

75 *Gilbert-Ash, the Bovis lump-sum contract division, undertook many reconstruction contracts such as this building in Whitehall Place finished in 1952.*

end of the weekend, Sidney asked me what I was going to do after I left the army. I said I didn't know, and he said "Well, I'm the chairman of Bovis, how about joining us?" and I said "Yes, when can I start." I rushed upstairs and told my wife I had a job, and she said "Marvellous, who are you with?" When I said Bovis, she said she thought it was something to do with the beef extract, and I said no, that's Bovril, and it can't be brown bread, that's Hovis. I don't know what they do! Anyway, we made a few enquiries and found out that they were builders.

Despite this opportunistic debut, Peter Trench's card was marked for higher things. The company put him on a fast-track management programme, and he completed his basic training and CIOB exams in just twelve months. On the formation of Bovis Holdings in 1949, Peter Trench became assistant managing director of Bovis Ltd, reporting to V. E. Vincent, and was the latter's natural successor in 1951 when he retired. In that year the rest of the main board directors were: Sidney Glyn, Paul Gilbert, the Earl of Albemarle (formerly Lord Bury), William Ide, Sir Keith Joseph, Harry Vincent, Charles Collett, and G. G. Thompson.

The fortunes of the Bovis System began to revive and long-standing clients of the 1930s returned. Marks & Spencer, United Dairies, Owen Owen and Times Furnishing awarded building programmes to Bovis. The company built seven new stores for Marks & Spencer and altered many existing premises between 1950 and 1954. M&S jobs brought some notable innovations to the construction industry, often at the insistence of a very particular client, Sir Simon Marks (later Lord Marks). Peter Trench recalled that Sir Simon lived in Sunningdale and had the habit of calling in on M&S projects on the 'royal route' from his house to Baker Street. 'He saw the men on site eating their lunch in pretty awful conditions and asked me why we didn't have a decent canteen. I told him that we would have one, but he would have to pay for it. He said, "I know that, and I'll pay".'

This set a trend for much better facilities on M&S sites, as well as on other Bovis projects around the country. It was not haute cuisine, but a very welcome innovation. Sir Simon also popularised the use of skips on site. Once, while he watched a gang at work he questioned the economics of shovelling rubbish into the back of a lorry. Somebody discovered that a transport contractor called George Cross had introduced a detachable skip to shift waste in a Brentford factory. Sir Simon ordered them for every M&S site, and in doing so turned the skip into a ubiquitous feature on modern building sites.

Many M&S contracts were extensions to existing stores where the amount of room on site was very limited. Legend has it that Sir Simon visited one project and was appalled by the untidiness surrounding the concrete mixer, cement silo and their attendant heaps of sand and aggregates. He suggested ready-mix concrete as an alternative. Today ready-mix is such a common building material, it is hard to believe that in the early 1950s there was only one ready-mix plant in the country, tucked away at Bedfont in Middlesex. The subsequent dictat from the same client that ready-mix concrete should be supplied to all M&S building sites 'as and when it became available' is a very significant moment in the history of this building material. Bovis soon decided to pour ready-mix wherever practical, and ready-mix concrete was arguably the most successful new building material introduced in this period.

In the 1950s Bovis also scored its first serious commercial hit in prefabrication with Intergrid, a pre-stressed concrete system designed by Building Design Partnership and patented by Gilbert-Ash. The first Intergrid project was a technical school at Worthing in 1955. Bovis built the school quickly and within budget, and the Ministry of Education liked its appearance. When Herbert Cruickshank was recalled from South Africa in 1956, he took charge of selling the Intergrid system to local authorities; over the next ten years Gilbert-Ash built more than one hundred schools and two universities using Intergrid.

Bovis adapted the system for commercial building, and built numerous office developments, including the redevelopment of the Bovis headquarters at Stanhope Gate in 1962. There was also a major extension to the West Middlesex Hospital at Isleworth and the Concorde test laboratory at Farnham. The Canadian Provinces of British Columbia and Alberta showed interest in the system, and Herbert Cruickshank made a visit to Canada in 1956. But Bovis abandoned this export initiative when he found 'the market for Intergrid schools was less than that for the London area alone'.

Gilbert-Ash had finally made its mark in prefabrication, but for Bovis the most

76 *Marks & Spencer introduced better facilities for site workers in the 1950s and revived its building programme. Bovis handed over this new Edinburgh store in 1957.*

76

important phenomenon of the post-war era was the rebirth of the Bovis System. Marks & Spencer was not the only pre-war client to return. Work for United Dairies generally consisted of building new pasteurising plants in the old dairies acquired by the group. Bovis built a new store for Owen Owen in the war-damaged Southampton city centre. The Owen Owen premises in Coventry was also completely reconstructed, attracting praise in the architectural press for both its design and the speed of construction which was attributed to the integration of the building team fostered by the Bovis System.

Yet clients still often regarded the Bovis System as a maverick alternative to lump-sum tendering, and the pre-war controversy erupted again. *The Builder* carried an article in 1952 under the heading 'Building for a fee – The Bovis System'. It credited Bovis with introducing 'an entirely different approach to building which is a good thing, both for the industry and the people it serves'. A magazine called *The Statist* featured Bovis in an article entitled 'The Professional System in Building' and *The Recorder* examined the advantages claimed by the Bovis System in 1954.

Under Peter Trench's leadership Bovis Ltd taught a new generation the mantras of the Bovis System. Maintaining the goodwill of clients was impressed on staff as a moral imperative. So too was the necessity of keeping the goodwill of the professional firms that served the clients. Relationships with professionals were important both for rapid progress on site, and because personal recommendations were often the means of securing contracts.

It is not always possible to pin down the precise reason for winning a job. Fred Cosford told of one example: 'We'd finished the Cyclotron Chamber job at Liverpool University, and one day Mr Shennon, the architect said to me: "I'm taking you to see your next job. It's at Peterlee in Durham." We set off by road and stopped for dinner. Shennon told me that the job was a factory and started drawing on the table cloth. I asked him where the drawings were and he gave me the table cloth!' This was the first factory to be constructed in the new town of Peterlee, and Bovis subsequently built two more. It proved the speed of design and construction achievable with the Bovis System, and marked a breakthrough into the public sector for Bovis Ltd, whose work had previously been confined to private contracts.

Selling the Bovis System to a sceptical client-base was an ongoing campaign and Peter Trench maintained a high public profile. He was a natural speaker, with an easy charm and an unshakeable faith in the Bovis System, and was in constant demand for public events, industry committees and press interviews. His team leadership skills were also very strong, and he was well served by several able lieutenants. Frank Holland assumed responsibility for Marks & Spencer's contracts on the retirement of Gerry Munn, the Wood Green store pioneer of 1926. Fred Cosford was placed in charge of all work for clients, except Marks & Spencer. And Ted Chandler, a Bovis employee from 1935 and head of estimating since the war, was 'the money man' in Bovis Ltd.

It was a formidable line-up of talents, and throughout the 1950s the company's workload and reputation grew in leaps and bounds, greatly aided by the renewed expansion of Marks & Spencer. In addition, there was a new crop of retail clients to boost the order book, in particular United Draperies, James Beattie and J. Sainsbury and Sons. A youthful Timothy Sainsbury spent a period in the Stanhope Gate offices being indoctrinated into the rigours of the Bovis System. Bovis also won significant new non-retail clients at this time, such as De Havillands, George Angus, Humphries

Film Laboratories and the glass manufacturer Pilkington. The difficulties encountered with the first job for Pilkington are a good demonstration of the integrity of Bovis Ltd and of the Bovis System serving a client well.

Peter Trench told the story: 'The Pilkington's laboratory at St Helen's was one of the few jobs on which we had industrial relations problems and a strike. The effect of the strike resulted in the cost of the job exceeding the estimate by 25 per cent. I went to see the Pilkington's director, and told him that I thought it unfair that Pilkington should pay because industrial relations were our responsibility and that I was going to deduct the 25 per cent. He said "You can't do that Peter." but I did. Everybody at Stanhope Gate agreed with me. Two weeks later we were awarded a Pilkington's factory in Liverpool, of which I had no prior knowledge.' This relationship with Pilkington has continued to the present day, and most recently Bovis completed an award-winning contract for a major new glass factory in Poland.

An additional source of contracts for the Bovis System came from the early development of commercial television. In 1955 Bovis Ltd was selected to convert the Air Ministry's former headquarters in Kingsway into Britain's first independent television studio. Bovis executed the contract at such a pace that the *Daily Mail* described it as '230 days of Tele-Hustle'. But the outcome was obviously satisfactory, as a similar 'Tele-Hustle' followed in 1956 to convert the Granville Theatre in Fulham into a television studio.

Before his resignation from Bovis in 1958, Peter Trench secured the largest contract to date – the construction of new offices for the Thorn Electrical Group in Upper St Martin's Lane. Thorn House was the first high-rise office building erected in London after the war. Winning the contract was definitely a personal triumph for Peter Trench, as Jules Thorn came to see him just as Thorn was about to sign the contract with another major contractor. Peter Trench recalled: 'He looked around Stanhope Gate, and then asked to see our plant yard. I took him up to Oxgate but there wasn't much to see, just a few concrete mixers. He said "There isn't much here" and I told him that was because we were so busy. He liked that and we got the job. Afterwards I asked him why he had chosen Bovis. He told me that he had gone to visit the head office of the other builder. While sitting in their waiting room, he had noticed a large crack in the plaster running down the wall. "I said to myself, if they can't look after their own place, I'm not sure I want them to be looking after mine".'

In 1957 *The Evening News* commented on the merits of the Bovis System in the construction of Thorn House: 'Such speed of construction is of immense value to owners whose new building is to be a revenue-earning asset, which must be brought into productive use as soon as possible.' This newspaper was acknowledging something that Marks & Spencer had appreciated years earlier. The construction market was still generally unaware of the paradox presented by the rival competitive tendering system. Clients were usually eager to get their buildings as fast as possible, yet they wasted precious time going through a tendering process.

At the end of 1958 Peter Trench departed to become director general of the National Federation of Building Trades Employers. As often happens the resignation of a strong personality triggered a wave of changes across the group. Peter Trench was replaced as managing director by Fred Cosford, Frank Holland became assistant managing director, and Bernard Heaphy and Freddie Downing joined the board.

In May 1959 seventy-one year old Sidney Glyn – the man who bought C. W. Bovis in 1908 – announced that he would be retiring as chairman, and would also cease to be a managing director of Bovis Holdings in January 1960. Sidney Glyn was forced into retirement by ill health. According to his son John, a ship's doctor wrongly diagnosed him as suffering from bronchial asthma on a voyage to South Africa and gave him large doses of adrenaline that greatly aggravated his actual condition of cardiac asthma. This episode left the man who bought C. W. Bovis & Co in 1908 a shadow of his former self. It was an unhappy conclusion to over half a century at the top of Bovis, although Sidney remained on the board as a director and was the group's first president.

Already a managing director of Bovis Holdings, Paul Gilbert was appointed chairman to replace Sidney Glyn and Harry Vincent was promoted as a further managing director of Bovis Holdings. The board also appointed two employee directors, Roger Dawe and Alec Emmel, who became finance director after the resignation of A. L. Scott. Furthermore, in the same year David Woodbine Parish (later Sir David Woodbine Parish) became a board director, and chairman of Bovis Ltd, and Charles Collett retired due to ill health in May 1960. Yet this was not the team that would take Bovis into the swinging sixties. Paul Gilbert was the first chairman of Bovis from outside the family, but his tenure was cut tragically short. In May 1960 Paul Gilbert and his wife travelled to the South of France for a holiday, and while unpacking he died of a heart attack. He was only 60 years old, and had spent a lifetime with Bovis, taking charge of landmark contracts such as the Swynnerton munitions factory in the Second World War.

Harry Vincent was elected chairman. His first board meeting as chairman opened with a short silence in memory of Paul Gilbert. The minutes recorded the following tribute: 'Paul Gilbert served the company well over a period of some 37 years, and its present position of high regard in the industry is due in no small measure to his sound judgement and powerful driving force. He devoted his untiring energy without cease in furthering the interests of the company.'

The new chairman was 47 and belonged to a different generation. He was very ambitious for the group and full of new ideas. His first board meeting as chairman approved a name change, in principle, for Bovis Holdings to become B. H. Group 'to avoid the continuing confusion arising at present between Bovis Holdings Ltd and Bovis Ltd'. And at the next meeting the board agreed to a rights issue of 500,000 new shares to raise new funds, and to the listing of Bovis shares in the *Financial Times*.

'Harry Vincent loved the good life and always seemed to have a glass in his hand', remembers future Bovis managing director Chris Spackman. 'He used to let junior staff borrow his flat near Cannes and speedboat out of season. My wife and I had a great time. Harry was a flamboyant character and liked nothing better than to throw a party at the Roof Garden in Kensington.' But he was also a paternalistic employer. Barry Holmes, later a Bovis Europe main board director, recalled the way Harry Vincent used to interview all apprentices personally, and how they were all marked against a score sheet. Such human touches were appreciated. Holmes' own report is marked 'Excellent – very well done H.V.' and he still has it after 45 years.

But Bovis was moving into a different era and the board announced two new appointments from outside the industry – Sir Richard Powell and the Honourable David Montagu. As managing director of Samuel Montagu & Co Ltd, David Montagu was recruited because 'his experience and knowledge in the financial world would be of value to the group'. And Harry Vincent notes in his first report to shareholders: 'Your board has decided that its deliberations would benefit from the counsel of persons with knowledge and interests outside the world of building and civil engineering. Their participation in our affairs has already been of great value.'

What the presence of these two gentlemen really signalled was that Bovis was about to become more involved in property development, and embark on a series of acquisitions. Greater activity in property development had been under discussion for a long time. The Gilbert-Ash and Leslie subsidiaries were already involved in property schemes where deferred payments were offered in exchange for negotiated contracts. And in the late 1950s the Audley Properties subsidiary undertook small retail developments at Hornchurch, Stanmore, Rickmansworth, Harringay, Peckham, Brighton, Wardour Street and Hatton Garden.

It is unfair to Paul Gilbert to suggest that the push to increase property development was entirely due to Harry Vincent. However, Paul Gilbert was a more conservative and cautious character, and would not have been as enthusiastic about the idea. The last board meeting chaired by Paul Gilbert in May 1960 took the initial steps into property. At this meeting he reported on discussions with the Scottish Widows Fund and Life Assurance Society about the formation of a joint venture property company.

The agreement with Scottish Widows, which became an important client, marked a breakthrough into large commercial developments. Bovis entered into two joint development property companies: BK Developments Ltd with Highland Engineering and Bofield Properties Ltd with Norman Hirshfield and Partners. Bovis built a twenty-storey office block in Manchester, and further offices in Glasgow, Park Lane, Reigate, Stoke and Curzon Street. In 1962 Bovis completed a block of flats in Hill Street, Mayfair.

Harry Vincent loved travel and visited America and the West Indies in 1959. He went to Australia and New Zealand in 1960 and discussed property development opportunities in these countries. The volume of work Bovis was obtaining from property companies no doubt also influenced his thinking. Harry Vincent must have seen property development as a means of obtaining better profit margins than construction. In some ways it was a return to the past, and the days of C. W. Bovis & Co doing a little speculative house building to increase profits, or the three directors speculating in retail construction on housing estates and building luxury apartment blocks in the 1930s.

Improving profits became even more of an imperative after an unsatisfactory set of financial results for 1961. Profit before taxation plunged from £261,603 to £77,052. Harry Vincent's report pointed the finger at 'trading deficits arising from increased costs on certain large firm price contracts being carried out for Government and other Public Authorities by Gilbert-Ash Ltd and Leslie and Co Ltd'. Rising building costs on 'firm price' contracts were squeezing Bovis's profits. The main offending contract in 1961 was the Chelsea Barracks. At £2 million, this was the first £1 million-plus project ever won in open tender by Bovis subsidiary Gilbert-Ash, and was awarded at a time when Prime Minister Harold Macmillan boasted that Britain had reached a 'plateau of prices'. The plateau was short lived and Bovis completed Chelsea Barracks against a background of a building boom and spiralling costs. At one point the Bovis board seriously considered closing Gilbert-Ash. It was only the legal responsibility to finish the Chelsea Barracks, and the success of the Intergrid system that saved the lump-sum tendering subsidiary. Eventually the Ministry of Public Building Works paid Gilbert-Ash an *ex gratia* payment of £100,000 for the Chelsea

Barracks 'in recognition of the difficulties of the job and the honourable way in which the project had been completed'.

John Gillham recalled how he took Sir Donald Gibson, general controller of the then Ministry of Public Building and Works, to lunch at the Reform Club to explain the predicament: 'I explained that the company was bleeding due to unforeseeable circumstances, particularly spiralling labour costs. I added that it was our intention to pursue the contract with the utmost vigour and complete the contract on time, but we would appreciate consideration of an *ex gratia* payment. Sir Donald arranged for me to meet the director of contracts, and a few days later we received a letter agreeing to the payment subject to completion on time.' John Gillham believes that this initiative turned defeat into victory, as from now on the Ministry viewed Bovis in a more favourable light, and later awarded Gilbert-Ash important prison contracts and a series of army barracks at Aldershot. The latter achieved twice the national average productivity rate using prefabricated building methods, and received both the Concrete Society and Civic Trust awards.

Despite the pressure on profits, there was no shortage of contracts, and the offices at Stanhope Gate became cramped. In 1960 Bovis took a number of satellite offices in the vicinity, but this proved a temporary expedient and the company acquired leases on two new adjacent office blocks in Notting Hill Gate. In late 1961 the group transferred operations to Notting Hill Gate, and commenced the redevelopment of Stanhope Gate. But the unremitting growth of the company soon put a premium on space at Notting Hill Gate. So Bovis built new offices over the Classic Cinema next door, and Gilbert-Ash found new premises in Woking. Meanwhile, David Woodbine Parish reported to the board that 'the existing capacity at Oxgate Lane is unlikely to prove sufficient for future requirements'. To free space at Oxgate, part of the operations were relocated to the premises of Barker of Hitchin, a joinery company purchased by the group.

Harry Vincent commissioned management consultants Urwick Orr and Partners to study and make recommendations on the management structure of the group. The board accepted its advice, and restructured Bovis Holdings into three divisions in February 1962: construction headed by David Woodbine Parish, administration under Roger Dawe and finance run by Alec Emmel. Urwick Orr's second major recommendation was to split the Leslie subsidiary into two parts. Staff engaged on fee-based contracts were transferred to Bovis Ltd, and those employed for tender work went to Gilbert-Ash. The Leslie offices in Kensington were let. There were good financial reasons for streamlining the group, but it also helped to clarify the public image of Bovis Holdings which had become a matter of some concern.

In a board meeting in July 1963 Harry Vincent referred to 'the need for determining a policy defining the image of the group and its constituent parts which it is desirable to project to the various publics'. And in his 1964 annual report he said: 'I am frequently asked why we have two main building divisions, both apparently performing the same function. The answer is the Bovis Fee System, which, as far as I know, is unique in the world and certainly in this country.' Two new appointments to the main board in March 1964 showed a new sharper focus to the group. Fred Cosford became managing director of Bovis Ltd and Herbert Cruickshank became managing director of Gilbert-Ash. Yet observers remained mystified about how Bovis maintained such a large order book, and yet took part in relatively few tendering competitions. The magic of the Bovis System was baffling a second generation.

77 *Prime Minister Harold Macmillan (left) inspects the Chelsea Barracks with John Gillham (centre) and Herbert Cruickshank (right). Spiralling labour costs on the project left Bovis with mounting losses and John Gillham negotiated a £100,000 ex gratia payment.*

78

78 *The Granada cinema in Greenford, constructed by Bovis in 1937, was converted into this Tesco store by the next generation of Bovis managers.*

Bovis Ltd grew rapidly. Branch offices were opened in Bristol under future managing director Chris Spackman, and in Glasgow, and Leslie's Bradford office was transferred to Bovis Ltd. Satellite offices were created in Croydon and St Albans, but the company needed more space and a new headquarters. The opportunity to move presented itself in 1965 when a Bovis-built speculative office block in South Harrow lay empty for a time, and the company decided it would be an ideal base. Bovis Construction Ltd is still there.

The list of Bovis System clients mushroomed to include: Guardian Royal Exchange Assurance, Smiths Crisps, WH Smith, National Spastics Society, Boots, the Automobile Association, John Smith's Tadcaster Brewery, Scottish and Newcastle Breweries, British Rail, Arndale Property Trust, Samuel Properties, Wessex Co-operative Society, Tesco and the House of Fraser. Sometimes contracts were for the conversion of earlier Bovis projects. The Granada cinema in Greenford, built by Bovis in 1937, was converted into a Tesco store. And alterations to the Union of Canton Building in Threadneedle Street, constructed by Bovis in the 1920s, were carried out for Guardian Royal.

Prestige clients included the Royal Opera House in Covent Garden, Wembley Stadium, King's and St Catherine's Colleges in Cambridge and Trinity College, Oxford. It is impossible to omit Marks & Spencer. In 1966 the opening of the Argyle Street, Glasgow store was commemorated with a plaque noting that this was 'the six hundred and seventieth contract given by Marks & Spencer since their first association in 1926. . .and the first contract to be completed at a building cost in excess of one million pounds'.

Sir Brian Horrocks joined the board after retiring from the office of Black Rod in the Houses of Parliament, and the Labour victory at the general election in 1964 meant that Sir Keith Joseph lost his ministerial position and returned to the board. One tricky item on the new board's agenda was what to do with the Compactom subsidiary. Its venture into partitioning and false ceilings had been a success, notably on a contract for '16 miles of partitioning' in the new Shell headquarters building on the South Bank. However, competition was intensifying, and in 1964 Compactom supremo Edward Pinto retired after 43 years of service, and so did his right-hand man John McGeorge. Losses were forecast for 1965, so the board decided to sell Compactom, and eventually sold the operation to Unilock Partitions.

The patriarch Sidney Glyn passed away on Christmas Day in 1965. He was seventy-seven, and had left the board just two years earlier. His obituary appeared in the leading newspapers and periodicals. The *Bovis Weekly Diary* spoke for many when it wrote: 'A man possessed of great character and sound judgement, though himself modest and retiring, Mr Glyn had a rare capacity for creating around him a loyal and enthusiastic team. All of us who knew and worked with him will always remember him with great respect and affection.'

Yet by the mid-1960s the financial problems of 1961 were history, and the refocusing of the group was starting to produce excellent results. In 1965 there were 105 Bovis System contracts underway, of which 25 were for Marks & Spencer, more than ever before. Strict guidelines were in place for ensuring profit margins in contracts won by tender. And Gilbert-Ash was enjoying remarkable success with the Intergrid construction system. This improved financial performance allowed an

79 *Oxford University's Trinity College, a prestigious new client won in the late 1960s. Bovis also built St Catherine's College in Cambridge.*

increase in authorised capital from £1.25 million to £1.75 million 'to bring it more into line' with the net assets of the company. It also foreshadowed a phase of acquisitions. Bovis bought two related companies in Northern Ireland, P. Carvill & Sons Ltd, and Carvill (Engineering) Ltd. The Carvill companies became Gilbert-Ash (NI) Ltd, and Pat O'Brien was transferred from Woking to run the operation. Later the discovery of a trading deficit caused some problems, but profits had been guaranteed by the Carvill family.

More significant was the 1964 decision to 'proceed with the acquisition of a 30 per cent interest in Malcolm Sanderson (Developments) Ltd', an estate agency turned house builder. It was owned by Frank Sanderson. Harry Vincent's younger brother Neville had introduced Frank Sanderson to Bovis and Sanderson was destined to play a major role in the company's future as chairman and managing director in the early 1970s. In 1965 the group formed a new company, Audley Estates Ltd, for speculative house building headed by Philip Warner, then a rising young star who would later become the head of Bovis Homes (*see chapter eight*).

Neville Vincent was rewarded for his part in this acquisition by his appointment to the board as the director responsible for property in early 1966, and he would figure prominently in the future of the company. A barrister by training, with a mischievous wit, Neville Vincent was a completely different character from his flamboyant brother Harry. He loved to champion causes, notably his home for battered wives in Chiswick, Amnesty International and the *New Statesman* magazine. His Apex Trust employment agency for ex-prisoners is also well remembered at Bovis, although in this case Neville Vincent's faith in human nature was somewhat misplaced and ex-convicts often proved unreliable employees.

After the death of Sidney Glyn in 1965, Lord Albemarle became president of Bovis. There were further additions to the board in 1966. David Woodbine Parish resigned, and Herbert Cruickshank took his place as managing director of construction operations. Fred Cosford became an assistant managing director. And Sir Sadler Forster joined the board, a further appointment from the wider world of commerce and industry. Then in a remarkable turnaround, Harry Vincent was elected chairman of the executive of the London Master Builders' Association, the same organisation Bovis had sued 40 years earlier.

The policy of growth by acquisition stepped up a gear with the purchase of R. T. Warren (Builders) Ltd, a private house builder with a large land bank. Then the group bought the outstanding 70 per cent of shares in Malcolm Sanderson (Developments) Ltd. Frank Sanderson joined the board as chairman of Audley Estates Ltd to supervise the housing division, with Neville Vincent as managing director and Philip Warner running day-to-day operations. The aim was to build 500 houses a year. Acquisitions continued with a deal to buy Gloucester-based H. W. Tily and Sons. In these heady days, even a French house-building subsidiary was formed with offices in Paris.

The board considered diversification into fields related to the building industry, such as estate agency and merchant banking, and decided against it. But the directors did agree to acquire two firms, Woodward & Co (Engineers) Ltd and David F. Wiseman and Sons Ltd, to expand into heating, ventilation, mechanical engineering and plumbing. Bovis also purchased a Westbury-based civil engineering contractor, A. E. Farr, in 1968 to allow the group to compete for major civil engineering projects.

Larry Webb (Plant) Ltd was also bought from an ex-Bovis project manager, who had left to start his own business. And in 1970 Bovis acquired the northern firm of

80

80 *In the mid-1960s Prime Minister Harold Wilson opened this school in Lancashire built by the Bovis lump-sum tendering subsidiary Gilbert-Ash.*

builders and property developers, Ackroyd and Abbott. Barry Abbott was made chief executive of the Bovis property division. But a bid for the construction company Cementation Ltd was withdrawn in 1970, because 'the price was too high'. There were even a number of foreign ventures. Harry Vincent liked the tourism and leisure potential of the Virgin Islands and formed Bovis (VI) Ltd in 1968. And a 52 per cent stake in Gunnar Mining of Canada was purchased in 1969 and rechristened the Bovis Corporation.

On the property side, Neville Vincent formed two new companies in 1967: Bovis Investments Ltd and Bovis Developments Ltd. In his 1967 report to shareholders, Harry Vincent explains: 'We are expanding our property division, and we have secured additional mortgage facilities of £5 million, making a total amount on which we can draw of £8 million'. The following year, he added: 'We are active in shop and office schemes and a substantial industrial development which has already been let.' This was probably referring to Avonmouth where a 25,000 square metre industrial building was under construction. In his 1970 annual report Harry Vincent mentions 'the 1968 decision to switch the emphasis of property activities from investment to development and dealing'. This dealing activity involved the purchase of 400 flats in St John's Wood, Notting Hill Gate and Roehampton for resale to individuals, and there was also the acquisition and sale of 104 houses in Tottenham.

Bovis Construction was significantly overhauled at this time. Bernard Heaphy later recalled: '1968 was significant for the fee system. Then managing director Frank Sanderson said bluntly that for all the effort Bovis people put into making their several hundred thousand pounds annual profit, everybody would be better off making tea'. Two years later thanks to 'a single minded concentration on the fee system' and profits from acquisitions, Bovis Construction was making over £1 million.

As the swinging sixties drew to a close Bovis was enjoying unparalleled success. The renaissance of the Bovis System had provided capital for the diversification of the group and pre-tax profits had grown steadily from £77,052 in 1961 to pass the £1 million mark in 1968. A record £3.34 million pre-tax profit was posted for 1970 and a breakdown of divisional operating profits was published for the first time. Construction contributed £1.3 million while house building made £710,000 and property earned £1.2 million. The independent stockmarket-quoted Bovis must have caught the eye of predators waiting for the company to over-stretch itself. They would not have long to wait.

81 *In 1969 Bovis converted a petrol station in Southport into this Safeway Foods supermarket, its first Safeway contract. Safeway Foods remains a major client and celebrated its thirtieth anniversary with Bovis in 1999.*

81

95

CHAPTER 7

P&O takes control

Many people remember Prime Minister Edward Heath's government for its savage boom-to-bust business cycle. It featured a rapid inflation of property prices and a wave of new ideas from aggressive young businessmen that was cruelly deflated by a sudden massive increase in oil prices. This was a time of rampant house price inflation, the so-called whizz-kids and the oil price shock. It was a roller-coaster ride for the nation, with great excitement about the future quickly turning to disappointment and financial failure.

As a construction, housing and property group, Bovis found itself caught up in this whirlwind of change, at one time setting the agenda, and then being overpowered by the very forces it unleashed. Rapid innovation and corporate expansion went horribly wrong for Bovis in the early 1970s. Indeed, the liquidation of the whole group was only narrowly avoided in 1974. In a matter of fifteen months a deal to install Bovis management at the shipping group P&O was turned on its head into a P&O takeover of Bovis. Nine decades as a successful independent company came to an end. And at that moment few would have predicted the brilliant future for Bovis which followed under the P&O flag.

With the benefits of hindsight, the events leading up to the P&O Group takeover of Bovis are a microcosm of everything that went wrong with Britain in the early 1970s. Bovis had succumbed to the get-rich-quick philosophy of a housing and property developer, fatally chose to acquire a secondary bank and displayed a naive faith in the ideas of younger executives. It was the business equivalent to the Flower Power era, although it probably looked sensible enough in its day. Without the oil price shock perhaps historians would be kinder. On the other hand, the economic bubble might well have grown bigger before it burst.

At Bovis the first signs of danger came in June 1969. Harry and Neville Vincent reported the appointment of 'three young executives of high calibre'. Some months earlier Bovis placed an advertisement for one young executive at the then outrageously high salary of £10,000 per annum, with the stipulation that the applicants should have 'founded and run a successful company'. In fact, the company recruited three whizz-kids – Jim Holding, Paddy Naylor and Dr Brian Baird – although doubts about the profitability of Jim Holding's software company soon surfaced. The board instructed the three to form a special executive and to make recommendations about the future of Bovis. It was typical of this period to seek advice from those with the least experience, and then charge ahead regardless, despite

82 *Woking Town Centre is typical of 1970s architecture and received little praise from the general public.*

83

83 *Frank Sanderson's acquisitions turned Bovis into the UK's second largest house builder and he almost succeeded in engineering a reverse takeover of the P&O Group. A Bovis boardroom rebellion led by Neville Vincent forced his eventual resignation.*

the quite justified misgivings of many of the older members of staff.

The whizz-kids presented their report to the board at the end of 1969. They proposed a new group structure with four divisions. Neville Vincent would supervise property, but the three new executives allocated themselves the plumb jobs – construction went to Paddy Naylor, housing to Brian Baird and a grandly titled 'new business and acquisition's division' was created for Jim Holding. All three whizz-kids became main board directors in July 1970 to the dismay of older members of staff who resented their high salaries and quick promotion. There were some other important changes at the top of the company as the 1970s dawned. Sir Keith Joseph and Herbert Cruickshank became joint deputy chairmen. Most significantly, Frank

Sanderson took over day-to-day control of the group as managing director.

Again it is possible to spot a portent of future danger with the benefit of hindsight. In March 1970 Frank Sanderson asked the board to release him from his existing service agreement owing to 'outside interests'. Sanderson said that he had been advised that a company should be formed to implement certain transactions with which he was involved. His service agreement prevented him forming another company and the board quickly agreed to release him from it. With hindsight, this is the first indication we have that Sanderson was acting for interests other than Bovis. A less starry-eyed board might have thought this was a conflict of interest, particularly for the group managing director.

The last board meeting of 1970 provides some evidence of concern about the diversification of the group and 'management problems in certain divisions'. For example, a new management development manager had been employed and then rather rapidly dismissed. Sir Richard Powell requested an improvement in communications to outside directors who felt they were not hearing about important matters 'until they read about it'. And the profitability of the recently acquired Larry Webb (Plant) was also 'under investigation'.

In 1971 two of the whizz-kids resigned and left the company. Brian Baird left the housing division under acrimonious circumstances and Fred Cosford took over. No letter of resignation is lodged in company records. Meanwhile, the board closed down

84 *TUC general secretary Lord 'Vic' Feather received a spontaneous standing ovation at the Guvnors' Club in January 1971. He is standing between Bovis chairman Harry Vincent (left) and John Gillham (right).*

85

85 *Bovis Construction picked up many new clients in the early 1970s; it built new headquarters for the Automobile Association in Basingstoke.*

86 *Marks & Spencer remains a consistent and faithful client. Bovis completed this new store in Bolton in the early 1970s.*

86

the new business division after Jim Holding's resignation by mutual arrangement. His 'successful' company 1900 Programming Ltd, which he had sold to Bovis, was losing money and put on the market.

There were further boardroom changes in 1971. A. C. Richards resigned as finance director, and Malcolm Paris was appointed in his place. Company secretary Sidney 'Jef' Jefcoate was also given a seat on the board. In addition, after barely six months as chief executive of the property division, Barry Abbott joined the board in recognition of 'an outstanding contribution to the group's activities'. Sir Sadler Forster resigned from the board at this time and Herbert Cruickshank was seconded to the Civil Service Department, ending his 40-year career with Bovis. Finally, there was the death of V. E. Vincent at the age of 78, although he had not been active in company affairs for more than 20 years.

Bovis Construction Ltd continued to make significant progress with the completion of the first-ever British management contract project in Nottingham for John Player and Son. As with the Bovis System and Marks & Spencer, an imaginative client was behind this major innovation, although both Bovis and the architects Arup Associates had visited the United States in the late sixties to study management contracting. Management contracting involves competitive tendering for all the sub-contract packages, but the close relationship between client and contractor is retained as in the Bovis System. As *Architectural Design* commented: 'Considerable time was saved because the design and construction periods were overlapped, and construction time was only two years, yet Players derived the full advantage of competitive tendering on all sub-contract works.' Management contracting would later turn out to be as important as the Bovis System to the future development and on-going success of the company.

Indeed, away from the boardroom dramas Bovis Construction was doing very well in the early 1970s, adding Safeway Food Stores as a major client. Offices were built for the new credit card company, Access, in Southend on a 24-hour-a-day works programme, and a new headquarters was built for the Automobile Association at Basingstoke. Bovis Construction modernised Grosvenor House, reconstructed Eaton Hall as a new family home for the Duke of Westminster and remodelled the Kingsway television studio it had converted in 1955 into modern offices. There were also dozens of new commercial building developments, and many more projects for Marks & Spencer, one of the firm's oldest clients.

Bovis made two highly significant acquisitions in 1971: the secondary bank Twentieth Century Banking Corporation, and the substantial house builder Page-Johnson Builders Ltd. Of the first purchase Harry Vincent commented: 'It gives us a sound and a profitable base in industrial banking, an industry which for some time we have seen as a logical extension of our operations in construction, housing and property.' Unfortunately the 'sound and profitable base' would prove to be built on rather less than secure foundations.

'Neville Vincent and I had lunch with an unconventional character called John Black who was working for the property developer Pat Matthews,' recalls the then finance director and later managing director, Malcolm Paris. 'He told us Matthews wanted to sell a finance company in Brighton and Neville immediately said "I always wanted to own a bank." Within two hours we were sat in their offices in Brighton, and they had drawn up a contract while we were on our way. Neville agreed the deal for £6 million that day, although I managed to stop him signing anything. It was an awful lot of money then.' The second acquisition was Page-Johnson Builders Ltd. Harry Vincent said this house builder boasted an 'excellent landbank' and would allow 'a substantial increase in our housing activities at a most opportune time'.

To fund these two acquisitions, a £5.3 million rights issue was undertaken in June 1971, and was 'an unqualified success'. Malcolm Paris noted the 'healthy financial state of the company' at a board meeting later in August.

The long-running dispute over the company name was also settled. BH Holdings reverted to Bovis Ltd, and the construction company using the Bovis System was rechristened Bovis Fee Construction Ltd. This acknowledged the prestige attached to the Bovis corporate identity, and the board decided to extend the use of the Bovis name to most of its subsidiary activities. The May issue of *Bovis Post* explained: 'Bovis controls potential advertising space worth hundreds of thousands of pounds on sites all over the country. But out of a total of nearly 1000 site boards, there are over 700 which do not even mention the name Bovis. This represents 700 lost opportunities to publicise the group.' So the Sanderson housing companies were transformed into Bovis New Homes, and even Gilbert-Ash was now to be referred to as Bovis: Gilbert-Ash Division.

The board also decided to find a group symbol as a part of this drive for a clear corporate identity. Design group Wolff Olins was briefed to produce 'a memorable, attractive, flexible' logo, which would 'look good on a letterhead, a Motorway site, plant and give-aways from diaries to cufflinks'.

Three main contenders emerged, all on an animal theme. There was the Bovis bull, as Bovis is Latin for bull. There was the Bovis beaver, a constructive rodent. And there was the winner, the hummingbird, a symbol of speed, energy and versatility. From 1971 the hummingbird hovered on boards above Bovis sites. The hummingbird's nest is a perfectly formed building structure delivered just in time for its eggs, although Bovis executives seem to have discovered this appropriate ornithological analogy after adopting the logo. Yet the hummingbird logo was not entirely successful. Earlier versions of the logo featuring the hummingbird in a steep dive were soon abandoned as the image seemed to suggest the firm was unstable.

It was a good period to be working for Bovis. At the start of the year Frank Sanderson said: 'We are confident that the company will continue to perform increasingly well and 1972 will be a further big improvement over 1971 and this implies constant progress in stock market terms.' His remarks followed a *Sunday Telegraph* survey rating Bovis the '16th fastest growing company in any industry in Great Britain'. It showed profits had soared from £750,000 in 1967 and were forecast to reach £13 million in 1972 thanks to the housing and property boom.

The year started quietly enough. Mr V. H. 'Johnnie' Johnson of newly acquired Page-Johnson joined the board and the Earl of Albemarle was congratulated on reaching his 90th birthday and having been on the board since 1923. Harry Vincent reminded the meeting of his impending retirement as chairman and recommended Frank Sanderson as his successor. This motion was carried. And on Harry Vincent's retirement, Sanderson became the first person in the history of the company to combine the roles of chairman and managing director. However, Sanderson guarded even greater ambitions. Perhaps he realised that Bovis's profits were about to peak, and wanted to use its high stock market value to engineer a merger with a group with a more solid asset base. Or from a personal point of view, maybe he wanted to use his new position at Bovis to hijack an even better job. Both motives seem to explain his

87

87 *The hummingbird hovered above Bovis sites from 1971. Design group Wolff Olins proposed this symbol of speed, energy and versatility.*

actions, although events and opportunities must have played an equal role.

In May 1972 a special board meeting was convened to keep directors 'informed on the proposals regarding Harbour', the code name for a takeover bid. Frank Sanderson reported that the 'stage had been reached where terms such as price would be discussed, and he required authority from the board to negotiate on what he considered to be the best terms possible'. In July Sanderson reported back, and was given the authority to negotiate final terms. On 10 August the shipping group P&O made a £130 million agreed bid for Bovis. However, this was to be what later became termed a 'reverse takeover'. For while P&O would be the new owner of Bovis, part of the deal was that the Bovis management would be installed at P&O. Frank Sanderson was to become joint deputy chairman and chairman of an executive committee running the group day-to-day, and heir-apparent to the P&O chairman Ford Geddes.

Then a succession of P&O shareholders and directors rumbled the deal and revolted. A spectacular one hundred days in the Square Mile followed. First P&O shareholders raised doubts about investing in construction and pointed out the dilution of asset backing per share. Next the P&O non-executive director Lord Inchcape concluded that the Bovis deal would be in the 'worst interests of P&O shareholders'. And when two P&O executive directors opposed the bid in mid-September, the Stock Exchange was forced to temporarily suspend P&O shares.

The situation became farcical at a press conference where a P&O director maintained it was impossible to put a value on its ships, and then another director turned against the Bovis takeover. To top the lot, Lord Inchcape emerged with a £230 million bid for P&O from the Inchcape group of companies, which was 250 per cent higher than the value put on P&O in the Bovis deal. Bovis now offered revised terms to P&O, increasing the latter's share in the combined group from 59.5 per cent to 63.5 per cent. It was a highly unusual thing to do, and added to P&O shareholders' suspicions that Bovis was really behind the deal.

In the event P&O shareholders voted against the Bovis takeover by five to two, and both Ford Geddes and Lord Poole resigned from the P&O board. Lord Poole was chairman of Lazard's merchant bank and his role as a Bovis advisor and a director of P&O since May 1972 put him in a highly questionable position. Lord Inchcape became the new chairman of P&O on the understanding that he withdrew his bid. But of great future significance was the fact that P&O now owned 2.36 million shares in Bovis, representing ten per cent of the company's equity.

After shareholders had voted against the proposals, Frank Sanderson held a press conference at the Savoy Hotel. An article in *Investors Review* tells what happened: 'For over an hour Sanderson talked of his regret that a good deal had fallen through, denied that Bovis was vulnerable as a result, and finally let slip one remark in public which brutally revealed what many had suspected all along behind the tinselled talk of asset redevelopment, cash flow benefits and the natural marriage of assets and earnings: "We wanted to find a company with good assets and rotten management. We found it in P&O".'

Frank Sanderson made a short film to circulate to Bovis offices about the failure of the deal. In it he took full responsibility, saying 'I am the one with egg on my face', although he could not resist complaining that he did not know how City institutions would gang up against an outsider. Nonetheless, Bovis Construction staff were extremely busy at this time, and were not very concerned about the outcome of the

88

88 *P&O chairman Ford Geddes negotiated a reverse takeover of P&O by Bovis. When P&O shareholders rejected the deal, he resigned. But the positions were soon reversed and within fifteen months Bovis was bought by P&O.*

89

89 *Lord Inchcape scuppered the reverse takeover of P&O by Bovis with his rival offer. He became the new chairman of P&O on the understanding that he withdrew his bid. This debacle left P&O with a ten per cent stake in Bovis.*

90

90 *The aesthetically challenging Fulcrum Centre in Slough, constructed by Bovis in the early 1970s.*

91 & **92** *Safeway Foods supermarkets in the Cross Keys Chequer in Salisbury and another at Black Fenn in Kent.*

bid. The general feeling was that being part of P&O would have been good for the order book, but it was not that important. In fact, P&O was not Frank Sanderson's first choice of target. He had only turned his attentions to this shipping conglomerate after a deal to buy the property group MEPC fell through. 'Frank just wanted to get bigger and bigger' says Malcolm Paris. 'He loved anything big and prestigious. But he had been an estate agent in Sidcup just four years earlier, and really had no idea what he was doing, let alone the management experience to run a big company.'

In the meantime, although the P&O affair was making the headlines, Bovis had been buying yet more companies and handling a tricky labour dispute. In June Bovis bought Ron Bell Properties Ltd in Devon and three associated companies, which pushed housing operations into a new area of the country. Then a national strike was called in the autumn, and met with limited success, bringing a sixth of Bovis sites to a standstill. This strike had a lasting impact on the Bovis Group. It sounded the final death-knell for lump-sum tendering, largely because the strike cost Bovis £1 million in time lost on fixed-price contracts. The Bovis board decided not to enter any more tendering competitions, and to work entirely on the basis of negotiated fees. Except for Northern Ireland, the Gilbert-Ash companies merged with Bovis Fee Construction into a new company, Bovis Construction Ltd, with Bernard Heaphy as managing director. There was bad feeling within Gilbert-Ash and a lot of the staff felt they did not have sufficient opportunity to prove themselves. The former managing director of Gilbert-Ash, Alan Ellett, moved to the property division as chief executive.

At this time Bovis had just completed the first phase of 1400 flats for the London Borough of Southwark's North Peckham housing development. This was the start of a very profitable relationship that lasted until 1980, with Bovis providing professional management for the Council's own direct labour organisation. Once again the

91

92

flexibility of the Bovis System in adapting to new clients was evident, and similar services were provided for other London boroughs such as Wandsworth.

On 15 September 1972, at the height of the P&O affair, Bovis issued an interim financial statement. Full-year profits were estimated at £13 million, more than double the £6.3 million achieved in 1971, and the chairman's statement noted that all divisions had 'substantially extended the growth pattern which has characterised progress over the last six years'. The property division boasted 'a £100 million development programme over the next four years'. Construction activities were growing in profitability because of an 'increasing emphasis towards low-risk areas' and private housing was 'showing excellent returns'.

The first indication of the trouble that lay ahead came at a board meeting in December 1972. A paper written by Barry Abbott was discussed by the board, and although the minutes do not record the content of the paper, press reports claimed that it proposed splitting the roles of managing director and chief executive, both held by Frank Sanderson, and that Barry Abbott should become chief executive. The board immediately rebuffed Abbott's attempted coup and the minutes note 'even had Mr Abbott not offered his resignation, he would have been requested to resign by all board members'. So another high-flier crossed Sanderson and was out.

A strengthening of the board followed in January 1973. Neville Vincent became deputy chairman and Malcolm Paris was promoted to assistant managing director. Jef Jefcoate became commercial director, handing over as company secretary to Roger Dawe. However, there was a mounting unease about the way board meetings were being conducted. Full board meetings were only held every two months, and many key decisions were taken by an executive board. Press reports criticised Frank Sanderson's style as a one-man-band, and pointed to his reputation for firing top executives or causing them to leave the company.

The last of the three whizz-kids, Paddy Naylor, was stripped of executive responsibility for the construction division in the summer of 1973 and Bernard Heaphy joined the board as the head of construction. Philip Warner and Ray Whatman became jointly responsible for housing, a post left vacant since the previous year when whizz-kid Brian Baird left after a blazing row with Frank Sanderson. Matters came to a head at the board meeting in September. Neville Vincent had written a letter to Frank Sanderson highly critical of his management style and recommended that Sanderson become a non-executive chairman and give up the role of managing director. Frank Sanderson vacated the chair in favour of Sir Richard Powell for the board meeting while directors discussed the issues raised in the letter.

Neville Vincent then proposed that Frank Sanderson should cease to be managing director, which was seconded by Paddy Naylor and a secret vote taken. By nine votes to five, the board voted against Frank Sanderson. He immediately left the meeting and resigned as chairman. The board then elected Neville Vincent as chairman and Malcolm Paris as managing director. It was a spectacular fall for Sanderson, although the full impact of his governance was yet to be appreciated.

After the September debacle, Frank Sanderson was still a non-executive director, and he attended two further board meetings. The first discussed the activities of housing co-chief executive Ray Whatman and a series of actions deemed 'not consistent with those of a director of Bovis Ltd'. One of the charges was that he was recruiting Bovis staff for his own company First Eleven Ltd. Whatman was not present at the meeting, having stated 'he was too ill to see the chairman, either at the office or in Mr Whatman's own home'. The meeting resolved that he would be asked to resign from the board.

At the same meeting Frank Sanderson was quizzed about his involvement with First Eleven Ltd after an article in the *Evening Standard* had raised the possibility of a 'conflict of interest'. Sanderson denied any conflict of interest, but refused to give an undertaking not to recruit Bovis staff. He resigned as a non-executive director on 12 November and Whatman submitted his resignation two days later. The obvious implication is that Whatman, who was Frank Sanderson's half-brother, had been operating on his behalf the whole time.

Nonetheless, both Frank Sanderson and Ray Whatman attended the November board meeting, and the minutes paid tribute to Sanderson's 'great services over the past seven years in leading the build up of Bovis to its present position of strength and prosperity'. Whatever these relatively minor 'conflicts of interest', and the lack of management skill in handling a rapidly expanding group, Sanderson was a modernising force, and left Bovis reporting record profits. It was only later that his true legacy became apparent.

It is tempting to blame a flawed character for Sanderson's downfall. Frank Sanderson once explained Barry Abbott's resignation by claiming that he was not a good company man and was 'too entrepreneurial'. Maybe the same could be said of Sanderson. But if he had succeeded in the reverse takeover of P&O Group, things might have been very different. On the other hand, who knows what would have happened to P&O with Sanderson in charge. Malcolm Paris thinks it would have been 'an absolute disaster'.

The next board meeting proceeded smoothly in December. It agreed the basis for a financial settlement with Frank Sanderson, and a motion introducing service agreements for members of the executive board and senior staff was carried. A subcommittee was also formed for directors' remuneration and severance payments, and a resolution passed to raise 50 million French francs for a newly formed Netherlands subsidiary Bovis Finance NV.

The only hint of the financial iceberg was in the memorandum tabled by Malcolm Paris outlining the group cash requirements for 1974. It noted 'that secondary banks were coming under pressure, and main banks were restricting their lending'. The board responded by deciding to sell completed properties rather than keep them for investment, and 'to dispose of the large numbers of flats held, and not to continue in the business of buying and selling flats'.

The Bovis subsidiary Twentieth Century Banking Corporation was a secondary bank which made its profits from borrowing in the money markets and lending to finance business deals, usually property development schemes. This was comparatively easy in a booming market, and in the Barber-boom of the early 1970s developers became so confident that construction often started before any attempt was made to pre-let an office building. Commercial rents were rising steeply, and it seemed sensible to delay letting until the last possible moment.

The oil crisis of 1973 burst this investment bubble. Recession set in and the demand for new buildings evaporated. That left developers with partly completed buildings that nobody wanted and the secondary banks with non-performing loans. As secondary banks borrowed on a short-term basis in the markets and lent long term, their loans were called in by lenders.

By the Bovis board meeting on 11 December 1973 Twentieth Century Banking

93 *Bovis subsidiary Audley Properties spawned a series of functional developments such as the Trident Centre in Dudley.*

93

Corporation was already in discussions to form a consortium to convert £10 million of its short-term finance into medium-term borrowing. National Westminster Bank examined these plans, and on 14 December told the Bovis Group to abandon the consortium, as it would provide the £10 million.

However, when Neville Vincent and Malcolm Paris met NatWest directors for lunch on 17 December, the Bank had examined the books and come to a different conclusion. NatWest reckoned Twentieth Century Banking Corporation would require £30 million, and not £10 million. The chief executive of Twentieth Century, Peter Gordon, joined the meeting. He remonstrated that £30 million would only be needed if all the depositors withdrew their money, and there was no reason to think that would happen.

Without notice or warning the Bovis Group faced closure within twenty-four hours. The Bank was adamant. It would not extend any further credit to Bovis 'after the day following the meeting'. NatWest had saved a number of secondary banks, but was not willing to help any more. It would liquidate Bovis to get its money back. Perhaps NatWest's hands were tied by the Bank of England. Neville Vincent was physically sick after the lunch, realising that his 10,000 staff would not be paid that week. Whatever the behind-the-scene shenanigans, the Bovis Group had reached the end of the road as an independent company; later that day Neville Vincent and Malcolm Paris 'held discussions with the chairman, managing director and finance director of another company'. The Bovis directors reported to NatWest that they had a possible buyer for Twentieth Century. NatWest then established that the rescue operation involved the whole Bovis Group and delayed closure until 4 January.

Not until the New Year was the identity of the rescuer revealed. It was none other than the P&O Group. As a major shareholder with 2.36 million shares, P&O had a big incentive to save Bovis from liquidation. But in the circumstances it expected a bargain, and offered £25 million for the Bovis Group compared with the £130 million it would have paid fifteen months earlier. The offer was set to close on 4 March. 'NatWest originally gave us seven days to agree a sale,' explains Malcolm Paris. 'But P&O dithered about for three months, and we fobbed off the bank for three months. We had a real problem when several directors started talking about leaving, and the bank made us get them to sign pieces of paper to say they were staying. It was a pretty desperate time, and poor Neville also had to cope with all the family shareholders who were worried about losing their money.'

Frank Sanderson also returned to haunt the board and was highly critical of the P&O takeover. He claimed to have the financial backing to make a counter-bid himself, which never appeared. And the Bovis board considered taking legal action after a critical article appeared in the *Daily Telegraph*, but decided against it.

Even at this troubled time, the Bovis Group continued to make acquisitions, although of the mopping-up variety. For taxation reasons Bovis increased its holding in Varney (Holdings) Ltd, a London-based company with extensive housing interests in Scotland, from 65 to 100 per cent. It was merged with existing housing and construction operations in Scotland to form the group's first geographical unit. Another notable event was the resignation of Paddy Naylor, the last of the notorious whizz-kids, who said he was taking a year's sabbatical to write a novel. He never returned to Bovis and nothing further was heard of his literary career.

On 25 February Neville Vincent sent a letter to Bovis shareholders urging the acceptance of the P&O offer, which he explained was a 'share exchange, not a bid'.

94

94 *A barrister by training, Neville Vincent 'saved Bovis' according to Lord Joseph's testimony. He persuaded P&O to take over Bovis after the National Westminster Bank pulled the plug on its secondary banking subsidiary and decided to close Bovis down.*

95 *P&O managing director Alexander 'Sandy' Marshall led the P&O dissidents in the Bovis affair. Yet he chaired the first Bovis board meeting as a subsidiary of P&O.*

95

The extreme nature of the liquidity crunch at Twentieth Century was revealed to shareholders. Short-term deposits had been withdrawn from the secondary bank, which was relying on £19 million of emergency support. This amount was expected to increase, and the Bovis Group had made cross-guarantees for borrowings of up to £45 million. There was no way the Bovis Group could survive as an independent company with a debt of £64 million.

Not surprisingly, there was massive support from shareholders who were presented with the choice of P&O shares or nothing. So for the second time in 88 years the Bovis Group found itself under new ownership. Lord Joseph maintained that 'Neville Vincent had saved Bovis'. Neville Vincent and Frank Sanderson never spoke again. The new owners made few demands, except for an assurance from Marks & Spencer that it would continue as a client. All the same, it was a bizarre twist of fate that had landed Bovis in the arms of P&O. If Bovis had not acquired the Twentieth Century Banking Corporation, P&O might well have quietly sold its shareholding and never have been heard of again. As it was, the advantages present in Frank Sanderson's original reverse takeover still remained. The construction and shipping business cycles are complementary and, at a fifth of the original takeover price, the Bovis Group was a wonderful buy. Would it have been any different if Frank Sanderson had still been in charge? Most likely not. The problems at Twentieth Century would have been the same, and obviously Frank Sanderson would not have lasted long under the P&O flag.

On 22 March 1974, the Bovis board held its first meeting of Bovis as a subsidiary of P&O. The managing director of P&O, Sandy Marshall, and finance director Oliver Brooks were welcomed to the board. A further P&O director, Clifford Nancarrow, also joined the board but was absent that day. It was a sombre occasion. The minutes recorded the resignations of the Earl of Albemarle, Lady Sharp and V. H. Johnson, and John Nicholson also announced his intention to resign. The new owners reported two developments. Oliver Brooks told the meeting he had become chairman of Twentieth Century, and that it was no longer a Bovis subsidiary. Few tears were shed. And Sandy Marshall informed the board that the P&O and Bovis property portfolios would be combined. It was soon evident that P&O was not interested in the day-to-day running of Bovis Ltd, but would require its approval for capital expenditure. From now on the parent group would have to sanction land acquisitions, property development schemes and acquisitions, although in practice Bovis had a fair degree of autonomy. Similarly financial guarantees would need P&O's agreement.

The days when the board met to rubber stamp Frank Sanderson's latest deal or acquisition were over. From 1974 onwards the Bovis Ltd board was a reporting forum for the chief executives and a place to discuss profit projections. The next decade would be a more sober period, with acquisitions off the agenda and a cautious parent group watching over Bovis Ltd.

CHAPTER 8

Bovis Homes

In the late 1960s and early 1970s Bovis earned most of its profits from house building, although construction remained a vital component of the group. But Bovis was a late starter in the housing market. Famous companies such as Wimpey and Laing were long established house builders by the time Bovis decided to take up the trowel. As earlier chapters have shown, the group avoided volume house building in the interwar years, and concentrated on reviving the Bovis System for commercial building immediately after the Second World War.

It was not until the early 1960s that Bovis began to operate as a speculative house builder. Yet this late start did not prevent Bovis Homes becoming the second largest house builder in the United Kingdom by 1972 with 18,000 housing plots in its land bank and 2659 completions in 1973. This astonishing turn of fortunes was largely the work of one man, Frank Sanderson, although his ambitious growth strategy eventually cost Bovis its independence in 1974.

While some repetition of events is unavoidable, it is right to consider the history of Bovis Homes in isolation from the rest of the company for two reasons. First, house building was the most important division before the property crash in 1974 and deserves special consideration. And secondly, from the P&O takeover in 1974 to the stock market flotation of Bovis Homes in 1997, the house building and construction divisions had totally separate management structures and lines of reporting, particularly after 1985 when Philip Warner and Frank Lampl were appointed to the P&O board. So the full history of Bovis Homes, up to the present day, will be analysed in this chapter.

Although the appointment of Frank Sanderson to the board of Bovis in 1967 is generally seen as the founding moment for the housing division, the group had actually been involved in house building for some three years. Twenty-eight-year-old Philip Warner, the future chairman of Bovis Homes, was seconded to the property division, Audley Properties, in 1962. By 1964 the division had secured eight sites with planning consent for over 500 homes and a further 500 plots on white land spread from Cheshire in the north to the Isle of Wight in the south.

Audley Properties also had a financial arrangement with a Middlesex house builder, Denham Construction. It took a 50 per cent share of profits from developments totalling 200 houses in Hampshire and Kent, of which 70 had already been sold by May 1964. Alan Morris was the head of the property division at this time, and records show that by May 1964 the company already had thirteen projects under development, ranging from a mixed-use scheme in Mayfair to a 180-acre farm outside Rugby. This was also the year

96

96 *Bovis originally seconded Philip Warner to its property division in 1962, and he became chief executive of Bovis Homes after Frank Sanderson's resignation in 1973. He retired in 1996 at the age of 60, after 41 years with the company.*

97 *Stone houses in Churchill Gate, Woodstock, further established Bovis Homes' reputation as a quality house builder.*

that Bovis took a critical 30 per cent interest in Frank Sanderson's company Malcolm Sanderson Developments. Malcolm was Frank's second name and he was introduced to the company by Neville Vincent, who was then a close friend and had a financial interest in Malcolm Sanderson Developments.

To some extent it appears that Bovis drifted into house building. Philip Warner explains: 'There was no defined plan, either strategic or geographic, for Bovis's entry into house building, only a belief by the Bovis board and Harry Vincent in particular, that this was a profitable business to be in, and that Bovis should make haste to join the club. Not until 1966, after Neville Vincent's appointment to the Bovis board as the director responsible for housing and property, did Frank Sanderson take a critical and direct involvement in the running of the housing arm of Bovis.'

By 1966 Bovis had already concentrated all of its house building interests into a separate company called Audley Estates. Its directors were Philip Warner, Frank Francis and Neville Selkirk, and Audley Estates took new offices at Vauxhall Bridge Road to help establish a separate identity from the rest of Bovis. At the end of 1965 the board asked Frank Sanderson to review the activities of Audley Estates. His report concluded that its geographically diverse programme for the development of cheap land was fundamentally wrong, and that 'the executive staff had set itself problems that would tax the ingenuity of even the most experienced team'. Frank Sanderson was already beginning to make his mark.

In June 1966 Neville Vincent became managing director of Audley Estates and Frank Sanderson became chairman, although the day-to-day running of the company remained with Philip Warner. The board adopted Frank Sanderson's recommendations and agreed a new strategy for concentrating the company's activities, as well as approving the acquisition of further land in London and the Home Counties. In the previous chapter we saw the boardroom battles that climaxed in the fall of Frank Sanderson. But it is worth looking at the skills that he brought to the Bovis board in 1966 which go a long way towards explaining his rapid rise in Bovis. Sanderson was a wealthy, successful estate agent turned developer from Sidcup in Kent, who had honed his housing operation into a profitable business. It was his strategy that established the future business plan for a decentralised Bovis Homes of the future, a model copied by many other house builders.

98 & **99** *A show home from the late 1960s and its equivalent thirty years later. Only the fashion for Chinese rugs appears to have stood the test of time!*

98   99

Firstly, his policy was to buy building land within a tightly defined geographic area where new homes could be marketed and sold by his own estate agencies. Secondly, he built homes to standard repetitive designs, so that costs could be kept under strict control by a dedicated management team, and the company employing tried-and-tested sub-contractors. The unsung heroes of the house building industry were, and probably still are, the site managers who took overall responsibility for all trades and activity on site from start to finish.

Thirdly, by engaging what amounted to an in-house lawyer – who was able to act for buyer and seller at this time – the legal process of each sale was expedited in the minimum time. A standard form of conditional contract was widely used by his sales staff. The only thing remaining for the purchaser to do was to get a mortgage. And to ensure that mortgage funds were available, Frank Sanderson maintained excellent contacts with the Woolwich and Abbey National building societies. In the 1970s and 1980s all major house builders negotiated block mortgage funding to cover a significant part of annual turnover so that their buyers would have mortgages available. It was a critical part of the business. This cosy arrangement – which reached £60 million at Bovis in the mid-1980s – suited both builder and lender.

By contrast land-bank policy altered dramatically. In the mid-1960s Frank Sanderson was not in favour of holding a large land bank for future housing, and avoided the large cash lock-up of a typical three-year land bank. His estate agencies were useful in locating and securing options on parcels of land in a relatively limited suburban area. But Frank Sanderson's operations were at that point comparatively modest. In that year, to the end of June 1965, Malcolm Sanderson Developments sold around 150 homes. Not surprisingly, this land-bank policy changed as Bovis expanded its housing operation to thousands of completions a year, which required a much more intensive and long-term land strategy.

Philip Warner remembers a very different Frank Sanderson from the corporate raider whose reverse takeover of P&O later went badly wrong. 'Like many powerful and successful men, Frank Sanderson had great charm and charisma as well as a ruthless streak that was seen only by his adversaries or those employees with whom he parted company. He was a good listener, but was seldom moved away from his own instinctive course of action. I suppose those of us who were close to him saw him as a sort of guru. I never encountered the arrogance that was seen by his co-directors on the Bovis board and was fortunate not to have been involved in the unedifying dispute with Neville Vincent that finally led to his departure from Bovis.'

In February 1966 Frank Sanderson began the dynamic expansion of the housing division with the acquisition of R. T. Warren Developments. It owned substantial land holdings within the London commuter belt of Hertfordshire, Surrey and Buckinghamshire, which included a site for 1000 homes at Camberley. R. T. Warren was brought to Bovis's attention by a solicitor and old friend of Harry Vincent who knew the family owners wanted to sell. As a family company R. T. Warren produced a steady income, rather than operating to maximise profits, and thus represented an ideal purchase for Bovis. All the same, its universally liked managing director Bill Hughes-Lewis continued to run the company for four years until his retirement. Senior directors remember how Bill Hughes-Lewis would entertain them on the piano at management conferences and demonstrate his musical rather than commercial talents.

Bovis acquired the outstanding 70 per cent of shares in Malcolm Sanderson Developments in March 1967. Then Frank Sanderson presented his four-year expansion plan for the housing division. The three growth engines were to be Audley Estates, Malcolm Sanderson and R. T. Warren, with further acquisitions also required. Frank Sanderson confidently predicted a 25 per cent annual compound rate of growth and pencilled in a rise in house sales from the 640 units achieved in 1967 to 1600 in 1971. Although this meant a considerable expansion of these three semi-autonomous companies, he also proposed setting up a holding company and the creation of a number of central departments, namely land finding, technical services (architecture, engineering and surveying) and a central estate agency to look after both site sales offices and the agency branch network. The conundrum of decentralisation versus centralisation was a classic problem for an expanding company.

'Frank Sanderson was no control freak and ideally wanted all his managing directors to operate with their own entrepreneurial flair,' says Philip Warner. 'At the same time, however, he liked the idea of standardising house types, costing, sales and marketing methods to maximise profits. This was a dichotomy that would plague the housing companies for the next two to three years.' Part of Frank Sanderson's plan was achieved with the location of the holding company and central services in Audley Estates offices, Audley House, in Vauxhall Bridge Road, Victoria.

Meanwhile, his regional expansion plans were partly satisfied in late 1967 with the acquisition of H. W. Tily, a Cheltenham-based house builder and contractor, with 20 projects under way in Gloucestershire, Somerset, Bristol and South Wales. One of the main attractions for Bovis was H. W. Tily's site for 200 homes in Stroud, although its contracting operation competed with Bovis Construction's new office in Bristol, which was in the hands of later managing director Chris Spackman. Frank Sanderson sent Philip Warner down to Cheltenham as managing director of Tily, and he immediately set about rationalising the business and developing its housing side. Back in London Frank Sanderson appointed Harry Vincent's 23-year-old son Anthony as a director of Audley Estates and shifted its offices to Esher to clear Audley House for the staff of Malcolm Sanderson Holdings.

In mid-1969 Frank Sanderson asked Anthony Vincent to go to France to enter Bovis Homes in a design competition for a small township of 7500 homes. He was not successful, but came back enthusiastic to start a French housing company modelled on a UK housing subsidiary. Anthony Vincent then set about recruiting a management team and acquiring sites. By November 1974 Bovis SA was building on five sites within 35 miles of Paris, and appeared to be having some success in converting the French to the merits of commuting. Yet as so often with foreign ventures, there were hidden problems which made the market tougher than expected. For example, although land prices were lower in France, local communes often required the provision of amenities before they would give planning consent. Amenities could even include the provision of a school, and send costs spiralling. Even before the P&O takeover in 1974 the Bovis board had resolved to sell on the land and work-in-progress to another developer.

Frank Sanderson's relentless ambition pushed the housing division forward rapidly in pursuit of its 25 per cent annual growth target, with expansion on all fronts. In 1969 he set about rebranding the group to establish a new identity. H. W. Tily became Malcolm Sanderson Western, R. T. Warren was rechristened Malcolm Sanderson Southern and Audley Estates changed to Malcolm Sanderson Projects. In April 1969 national coverage spread northwards with the formation of Malcolm Sanderson Scotland. It took over the private housing interests of Bovis Construction subsidiary Gilbert-Ash (Scotland), and acquired the Scottish housing interests of the London-based house builder Varney.

100 *New Ash Green in Kent was bought for £2.65 million in 1971 after the developer ran into difficulties. Building societies were unhappy with its innovative construction techniques so Bovis reverted to traditional methods and sold over 2000 homes on this model development.*

The next major corporate move was the purchase of New Ash Green, a giant project with consent to build a new village for 6000 inhabitants ten miles outside Maidstone in Kent. The scheme got into difficulties towards the end of 1969 as building societies were unhappy about the innovative construction techniques used by its developer Span. The consequent low levels of house sales forced Span into a cash-flow crisis. Frank Sanderson spent over twelve months in negotiations – doubtless allowing the cash-flow crisis to deepen – and bought New Ash Green for £2.65 million in early 1971.

The board appointed architects and planners Barton Willmore and Partners to reappraise the master plan and they made some changes to the layout. But critically, they made many changes to the specification of the houses, including the reversion to traditional cavity wall construction, to satisfy the building societies. New Ash Green ultimately became something of a planner's model village, and was a very profitable venture for Bovis Homes which built 2000 homes and supporting facilities on the site.

House building was by now the major profit centre of Bovis Holdings, and on Harry Vincent's resignation in 1970, Frank Sanderson became group managing director with responsibility for all operations. He continued to expand house building as rapidly as practical. In July 1970 Bovis Holdings bought the Canadian company, Gunnar Mining, thereby acquiring its McNamara housing interests in Ontario. Yet Frank Sanderson was

101

101 *The acquisition of Page-Johnson in October 1971 doubled the Bovis housing division at a stroke and also brought some history. This classic semi-detached house sold in the 1930s for £440.*

quite flexible. As a part of the new hummingbird corporate identity project, the board decided to rename the housing division Bovis New Homes in April 1971, and it dropped the Malcolm Sanderson title completely. A year later the word 'New' vanished. Bovis Homes has been the company title since then, although marketing efforts have since produced a friendlier logo with the name 'Bovis' in blue.

One notable character at this time was Frank Sanderson's personal assistant, Roger Warren-Evans, who had originally responded to an advertisement for trainee managing directors in the *Financial Times*. His background as a practising barrister with a double first in history and economics from Cambridge was unusual, to say the least. Later he became managing director of Bovis Homes Southern, and was instrumental in securing an 80-acre site from the Milton Keynes Development Corporation for 800 homes. But Roger Warren-Evans left in 1974 to become an adviser to Tony Crosland, then Secretary of State for the Environment.

In October 1971 Bovis Homes filled a big gap in geographical coverage with the £8.5 million acquisition of Page-Johnson Builders Ltd. The company had come to prominence under the charismatic and entrepreneurial executive V. H. 'Johnnie' Johnson, who took over the business from his father after completing his stint as a pilot trainer in the Second World War. The Birmingham-based house builder owned land for 13,000 homes in the Midlands, the North, Devon and Hampshire. It more than doubled the Bovis housing division overnight and also brought a foothold in the Australian market, since Page-Johnson had recently acquired Allen Homes (Western Australia), and had started building houses around Perth and Melbourne.

Australian chief executive Jim Cordwell remembers Philip Warner's first visit Down Under accompanied by his finance director Richard Dalzell. The visit was marred by Richard Dalzell's allergy to certain inoculations required by Australian authorities. Despite a letter from the company doctor, John Janvrin, alerting immigration officials to this problem, Dalzell spent the three days in a quarantine station, the only inmate of a 400-bed camp.

The Page-Johnson acquisition made Bovis the second largest house builder in Britain with over 18,000 building plots in Britain, France and Australia, and ten separate UK operating subsidiaries. As a part of the deal, the chairman of Page-Johnson, Johnnie Johnson, became chief executive of the Bovis housing division. But he only lasted four months. A series of senior executives also left, three of them to form another development company. It was a sign of prosperous times. In August 1972 Bovis Homes set up a new board to handle the expanded organisation. Its five members were Ray Whatman, Philip Warner, Reg Meakin, Alan Robson and John Swift. This was also the fateful month that Frank Sanderson became chairman and managing director of Bovis Holdings on the resignation of Harry Vincent.

The Page-Johnson takeover also had many lasting effects on how Bovis Homes functioned. In late 1973 Page-Johnson's former chief architect, Norman Jones, was asked to set up a centralised technical services division. It provided the group with expert architectural, civil and structural engineering and town planning services, which were later extended to include landscaping, mechanical and electrical services and land surveying. At its peak in 1988 Bovis Technical Services, as it was then called, employed 180 staff including 50 in the land surveying division under John Grant. Norman Jones reckoned this made his division the largest multi-disciplinary practice in the UK.

The acquisition of Ron Bell Properties in June 1972 was the last big deal of the Frank Sanderson regime. Ron Bell had started as a building contractor and had built up a remarkable business primarily building retirement bungalows in Cornwall. There were 20 sites spread across Cornwall and West Devon with names that read like a Cornish Odyssey: Porthleven, Gweek, Heamoore, Mylor, Warbstow, Petrockstowe, Mevagissey, St Agnes, Trebullet, Tregadillet, Lewannick and Porthscathow.

Philip Warner recalls some hair-raising plane trips to Perranporth for board meetings in the company's aircraft, a Piper Twin Navajo. Perranporth is an ex-World War Two airfield not without the odd pot-hole and was also used for grazing sheep. It was necessary for the aircraft to do a circuit above the airfield before landing in order to check that no sheep had strayed on to the runway. 'On one occasion we landed in a Force 8 gale,' says Philip Warner. 'And on take-off later in the day we caught an updraft over the sheer west-facing cliff beyond the end of the runway. That wiped the smile off our pilot's face and left his passengers redigesting their lunch.'

But Ron Bell only stayed with Bovis for six months before retiring to the Channel Islands. He found the level of reporting and financial control required by a bigger group totally frustrating, and his two lieutenants – Dennis Richards and Fred Hodge – took over. In the event replacing his land bank proved even more problematic which, combined with a more difficult retirement home market in the late 1970s, meant that Bovis Homes effectively withdrew from Cornwall.

The reason for the slowdown in Frank Sanderson's acquisition trail was simple. He had gone after a bigger fish and attempted a reverse takeover of the shipping conglomerate P&O. It was this deal that forced his resignation from Bovis (*see chapter seven*), and caused an exodus of 25 staff who joined his next venture. Charismatic and enterprising, Frank Sanderson went on to make and lose two fortunes. But his immediate legacy to Bovis was another acquisition, Twentieth Century Banking Corporation, which almost caused the liquidation of Bovis in 1974. It was then that P&O had to step in to rescue the company and Bovis Homes suddenly found itself part of the P&O Group.

After Frank Sanderson's resignation, Philip Warner became chief executive of Bovis Homes and assumed responsibility for regional and overseas operations. Finance director

Alan Robson stayed for a few weeks but left in early 1974. Rumours circulated that Frank Sanderson's departure was due to his housing policies, and that the housing division was going to be sold off. To quash these rumours Malcolm Paris and Philip Warner addressed a conference of Bovis executives at Mount Royal Hotel in London. Paris told the audience 'We have one clear intention, and that is to go on expanding profitably in this sector'. These were encouraging words at a time when Frank Sanderson was busy persuading Bovis executives to jump ship and join his own housing company.

However, shortly after Frank Sanderson left Bovis, the 1970s housing boom went bust. In the years 1971–3 UK house prices had surged by 102 per cent, and Bovis Homes entered 1974 with over 2700 homes under construction. A sudden increase in the mortgage rate to 11 per cent and an over-supply of new property led to a collapse in the market. There was no alternative but to shut down some projects completely, lay off labour and generally batten down the hatches.

At the time of the P&O takeover, Bovis Homes was building on 89 different sites, with over half its output coming from four large estate developments. These estates were at New Ash Green, Southcott Village near Leighton Buzzard, Amblecote to the west of Birmingham and Elton in Cheshire. Bovis Homes was completing 3500 houses a year, and was the only national house builder to operate through nine regional subsidiaries. Most large house builders have a regional structure like this today, but it was unique in 1974. A localised management structure allowed the flexibility and entrepreneurial spirit of a smaller unit, while maintaining the financial and technical advantages of a larger organisation.

Bovis Homes moved its headquarters to Cheltenham in 1974, alongside the regional subsidiary Bovis Homes Western. It also continued to use mortgage subsidies for first-time buyers, offering low and guaranteed interest rates – a pioneering innovation of

102 *Bovis Homes paid too much for the Lower Earley site at the top of the market in 1973. It became the largest housing development in the UK and required substantial investment in infrastructure.*

102

1973. On the other side of the world in Australia, Bovis Homes group completed 200 units. This was also a remarkably good time to be in the land buying market. With support from P&O, Bovis Homes was able to take advantage of the many receiverships and liquidity problems among other house builders, and enlarge its land bank. By the end of 1975 the land bank stood at 17,000 plots, almost back to its 1972 peak, and Australian sales were a credible 250 units.

The Community Land Act of 1976, which ironically Roger Warren-Evans had helped to draft while at the DoE, prompted Bovis Homes to negotiate package deals for sheltered housing with local authorities and housing associations. Five schemes were in train at the end of the year. But the recession took a long time to lift. There were two difficult years, and at the end of 1976 Bovis was left with 700 unsold properties that took some time to clear. Australia was the only hot spot with 400 units sold in Perth and Melbourne, although this successful operation transferred to P&O Australia in 1977. However, in 1977 the company still pushed on with two major new projects: Lower Earley, a new town on the outskirts of Reading, and a site for 1300 new homes at Stoke Gifford outside Bristol.

Lower Earley proved a major millstone to Bovis Homes due to the complications of dealing with a consortium of owners and problems with planning consent. Bovis had bought the land at the top of the market in 1973 and was the lead developer for a very ambitious scheme. Lower Earley covered an area of 1000 acres and comprised 6000 houses with five schools, a commercial centre, local sports centre and accompanying infrastructure. It was the largest housing development in the UK. But there were six miles of roads, bridges and underpasses to complete before any house building could commence. The difficult job of securing the necessary approvals fell to Philip Davies, land director of Bovis Homes Southern.

103 & **104** *This site for 2000 homes at Withymoor Village in Staffordshire was reclaimed from a former open-cast coal mine. It had to be carefully regraded and monitored for settlement over a two-year period.*

105 *This* Daily Express *cartoon makes fun at a marketing promotion offering a Bovis Home for a first hole-in-one at the British Open golf tournament. A Japanese player won the £40,000 house and promptly sold it.*

105

By 1978 the recession eased and Bovis sold a number of sites on the Lower Earley development to pay for its investment in infrastructure. In 1979 Bovis Civil Engineering completed the major road works, as well as building a giant Asda superstore in the centre of the development. House building did not commence until 1980. However, the strategic position of the site between Reading and the M4 meant that sales were assured, and ten national house builders were soon working on this enormous site. And from an unpromising start, Lower Earley provided Bovis Homes with an excellent and highly marketable site for the best part of a decade.

Another large and complicated site developed by Bovis Homes over the same period was Withymoor Village in the Black Country near Dudley. This 200-acre site was a former open-cast coal mine, and resembled a lunar landscape. It had to be carefully regraded and monitored for settlement by mining engineers over a two-year period, and was a core site for the Midlands region under managing director John Abbott. Eventually over 2000 houses and a Sainsbury supermarket were built on this classic piece of brown wasteland. Supermarket sites such as the one at Withymoor were hotly contested by major companies such as Sainsbury, Tesco, Asda and Waitrose, and the sites were a rich source of profit for the Bovis Group. Wherever possible the contract to build the supermarket was placed with Bovis Construction as a precondition for the land sale. Nevertheless, this level of co-operation between the Bovis contracting and house building arms was fairly rare, since few opportunities for a combined approach presented themselves.

In 1978 Bovis Homes made an unusual purchase, buying a well-established Midlands-based company which the Registrar of Companies had amazingly allowed to be called B-Vis. The firm was building homes in the West Midlands and had an attractive land bank. So B-Vis found itself incorporated into the Bovis Homes Midlands region and site boards were very quickly changed to avoid any confusion to Bovis house buyers in the future.

The late 1970s also saw an important strategic decision to move away from the first-time buyer market towards the trade-up section of the market. This took Bovis Homes out of the rat race of providing cheaper properties, and meant that the company was not tarred with the same brush as Barratt Developments, whose building methods were much criticised at the time. All the same, Mrs Thatcher's arrival in Number 10 in 1979 signalled another downturn in the housing market as interest rates soon rose to control inflation. But in the early 1980s the housing gloom began to brighten. House sales rose from 1703 in 1981 to 2045 in 1982, though sales in Scotland were difficult.

The board decided to close down Bovis Homes Scotland except for the development around Gleneagles Hotel, where Bovis was building luxury flats and houses on land owned by British Transport Hotels. Its 'Embassy suites' overlooking the Queen's Course were sold at unheard-of prices to the likes of IBM. And Bovis also gradually pulled out of the north of England to concentrate on developing its operations in the more prosperous southern half of the country. This proved to be an excellent strategic move. Indeed from 1981 to 1989 Bovis Homes contributed between 11 and 25 per cent of the total P&O Group operating profit, and its record results in 1983 helped P&O's successful efforts to rebuff the bid by Trafalgar House. A 60 per cent rise in turnover from the sale of 2689 units in 1983 marked the beginning of a boom of six consecutive years of record profits which ended abruptly in 1988 with the collapse of the British housing market.

The Bovis Northern Home Counties division was opened in the summer of 1981, and inherited one site in Milton Keynes and soon added a number of major sites in the surrounding area. Neville Tullah headed the company which produced some very innovative projects such as new thatched cottages in Milton Keynes designed by group architect Steve Lowe, and a range of three-storey Regency homes which proved popular with Japanese managers. In 1983 a scheme for 109 luxury apartments in Finchley, North London, was opened by Prime Minister Margaret Thatcher. Indeed, in a short time, it became the largest house builder in the region, and a major profit centre for the group.

106

106 From the mid-1980s the concentration of operations in the southern half of the country proved an excellent strategic move. The Hollies at Chorley Wood in Hertfordshire is typical of subsequent upmarket projects.

107

107 Margaret Thatcher, Prime Minister and MP for Finchley, opening the show apartment at Spencer Court, Regent's Park Road, in November 1983, accompanied by Philip Warner and Neville Tullah, the regional managing director responsible for the project

108 **109**

108 *New thatched cottages in Milton Keynes designed by group architect Steve Lowe and built by Bovis Northern Home Counties in the early 1980s.*

109 *The Regent's Gate development at Bishop's Stortford, Hertfordshire by Bovis Northern Home Counties.*

110 & **111** *Charlton Park, completed in 1987, features a variety of high-specification house types which is a hallmark of a Bovis Homes' development.*

112 *Finished in 1989, Holmewood in Redditch is a fine example of a quality development where the builder's name is now a selling point for second-hand homes.*

In 1981 Bovis Homes had decided to start building houses in the United States for the first time with the formation of Bovis-Brunning Inc in Georgia, and the US division sold its first house in 1982. Bovis-Brunning Inc was formed with Geoff Brunning, who was formerly managing director of three Bovis Homes' regional companies. He had actually moved with his family to Australia in 1975, and had been invited by a major Australian housing company called Hooker Homes to run its US house building subsidiary in Atlanta, Georgia. Philip Warner subsequently met up with Geoff Brunning in Atlanta, and persuaded him to set up a Bovis Homes operation in Georgia, with plans to open later in San Antonio, Texas and Orlando, Florida.

'Although the acquisition of land was not initially a problem, prices were high with roads and services already installed, unlike the UK,' recalls Philip Warner. 'The company's fortunes in Atlanta and San Antonio were mixed with thin margins, and a growing realisation that the US market can move very quickly from under to over-supply. This is due to the speed at which the industry can gear up and a very short build time of about fourteen weeks.' Bovis-Brunning specialised in the single family home market. Its average house on a fifth of an acre was at least 50 per cent larger than an equivalent UK home. And US sales took off rapidly, jumping from 48 in 1983 to 273 the next year. By 1986 sales peaked in Atlanta and San Antonio due to an over-supply of housing. This led Bovis-Brunning to close its operations there and concentrate instead on the Florida market, where the population was growing rapidly.

In 1987 Bovis-Brunning bought the assets of small house builder Laurel Homes in Orlando, which gave the company a flying start in the sunshine state. A former colleague of Geoff Brunning's from Hooker Homes, Arthur Tye, headed up the Florida operation. Geoff Brunning himself parted company with Bovis in 1989, and Arthur Tye went on to expand Bovis Homes Inc outside Orlando to West Palm Beach, Sarasota and later Jacksonville. The US sales volumes remained stuck at around 250 units and, at the time of the Bovis Homes flotation in 1997, P&O retained the operation. To mark the centenary of Bovis, Bovis Homes held a directors conference at Gleneagles Hotel in October 1985, where the board drew up its latest five-year strategic plan. The board

110

111

112

113

113 *Bovis-Brunning Inc developed homes in Florida from 1987 to the time of the Bovis Homes flotation in 1997, with annual sales of around 250 units.*

114 *The Gamston site in Nottingham acquired for £17 million from Nottingham County Council. It produced excellent profits for Bovis Homes.*

114

confirmed its objective of concentrating on the more profitable south-east, south-west and the Midlands, where 71 per cent of the UK population lived. This proved to be a very shrewd strategy during the great housing boom of the late 1980s. Indeed, in 1985 the recovery was already evident, with the average selling price of a Bovis house up from £34,184 in 1981 to £62,394.

Securing the right land in the right places became even more imperative, and in 1987 Bovis Homes tied up the acquisition of 195 acres of housing land at Gamston, Nottingham, for £17 million. Sealed bids for the site were required in 15 days for Nottingham County Council, requiring a tremendous effort from Philip Ashton, land director of Bovis Homes Midlands. The Gamston development went on to make excellent profits which included the sale of a superstore site to Safeway that also turned into another contract for Bovis Construction.

A further initiative to secure green land for housing came in the late 1980s with the formation of Consortium Developments Ltd by the ten members of the Volume House Builders Group. The idea of CDL was to take options on land in strategically located sites in the Home Counties where settlements of 4000 to ,000 homes could be built subject to planning approvals. After two failures, CDL seemed to have won a victory when Environment Secretary Nicholas Ridley said he was 'minded to approve' such a development at Foxley Wood in Hampshire. But sadly his successor Chris Patten revoked this tentative commitment for political reasons, and by then CDL had spent £1 million on four possible sites. CDL was wound up and green-field sites remain as scarce as ever, particularly in the south-east.

Production peaked in 1988 in a scramble to satisfy demand for new homes, and of course to maximise profits. House building, construction and development contributed a record £157.1m to P&O Group operating profits in 1988, of which Bovis Homes made by far the largest contribution. The average selling price of a Bovis Home was £111,000 in 1988, a 54 per cent rise on £72,000 in 1986. What house builders failed to anticipate was that the Chancellor of the Exchequer Nigel Lawson would raise interest rates from 8.5 to 13 per cent between June and November 1988. This pricked the housing bubble, and was compounded by a rush to beat the August deadline for the removal of multiple tax relief on single properties. Bovis Homes' cancellation rate for reservations hit an all-time high towards the end of 1988. Bovis Homes ended up with a very high level of work-in-progress the following year, partly because the company had begun a number of high-value Central London and Docklands' apartment schemes where sales dried up overnight. By March 1990 the Halifax variable lending rate of 15.4 per cent was at an all-time high. House prices in Greater London had risen in nominal terms by 67 per cent between 1986 and 1989 and then fallen by 17 per cent by 1993.

Buyers were hard to find, and Bovis Homes took its marketing campaign to Hong Kong and Singapore. South-east region managing director, and future chief executive, Malcolm Harris tied up a particularly complicated deal with Chinese buyers for block sales on the Sands Wharf Riverside scheme for 250 apartments in Fulham. There was also a renewed effort to break into the social housing market, and the south-east region was particularly successful in this respect.

The boom-to-slump cycle of the late 1980s also played havoc with land buying.

115 *Demand dried up overnight on several large Bovis Homes developments in London Docklands in the late 1980s, particularly for the very expensive penthouses.*

116 *Vestry Court in Westminster, London, was another scheme conceived in the heady days of the 1980s property boom and finished in time for the housing market slump.*

115 **116**

117

117 *Future chief executive Malcolm Harris tied up a complex block sale of apartments at Sands Wharf in Fulham to Chinese buyers.*

Between the springs of 1986 and 1989 land prices in the south-east trebled, while house prices showed a mere 84 per cent rise! When the market went into a nose dive, the effect was magnified in the other direction. Land prices slumped in the south-east from a peak of £720,000 per acre in 1989 to £238,000 per acre in 1993. Inevitably this meant that Bovis Homes had to make large provisions against the decline in value of its land bank which would severely impact on profits. As Philip Warner comments:

> The quest for land generates more excitement and causes more disappointment than any other activity within the company. Land is the ultimate prerequisite for any house building activity, and the principle supply-side constraint. There is immense competition among the major builders to secure the best sites and maintain a sound land bank. When it came to land transactions in Bovis Homes, communication lines were very short as all deals had to be cleared with the chairman and finance director as an absolute minimum, and larger transactions were referred onward to the P&O board for approval.

In the late 1980s and early 1990s the term 'negative equity' became synonymous with the anguish of homeowners who had taken out huge mortgages only to find themselves with houses worth less than their loan. At its peak in the first quarter of 1993 there were 1.7 million households with negative equity. The national press was full of cautionary tales of apartments in Docklands and Central London bought at astronomic prices only to leave the unfortunate owners with tens of thousands of pounds in negative equity.

P&O demanded the sale of surplus land to reduce capital employed, but supported the active pursuit of low cost land to dilute the average cost of the land bank. Hence in 1993 the P&O board supported the acquisition of a large tract of land north east of Swindon at Haydon, with a development programme which included the disposal of smaller land parcels to other house builders. This represented the biggest post-recession deal and South West managing director Peter Baker and his team burned the midnight oil putting it together.

In a further departure from post-recession caution, Bovis Homes decided to form an off-shoot in Germany in 1992 after a detailed appraisal of the housing market around Berlin by Neville Tullah, managing director and founder of Bovis Homes Northern Home Counties. He concluded that the market for good quality homes was under-supplied following the reunification of Germany and removal of the Berlin Wall. Furthermore, the Government was offering tax incentives to both investors and owner-occupiers to encourage house building, and the movement of the capital to Berlin boded well for future demand.

118 *Very Sheltered Housing for the elderly proved popular. Bovis Retirement Homes managing director Jim Ditheridge is shown playing cards with residents.*

Bovis Homes found a site for 300 homes 12 miles south of Berlin and agreed a contract conditional on planning consent. However, it took a long time to get planning approvals and permits due to the consultation process with the local community, and building did not start until late 1994. By then the market was cooling off, house prices were under pressure and the commercial development of Berlin was pushing construction costs upwards. Eventually plans to develop other sites were shelved and this bold investment had to be liquidated. Unfortunately, as with Bovis Homes' earlier French experiment, British house building failed again to make an impact on the continent.

The development of Very Sheltered Housing for the elderly was a more successful venture at this time. It was Lord Joseph, then a non-executive director of Bovis, who introduced Bovis Retirement Homes managing director Jim Ditheridge to Bob Bessell,

118

119

119 *Frank Sanderson introduced professional marketing for new homes in the late 1960s which continues to the present day.*

managing director of Retirement Security. Bob Bessell had pioneered the concept of Very Sheltered Housing for sale which offers residents a high level of support services. As a result of this meeting, the two companies co-operated on 12 successful Very Sheltered schemes around the UK, and the first was at Oxted in Surrey. This co-operation continues today.

The UK housing market stayed in the doldrums until 1995 when new house prices showed their first improvement in six years. For the Bovis Homes board this meant that cost reductions were of paramount importance in the early 1990s. In 1993 Malcolm Harris headed a fundamental review of his region's operations. This review led to three major initiatives in the south-east region: rationalisation of overheads, new value-engineered house designs and the introduction of standardised components and materials. Operating margins improved substantially, as the benefits of greater standardisation became clear. The board decided to spread the reforming ethos across the group, and in the second half of 1995, the Midlands, Northern Home Counties and

Northern regions were combined to form the Central region. This successful policy compounded the company's sound reputation for products and service in the market. The latter was acknowledged by the industry when a new award from *Building* magazine – based on a survey of 1000 clients, competitors, architects and industry professionals - voted Bovis Homes the best medium-sized house builder. Bovis Homes scored an impressive 10 per cent lead over runners-up Berkeley and Redrow.

Such a year of improvement was an optimistic note on which to retire, and after 41 years with Bovis, Philip Warner announced his retirement in January 1996, just short of his 60th birthday. His decision surprised the P&O board, and privately Lord Sterling joked that 'Philip Warner would be retiring at the end of June aged 60, and Sir Frank Lampl was offering himself for re-election aged 70!' It was also in January 1996 that press speculation about the future of Bovis Homes reached a crescendo with many commentators predicting that P&O Group would sell the company to reduce its borrowings. Such discussion prompted another major house builder to make a derisory offer for Bovis Homes, and caused considerable anxiety among its staff. Following representations from Philip Warner and Malcolm Harris, P&O announced its intention to 'float Bovis Homes in 1997, markets permitting'.

A management accountant by training, Malcolm Harris was the obvious heir-apparent, and he became group chief executive in July 1996 when Philip Warner stood down. Philip Warner's retirement was the occasion for a tremendous party for 200 colleagues and ex-colleagues at the Cheltenham offices. 'There was one chap I had not seen for 15 or 20 years, and I was most humbled and flattered,' he recalls. 'I wanted to make it clear how delighted I was that the company was being left in good and very experienced hands. I also asked them to remember the Bovis culture, heritage and dedication to quality that separates fine companies from the mediocre.'

The three-pronged initiatives from the South-east review were applied to the two other remaining regions, Central and South-west during 1996, and the Retirement Division also benefited from the rationalisation of its build costs and overheads. Administrative and overhead expenses as a percentage of turnover fell from 9.5 per cent to 7.9 per cent in 1996.

The company also made a modest acquisition, buying the house building assets of the small West Country firm Britannia Homes. Housing completions rose by 30 per cent between 1994 and 1996 to reach 2456 units, and operating profit rose strongly from £13.6m to £29.4m. In the same period total staff costs rose far less dramatically from £13.7m to £14.3m, indicating a substantial productivity gain across the company. Against this backgound, it was hardly surprising that the City greeted the Bovis Homes flotation in December 1997 with enthusiasm. Analysts like performance that can be measured in numbers, and Malcolm Harris had delivered the goods.

In its first year as an independent stock market-quoted company Bovis Homes saw its share price surge by over 60 per cent. This performance was partly down to an improving market for house builders combined with a 21 per cent rise in pre-tax profits to £45 million, but it also reflected a growing recognition of Bovis Homes' business strategy by financial institutions.

Perhaps too, it took time for investors to fully realise the value of a company that had previously been hidden under the umbrella of the P&O Group. Sadly the flotation meant the severing of links with Bovis Construction, besides a 999-year royalty-free licence to use the name Bovis, and continued membership of the Guvnors' Club for staff members. Only the common heritage remains.

120

120 *Malcolm Harris delivered the financial performance that ensured Bovis Homes an enthusiastic reception as an independent public company in December 1997.*

CHAPTER 9

Management contracting

From this point the history of Bovis will be considered almost exclusively in terms of the group's development as a construction company since 1974 and the P&O takeover. Inevitably the corporate party of the first half of the 1970s left a big hangover in the second half of the decade. There was a necessary reaction to the excesses that preceded the dramatic rescue by P&O. Indeed, the new owners wanted a solid return on their investment, and to make sure that the Bovis Group did not become involved in any more wild adventures. It was a change from radical to conservative corporate governance.

In late 1974 the commercial building market was in deep recession and so was the housing market. Moreover, after a period of whizz-kids, acquisitions and centralised management, morale was blighted across the group. The new managing director, Malcolm Paris was a very different character from his predecessor Frank Sanderson. Despite his love of fast cars, Paris was more of a professional manager than an entrepreneur, with a sureness of touch that was appreciated by the P&O Group. His success in reviving Bovis from the depths of its misfortunes in 1974 was acknowledged in 1978. At that point he became chairman as well as managing director on the retirement of Neville Vincent, and a P&O main board director. After the revolving doors of the early 1970s, Paris was a stabilising influence, remaining in the pole position for more than a decade.

'It took us about three to four years to sort out the mess of the early 1970s,' says Malcolm Paris. 'I tried to split the company into the good bits and the bad bits, and by 1978 we had got rid of most of the problems. P&O treated us more like a separate public limited company than a subsidiary, and kept us at arms length. My worst problem was sorting out the Canadian company, which was an absolute nightmare, and I hated commuting back and forth across the Atlantic.'

But Bovis was probably faster on the rebound than many other British contractors in the mid-1970s. One reason for this rapid recovery was its nimble switch from private- to public-sector contracting. The construction division was also quick to develop management contracting, the ambitious progeny of the Bovis System, which was destined to be the commercial saviour of the Bovis Group. By the mid-1970s clients were frightened by the high tender prices that contractors were submitting in a climate of rapid inflation of labour and material costs. One solution, vigorously marketed by the Bovis Group, was for clients to adopt the Bovis System, and at least get the contractor working on its side in the difficult environment that prevailed at

121 *Managing director Malcolm Paris, in temperament and character a completely different man from his predecessor Frank Sanderson.*

122 *Lord Rogers' controversial Lloyd's building in the City of London required the highest construction standards.*

123

123 *Wiggins Teape's headquarters in Basingstoke, an unusual mixture of offices and gardens, completed in the late 1970s.*

124 *Architect Lord Foster became an enthusiastic convert to management contracting after Bovis completed the spectacular Willis Faber Dumas building in Ipswich.*

the time. Alternatively there was Bovis's new fangled management contracting.

This was a logical development from the Bovis System, and was used successfully on the Nottingham project for John Player and Son. It offered the same unique relationship between client and contractor, with a negotiated fee, but included competitive tendering for subcontracting packages. Management contracting was to give Bovis a new lease of life in the second half of the 1970s. It was employed on projects such as the new headquarters for Scottish Widows in Edinburgh, offices for Wiggins Teape in Basingstoke and the spectacular Willis Faber Dumas building in Ipswich designed by Norman Foster. This famous architect became an enthusiastic convert to management contracting, and paid Bovis the compliment of insisting on its appointment as management contractor on the Visual Arts Centre at the University of East Anglia, despite the client's desire for a competitive tendering process.

Management contracting was also winning friends through its flexibility. One of the most challenging management contracts was a new bakery for J. Lyons in Barnsley. It had been awarded to a firm called Woodall Duckham on a lump-sum design and build contract in late 1972, and after twelve months Lyons was unhappy with progress. By awarding a separate management contract to Bovis, Lyons was able to keep its contractual relationships intact with both Woodall Duckham and its subcontractors, and get the job finished by its original completion date in 1975.

A further opportunity arose to demonstrate the flexibility of the Bovis System compared with the inflexibility of the standard form of contract, on the World's End housing project in Chelsea. Here the borough council and contractor had found themselves locked into a contractual straitjacket by the standard form of contract, and work on site was at a standstill. The council appointed Bovis to finish the project in 1973, and a team led by John Smith delivered the work on time and to budget, with a high quality of finish. Bovis had discovered a new market – rescue operations.

124

125

125 *World's End in Chelsea was rescued by Bovis when a contractual dispute between the borough council and its contractor brought the site to a standstill. Bovis took over the public housing project and finished it on time and to budget.*

One of the first jobs future chairman Sir Frank Lampl secured for Bovis was an unusual rescue situation. While attending his son's degree ceremony at Oxford University, Frank Lampl noticed a newspaper billboard outside the Sheldonian Theatre that read 'Pergamon burnt out'. He knew that the proprietor was Robert Maxwell, 'A man I did not know from Adam', and the next day rang him to express his condolences. Maxwell listened to his introduction, and then said: 'Are you a Czech? Well, come and see me at 3 o'clock this afternoon, and speak to me in Czech, and I'll probably give you the job'. True to his word, Bovis won the Pergamon contract, although Maxwell was a difficult client, and would visit the site daily at the crack of dawn to make changes.

Bovis clinched two further major projects in the early 1970s, both bigger than anything the firm had undertaken before, except for the Swynnerton munitions factory in the Second World War. The first was a new £20-million headquarters for EMI on the Tottenham Court Road in London, a huge office development by the

126

standards of the day. The second was the Royal Liverpool Teaching Hospital, another rescue job, but on a larger scale. Originally planned in the 1930s, the hospital was not awarded until after a tender competition in 1968. Within a year the project was hopelessly late, and then the contracting company got into financial difficulties and its parent group decided to close it down. The health authority's parent company guarantee was invoked, and another contractor brought in to finish the job on a cost-plus basis.

However, at the start of 1975 the parent company was able to wriggle out of its contract, and walk away from the half-completed hospital. It was at this point that the health authority approached Bovis to complete the project under the Bovis System.

126 *Robert Maxwell stands alongside Malcolm Paris (right) at the Guvnors' Club dinner in 1979. His Pergamon Press building was destroyed by fire, and rebuilt by Bovis, an early contract win for fellow Czech emigré Frank Lampl.*

127 *The £20 million EMI Centre in Tottenham Court Road, a huge office development by the standards of the time.*

127

It was an extremely demanding brief, and the job had to be taken over in September without Bovis being allowed on site beforehand. Yet Bovis had to commit itself to a programme for completion, and on the day of the takeover sign up more than 500 directly employed staff.

This mammoth task called for a management team of exceptional abilities, and Ron Peggs led the Bovis project managers. They had a tough job, particularly in the field of industrial relations. The Parliamentary Committee of Public Accounts later complimented Bovis on the cost control of the Royal Liverpool Teaching Hospital. More construction projects followed in Liverpool. The first-ever management contract awarded in the city was for the modernisation of the Royal Liver Building in 1977. The trades unions were initially suspicious of subcontracting all the work, but the relationship established by Bovis allowed the project to proceed without industrial disputes and it was finished on time. A third successful Liverpool contract was the rebuilding of the Marks & Spencer store, again a project which was completed in harmony with the trades unions.

One further spin-off from the innovative Royal Liverpool Teaching Hospital was the appointment of Bovis as the management contractor on a hospital at Chester, which became a double first for the company. It was the first of the new nucleus hospitals to be built, and the first hospital constructed under a management contract.

128 *Modernisation of the Royal Liver Building, the first-ever management contract in Liverpool. Bovis managers won the confidence of suspicious unions.*

128

Impressively, the scheduled seven-year timetable for design and construction was reduced to four years.

In 1977 Bovis split the construction division into building and civil engineering. A. E. Farr became Bovis Civil Engineering Ltd with Pat Hall as managing director. Both Pat Hall and Bob Heatley, the managing director of Gilbert-Ash in Scotland, joined the Bovis board. Then in December Clifford Nancarrow retired from the board and was replaced by the chief executive officer of P&O, Dick Adams. There were further significant boardroom changes in 1978 with Sandy Marshall's resignation and later in the year both Neville Vincent and Sir Brian Horrocks announced their intentions to retire. On his retirement as chairman, Neville Vincent became president, and his successor Malcolm Paris expressed: 'the thanks of the board for the guidance and leadership he had given during the most critically difficult years in the life of the Bovis Group. His manner and style had set a tone which generated affection and co-operation'.

With commercial building and private housebuilding in the doldrums, public sector contracts were crucial for the success of a contractor in the late 1970s. Aside from hospital and school contracts, Bovis won vast housing estate projects in Islington and Hackney, and was probably building, or managing the construction of more residential accommodation than any other contractor. Indeed, Bovis managed to push construction turnover to a record £100 million in 1978 at a time when rival firms were hard pressed.

Naturally, the large volume of work from Marks & Spencer, that most faithful and consistent client of the Bovis System, underpinned the development of management contracting. Marks & Spencer took Bovis to Paris and Dublin for the building of stores and warehousing, and both shops were so successful that Bovis was soon back to build extensions. There was also an enormous warehouse in White City for Marks & Spencer. In 1981 the managing director of Bovis, Bernard Heaphy, was honoured with an OBE. He said that the award was a recognition of everything the construction division had achieved during his decade in charge.

But while the construction division made a spirited recovery, house building languished in a parlous state. Bovis Homes saw demand recover briefly in 1976 with 312 houses sold in five weeks in April, but by November sales had slumped to 16 houses per week, and Bovis Homes' stock of unsold houses stood at 700. It was a similar story in 1978 when the market picked up, only to be dashed by mortgage rate increases. It would be the mid-1980s before Bovis Homes would return to the glory of its hey-day.

Meantime, Bovis was scaling the heights of British contracting. In June 1980 a Bovis team under John Smith was selected as management contractor for the City's most eclectic office project to-date, the Richard Rogers-designed Lloyd's building in Leadenhall Street. Its stunning stainless-steel exterior with elevators and services outside the building envelope and ultra-violet night lights, was soon acknowledged as a masterpiece of modern architecture.

The controversial Lloyd's building heralded a wave of projects in the City, as firms prepared for the Big Bang financial sector reforms promoted by Prime Minister Margaret Thatcher's first administration. It was an indicator of just how far the Bovis Group had come since its forced sell-out to P&O in 1974, and a sign that Bovis was now in the upper echelons of the British construction industry, working alongside architects like Richard Rogers and Norman Foster. Even the building of Regent

129

129 *The International Conference Centre in Westminster demonstrated the flexibility of management contracting when the financial collapse of a subcontractor failed to hold up work.*

Street in the 1920s was nothing by comparison. This was world-class construction for the most demanding of designers.

All the same, Bovis remained at the cutting-edge of contractual development, and was still busy persuading clients to use different forms of contract. Just as Sidney Gluckstein had pushed the Bovis System in the 1930s, fifty years later Bovis Limited was peddling its latest manifestation, management contracting, in the early 1980s. The successor to the Ministry of Public Buildings, the Property Services Agency, invited Bovis to discuss management contracting at this time, and over a period of some months the PSA's standard form of contract was transformed into a management contract document.

As usual with Bovis, the evolution of a contract format was linked to a specific job. In this case, the relationship with the PSA led to the appointment of Bovis as managing contractor for the International Conference Centre in Westminster, a terrorist-resistant fortress opposite the Abbey. This project amply demonstrated the flexibility of management contracting when the concrete frame subcontractor went into receivership. Bovis immediately took on its staff, ensuring minimal delay, and the whole job was finished on time. Under the Standard Form of Contract such a response would have been unimaginable.

In 1981 the Sports Council sponsored a competition for the design of a multi-purpose sports hall and, from 122 entries, the architect working with Bovis was declared the winner. This Standard Approach to sports halls resulted in almost thirty contracts, and showed how design and construction should be considered as a partnership rather than an adversarial relationship.

It soon became apparent that management contracting was well suited to the most complicated building projects. Hospitals, for example, which are extremely complex, were early candidates for management contracting. But in the 1980s Bovis adapted the concept to a broad range of projects, from a prison at Cambridge to the Renault factory at Swindon, another office development for Wiggins Teape at Basingstoke, the Royal Concert Hall in Nottingham, the London Docklands Arena, five hospitals for BUPA and the modernisation of London underground stations.

Rather belatedly, other British contractors began to form 'fee' and 'construction management' divisions. Imitation might be the sincerest form of flattery, but rival contractors did not really understand what the new approach meant beyond being a good way to win work. So they started poaching Bovis staff to head their new divisions and show them what to do. Bovis-trained managers thus spread across the British construction industry and achieved prominence at a much earlier stage of their careers than might have been expected. This phenomenon also promoted a certain mystique, with Bovis as the *alma mater* to a generation of young construction managers. But these were not whizz-kids, these were managers who delivered results.

However, the expansion of management contracting to the household names of British construction had an unforeseen effect. Clients began insisting on competitive bidding for management contracts. There was nothing wrong with this in principle and Bovis took part in many competitions. But in some cases the competition became a contest to see who submitted the lowest fee, although interview performance counted for a great deal. This was just the tendering system masquerading under another name and nothing to do with establishing a non-adversarial relationship between contractor and client.

Indeed, the dilution of the principles underlying management contracting was a source of much annoyance at Bovis, and equally insidious was the poor understanding of management construction documentation by professionals. Quantity surveyors in particular disliked management contracting because it undermined their role. Many opportunities to compete were turned away by Bovis because the documentation and attitudes were not concurrent with the spirit, or letter of management contracting.

Yet the luxury of being in a position to turn away work was another feather in the management contracting cap. In 1981 management contracting represented around half the workload of Bovis, while by 1984 the majority of contracts were carried out under this system. Increasingly, the company switched from being a large employer of direct labour to being purely a provider of management. In fact, the redevelopment of the Trocadero site in London's Piccadilly became the last project on which direct labour was employed, and from employing thousands of tradesmen and labourers, numbers dwindled to a few hundred.

Bovis had pioneered a revolution in the construction industry. Increasingly, contractors were regarded as managers of the construction process, as vital to a client's team as the designers. They were white-collar professionals rather than men in muddy boots, and tended to be university-educated instead of graduates of the school of hard knocks. Clients had come to realise the importance of their own role and no longer sat back relying on consultants. It now became normal practice for clients to select both the method and firm for a particular job.

In actual fact, contractual relations had come full circle in a hundred years. When

130 *Management contracting adapted to a wide range of projects in the early 1980s, including the Renault parts centre at Swindon.*

130

Charles William Bovis founded C. W. Bovis & Co in 1885, separate 'trades contracts' were common, and they persisted in Scotland and the north of England until the Second World War. By the time Bovis was appointed as 'construction manager' on the Broad Street station site next to Liverpool Street station in 1985 its role was to manage contractors appointed by, and in contract with, the client. Charles Bovis could almost have walked on site and taken over from the modern Bovis team.

Margaret Thatcher liked to proclaim her sympathy for Victorian values, and here was another example of restoring an earlier *modus operandi*, albeit under very different conditions. Construction management was the next big idea to hit the British construction industry. It offered previously unattainable targets of quality, speed and budgetary control by achieving an identity of interest between client, architect, contractor and subcontractors. But an industry finding it hard to understand management contracting found the concept of construction management hard to grasp, and not for the first time Bovis managers found themselves having to sell a new construction concept.

In parallel with the considerable impact of Bovis in the United Kingdom, the decade after the P&O Group takeover saw the first real successes in contracting overseas, partly as a reaction to the slump in new domestic contracts after the financial crisis of 1974. The lessons from the company's previous misadventures in pre-war Palestine and post-war South Africa seem to have been learnt, and the first overseas project was the Marriott hotel in Amsterdam. A new strategy for overseas contracting was agreed at a board meeting early in 1975. It noted that the group already had modest interests in ten countries: Singapore, Indonesia, Malaysia, Spain, France, Belgium, Holland, Canada, Egypt and Kuwait, but the meeting resolved to concentrate on Iran where Marks & Spencer had been approached for advice by a retail group. An office was opened in Tehran with Mike Walker in charge and Barry Holmes as operations director. At the same time, Bovis decided to form an overseas construction division under Frank Lampl.

This was the start of a remarkable career for Frank Lampl and would propel Bovis into the ranks of the world's leading contractors, an achievement his knighthood in 1990 would recognise. But if Frank Lampl's life were ever made into a film, this period would only be the third reel. Hopefully, nobody today will ever have to match his experience which represents an amazing triumph over the evil twins of the twentieth century, fascism and communism.

Frank Lampl spent his teenage years in the concentration camps of Auschwitz and Dachau, and first worked in construction as a slave labourer on an underground factory for BMW outside Munich. After the liberation he returned to his native Czechoslovakia and resumed his education in Brno. The inheritance from his murdered family brought him some prosperity, but this property was soon nationalised by the communist authorities. Denounced as an 'undesirable bourgeois', Frank Lampl was sent to the uranium mines of Jachymov where he served three years' hard labour out of a five-year sentence. A condition of his release in 1953 was that he took up a manual labouring job in either mining or construction. Having had enough of mining, Frank Lampl joined a state construction company in Ostrava as a labourer. By 1960 he was a site manager and three years later, as managing director of the construction company Pozemni Stavby Zavod Opava, he won a place at Brno Technical University to study construction.

Working his way up the hierarchy, he was in a senior position in a Moravian state

131

131 *Frank Lampl's success in winning overseas projects from 1975 onwards started his remarkable ascent to the top of the British construction industry.*

132

132 Riyadh's Olympic stadium, an early project for Bovis International in the late 1970s. Bovis worked in a joint venture with Philipp Holzmann.

133 Abu Dhabi Chamber of Commerce is a notable landmark on the Arabian Gulf coastline, built in the late 1970s.

contractor when the Russian tanks rolled into Prague in the spring of 1968. Unwilling to get caught up in another repressive regime, Frank Lampl and his wife left with one suitcase to visit his son Thomas, who was studying at Oxford University. They never returned and a career in British construction seemed the best option available to the new immigrant. At first, language was a problem. The future senior statesman of the British construction industry could read Shakespeare, but not understand Cockney. But these difficulties were soon overcome, although Frank Lampl's first employer would later write to him expressing amazement that he had never recognised his talent. Certainly, Frank Lampl's linguistic skills were useful later in the worldwide expansion of Bovis, which he joined in 1971 as an assistant project manager, and his Bovis career was meteoric.

Back in 1975 Bovis was only looking for a few lucrative foreign contracts to replace work lost in the commercial denouement of the previous year. That objective was quickly achieved. For Bovis, the commercial success of overseas contracting was definitely a case of third time lucky. The overseas division became a separate company, Bovis International, in 1978 with Frank Lampl as managing director. Its mission was to obtain work overseas on a fee-earning management basis. In its first three years Bovis International secured contracts in Saudi Arabia, Kuwait, Abu Dhabi, Iraq, Jordan, Nigeria, Congo, Luxembourg and California. However, in certain countries Bovis was obliged to bid for lump-sum contracts in joint venture with local contractors, although the local partner took most of the risk. Many of the projects

133

134

134 *Bovis International completed a five-star hotel, golf course, villas and apartments at Quinta do Lago on the Algarve in Portugal.*

were financed by the huge oil revenues which followed the oil price hikes of 1974. Even the oil-funded infrastructure boom was not without its bad days. In Saudi Arabia Bovis was left responsible for the completion of on-going projects when a local firm got into difficulties. Once bitten, Bovis International turned shy, and from 1981 all appointments abroad were solely on a fee basis.

It was ironic that the oil money financing the expanding Bovis International order book had also been the source of the financial crisis that had cost the Bovis Group its independence in 1974. Recycling petro-dollars was an essential part of bailing the UK out of recession. Bovis certainly reaped the benefit, and the new overseas division was profitable from its first year. Bovis International built a small palace, schools and houses in Saudi Arabia, and an Olympic stadium in Riyadh in joint venture with Philipp Holzmann. Its other contracts ranged from civil engineering projects like extensive sewage works in Abu Dhabi, roads and pipelines to schools, offices, hotels, apartments and shopping centres. The Iranian Revolution in 1978 caused the abrupt closure of the office in Tehran. The operations director Barry Holmes remembers how he and Bob Diamond were the last ones out. 'We drove to the airport and abandoned our car, and got on any plane. We ended up in Istanbul, and it took three days to get out. That was in Christmas 1978, and two weeks before the return of Ayatollah Khomeni.'

From 1981 to 1985 Frank Lampl with his lieutenants Mike Walker and Barry Holmes, hunted around the globe for new business, travelling as far afield as Chile, Venezuela, Bermuda, Morocco and Sri Lanka. In 1982 alone 22 contracts worth a total of £350 million were bagged, including a 400-bed hotel in Sri Lanka, 50 villas in the Algarve and a £25-million pipeline in Aden. The following year the failure of a contractor in Abu Dhabi brought in contracts worth £50 million, and contracts were also won in Yemen, Portugal and San Francisco. The California awards comprised the management of hotel, commercial and retail developments, and represented an important stateside debut. Bovis International Ltd (California) was formed and would be greatly enhanced by acquisitions later in the decade. An executive, Tony Farmer, was also seconded to a South African company to advise on management contracting.

By the early 1980s the United Kingdom was plunged into another oil price-induced recession, and the recession at home meant that Bovis International had no problem recruiting staff for its growing portfolio of overseas contracts. There was also a project management appointment to develop 3500 acres at Quinta do Lago on the Algarve in Portugal. It started with the construction management of a five-star hotel and golf course, and was rounded off with a Bovis development of villas and apartments.

In 1985 Bovis International's new appointments ranged widely again, from a 300-bed hotel in San Francisco to a consultancy in Zaire for the World Bank, and even work in Bangladesh. This succession of new overseas business did not go unnoticed, and Bovis International won the Queen's Award for Exports in 1984 and 1986. By any estimation the Bovis Group's days of speculation and disaster in foreign climes was over, and the highly successful growth of international contracting was a feature of the first decade under P&O's ownership.

Frank Lampl's outstanding performance was acknowledged by his appointment to the P&O main board in 1985, along with Philip Warner, following the retirement of Malcolm Paris on medical advice. Bernard Heaphy and Pat O'Brien also retired in 1985, and so did Jef Jefcoate following the P&O decision to close the Bovis property division. A life-long Bovis stalwart, and for many years in charge of work for Marks & Spencer, Chris Spackman was appointed as the new managing director of Bovis. Thus another Bovis old guard made way for the new, with Frank Lampl as chairman

135

135 *In 1977 the route for Her Majesty Queen Elizabeth II's Silver Jubilee procession provided Bovis with a marketing opportunity too good to miss.*

136

136 *In July 1984 Her Majesty Queen Elizabeth the Queen Mother and Bernard Heaphy OBE, chairman and managing director of Bovis Construction Ltd, toasted the success of the eclectic new Lloyd's building.*

of Bovis Construction and Philip Warner running Bovis Homes.

The year before had also seen a reshaping of the Bovis Group with management buy-outs at three divisions: Gilbert-Ash in Scotland, Bovis Civil Engineering and the site accommodation manufacturer Wyseplan. The Scottish sale reflected almost a decade of rearguard fighting by its directors, who had long argued against the ban on competitive tendering imposed in 1974, and had unsuccessfully asked for an MBO twice before. With a full order book and the success of the Cameron Toll retail centre in Edinburgh behind it, Gilbert-Ash Group was at last granted its request in December 1984, and became the GA Group, with the Gilbert-Ash name finally fading into oblivion.

The sale of Bovis Civil Engineering was due to problems with competitive tendering too, and a clash with the Bovis culture of fee-based contracting. Civil engineering was a very late addition to the Bovis Group, and arrived with the acquisition of A. E. Farr Ltd in 1968 which became Bovis Civil Engineering Ltd in 1972. The majority of its work was on roads and motorways, and a profit could only be made by pursuing claims at the end of contracts, which could take months or years. In 1978, for example, a budgeted profit of £650,000 became a loss of £349,000 at the year end due to claims outstanding on three motorway contracts.

By 1980 the Department of Transport was finding it increasingly difficult to get firms to tender, and Bovis suggested the introduction of management contracting for road contracts. Bernard Heaphy and Pat Hall were summoned to the Department, but failed to convince officials that management contracting was the solution. So the Bovis board decided not to tender for any more road contracts and Pat Hall resigned from the company. This ban was rescinded in 1983 to allow Bovis Civil Engineering to tender successfully for the Leatherhead to Reigate section of the M25, but the contract was a commercial failure. The Bovis board was not amused and at the end of 1984 a management buy-out was completed, and the company reverted to its former title A. E. Farr Ltd. Bovis was never happy as a civil engineering contractor and never tried to become one again.

In 1985, after a tough recession, only the most optimistic forecasters would have imagined the housing and construction building booms that lay just around the corner. The Bovis centenary dinner at the Mansion House on 20 March 1985 seemed to celebrate the company's return to financial health after a decade within the P&O Group. On the guestlist for that glittering night in the magnificent Egyptian Room were the Lord Mayor Sir Alan Traill, Lord Seiff, Sir Keith Joseph, Sir Jeffrey Sterling, Neville and Harry Vincent and Dr John Glyn. As the panegyric speeches infused the atmosphere with nostalgia, the presence of Charles Bovis, Sidney Glyn, Sir Samuel Joseph and V. E. Vincent could almost be felt. The Bovis tradition lived on, ready for a brighter tomorrow.

In an interview with *Building* magazine to mark the 100th anniversary of Bovis, Malcolm Paris gave an insight into future strategy: 'Bovis will stay fee-system orientated, although we are moving in the direction of design-manage-construct as well. It is generally believed that our competitors will go back into tendering when the economic conditions are right because they reckon they can make wider margins there. We won't. It cuts both ways. For the tenderer, the margins can be wider. But Bovis has the advantage in having always been fee-orientated. When a recession occurs, we don't have to restructure the way we work to survive.'

However, the previous two years had seen some highly significant developments at the parent group P&O, notably the dramatic emergence of Jeffrey Sterling as chairman in November 1983 at the height of a hostile takeover bid by Trafalgar House. It is hard to imagine what would have happened if Sir Nigel Broackes' shipping, construction and property conglomerate had succeeded in getting its hands on P&O. Maybe Bovis would have survived as a fee-based contractor within this corporate empire and Bovis Homes would have been subsumed into a larger housing division. Fortunately, this is just a matter for speculation.

As it was, a reference to the Monopolies and Mergers Commission gave Sterling a breathing space to put P&O's house in order, particularly in certain American oil ventures. With characteristic energy and verve, he produced the balance sheet and accounts for 1983 two months ahead of schedule, and by the time the MMC cleared the Trafalgar bid, P&O could justly claim to be financially robust. Trafalgar House realised what it was up against and withdrew its bid. Nigel Broackes took it on the chin. Quite apart from saving the group, the bid contest resulted in the installation of an ambitious and aggressive new chairman at the helm of P&O. This was exactly what Frank Sanderson had hoped to achieve in 1974, although casting himself in the role of captain. Now the Bovis Group could hope that a more adventurous strategy would be endorsed by the parent group. The omens were certainly good.

Sir Jeffrey Sterling, as he became in the New Year's honours list of 1985, was a natural entrepreneur and had started his career as a stockbroker, later founding the Sterling Guarantee Trust in 1969. His City reputation was sealed by his part in the rescue of Town & City Properties following the 1974 property crash, and he had been a director of P&O Group since 1980, as well as an adviser to the Department of Trade and Industry and confidante of Mrs Thatcher.

Interesting times lay ahead for the Bovis Group, whose former deputy chairman and scion of the family owners, Sir Keith Joseph, was one of the architects of the Thatcher Revolution. It was apt that Bovis should prosper under the business conditions that Sir Keith Joseph worked so hard to create, even if the boom was doomed to go bust.

137 *Jeffrey Sterling's (now Lord Sterling) emergence as chairman of P&O Group in 1983 signalled a new era in Bovis's development both in the UK and overseas.*

137

CHAPTER 10

Boom, bust and globalisation

History never entirely repeats itself but it is instructive to compare the boom-to-bust business cycles of the early 1970s and late 1980s. Both episodes were under Conservative governments, and followed an expansion of credit in the UK economy that inflated commercial property and house prices. For the construction industry there was a long period of massive profitability, mainly from windfalls on property development and house building. Then the bubble burst, leaving huge office schemes unlet and house prices substantially lower in real terms. The building industry plunged into the red, with the inevitable concomitant of several years of receiverships, redundancies and restructuring.

Of course, the parallels between 1971–4 and 1986–90 can be over drawn, but the property roller-coaster was a familiar ride to older hands. However, Bovis was a very different corporate animal in the second great post-war property crash. In the early 1970s the group was operating as an independent stock-market-quoted company, and became heavily involved in both secondary banking and property development. In contrast, in the late 1980s Bovis was a subsidiary of P&O and acting uniquely as a fee-based contractor and house builder.

As might be expected, Bovis Homes suffered considerably in the second housing slump. Chancellor, and then Prime Minister John Major's regime of high interest rates and low inflation meant that house price falls were not disguised by high general inflation as they were in the 1970s. That meant recent mortgages were often bigger than house values and left owners with real capital losses or negative equity. House builders found themselves with expensive landbanks and resorted to discounting and marketing incentives to shift their stock. Thus the easy profits of house price inflation had a very nasty sting in the tail.

The story for Bovis Construction was rather different. Still under the watchful eye of the P&O board, the company was not allowed to return to property development, let alone high finance. The nearest Bovis came to property development was working for P&O's property arm, which provided significant contracts such as Chelsea Harbour and Beaufort House in the City. However, Bovis did succeed in acquiring a unique range of skills from the London office building boom, especially in the fast-track construction of ultra-modern offices for the financial sector. The £800-million Broadgate complex in the City and £3-billion Canary Wharf development in London Docklands are the most memorable examples. There were many others. At times the Bovis name board seemed synonymous with the City of London.

Such complicated and fast-track building projects required the assimilation of best practice from around the world, and the Bovis team travelled the globe to learn how to achieve seemingly impossible time schedules, or certainly ones that had never been accomplished in the United Kingdom before. It was a combination of the market slump in Britain and the accumulation of Anglo-American construction expertise at Bovis that made globalisation a natural strategic step for chairman Frank Lampl. Globalisation is an ill-defined term. In essence it means the selling of goods and services on a worldwide basis, and the assembly of the people and office network required to deliver what has been sold. Coca-Cola, for instance, is the quintessential global brand with a global supply chain. Bovis was to become another global brand name in the 1990s. The alternative would have been a more savage round of redundancies for Bovis in Britain, and the break-up of even more of the talented teams assembled in the late 1980s. With his internationalist pedigree, Frank Lampl was the right man to pull off this very difficult strategy.

It certainly was a difficult objective. In the markets of the industrialised world, where Bovis was likely to sell its expertise, there were already highly advanced construction industries, usually with strong protectionist reflexes. A British building company was hardly likely to be welcomed with open arms if it was out to pinch work from local firms. Frank Lampl's vision was to see that the highly selective acquisition of local construction management companies was the key to opening this door. Whether this process represented the helpful globalisation of a local company, or a global foot-in-the-door for Bovis depended on where you happened to be standing at the time.

This 'local and global' strategy was not just a reflex reaction to the collapse of the building boom of the late 1980s, although the slump greatly accelerated the process. It was a thread running through the whole general management strategy of the period and a popular management concept of the time. In the context of Bovis this meant expansion from a strong base in the United Kingdom to create a worldwide network of construction management companies, and at the same time winning work from multinational clients which were in the process of globalising their own operations. It was a modern parallel to C. W. Bovis 'going where the work was' in London a hundred years ago. Only this time the work could be in Shanghai, Kuala Lumpur or Johannesburg, and Bovis was 'following the finance'.

Frank Lampl received exceptional support from P&O chairman Sir Jeffrey (later Lord) Sterling and its managing director Bruce (later Sir Bruce) McPhail, who trusted his judgement for a whole series of acquisitions around the world. This was the first time since the questionable acquisitions of the late 1960s and early 1970s that Bovis had embarked on such an expansive programme. The ultimate result was the hummingbird's arrival in more than 30 countries around the globe, and the creation of a global construction management service.

For Sir Frank Lampl, as he became in the 1990 New Year's Honours, it was a continuation of the process that began as chief executive of Bovis International in 1978. Then he was looking for work abroad to beef up an order book hit by a domestic construction slump. This experience meant that when the next boom went bust, Sir Frank already had his overseas expansion strategy up and running. Nevertheless, this summary puts the history of Bovis into fast-forward, and paints its analysis with a very broad brush. Reality demands a far more detailed appraisal of the period under discussion, although in the mayhem of the late 1980s events moved so fast at

138 *The Broadgate project in the City of London revolutionised British construction with its adoption of US construction management techniques. Bovis worked alongside Schal International and readily adapted to American fast-track building methods.*

Bovis that the underlying picture is often hard to discern.

First it is necessary to turn the clock back to 1985 and the Broadgate development, and to explore exactly why this project represented such a revolution for the British construction industry. *Building* magazine carried an unprecedented four articles on the Broadgate scheme, as the whole industry became fascinated by what Bovis was, quite literally, managing to achieve. As was often the case, the starting point was an extremely demanding client, in this instance Rosehaugh Stanhope, a joint venture between Godfrey Bradman and Stuart Lipton, two highly successful City property developers, whose principal representative was Peter Rogers, brother of the celebrated architect Richard Rogers, now Lord Rogers.

For the original bidding, contractors had to demonstrate how a 42,700-square-metre building could be at shell-and-core stage in twelve months. Bovis won the job, but a rival bidder from the United States, Schal International, ended up with the role of construction adviser, and brought an infusion of US construction knowledge with it. American ideas and innovations were adopted for the erection of the steel frame, such as the use of crawler cranes rather than tower cranes to lift several sections of steel at once. 'You do not have to lift one beam at a time, you can lift three at a time, like they do in America using the chandelier method,' one Bovis manager explained. 'You can have things like shakedown decks, where you take all the steel up to one level. It all saves time'.

And save time they did. Steel erection was twice as fast as the previous record of 120 tonnes per day notched up on the neighbouring Finsbury Avenue office project, also a Rosehaugh Stanhope development. One more American-inspired innovation was the adoption of something called value engineering. This process enables the contractor to inspect the design of the building as it is produced to see if there is any way it can be built more cheaply, or more quickly, and how lay out options impact on rental income. For value engineering to work on Broadgate there had to be a highly professional spirit of co-operation between the architect, Arup Associates, the construction team and the client.

Ian Macpherson, Bovis's project director on Broadgate, summed it up as 'a committed client, first-rate design, the right management structures and everybody pushing in the same direction.' There was also a new 'can-do' American attitude, which got everyone talking in the UK construction press. As the Broadgate director said: 'The Americans will tell you about the million things that can be done, and the one problem that they intend to solve. In this country it is a million reasons why it cannot damn well be done.' This positive approach caught the heady spirit of the times. In the mid-1980s the British financial sector embarked on a series of structural reforms known as the Big Bang that dramatically changed the way the City did its business. It was perhaps apt that the construction industry modified its approach to building offices in this atmosphere of reform. Bovis was in the driving seat, and envious rivals could only listen and learn about this remarkable increase in the speed of the construction process.

It was a dizzy experience. Former Bovis managing director Sir Peter Trench actually wrote a letter to *Building* magazine wondering whether the extra expense of speeding up the construction process was really worth it. Certainly, it seemed that for City traders, in desperate need of a new trading floor, the new fast-track methods were the answer, but Sir Peter had a point. The total cost of many projects is much more important than delivery time, although obviously this was not the case at Broadgate or Canary Wharf. On the other hand, where speed was the main objective, Bovis had secured itself a major advantage. And in the late 1980s, speed was what the highest spending clients wanted. But even as Broadgate captured the headlines in the mid-1980s, the efforts of Bovis International were bearing fruit, and export turnover passed £100 million. It was sufficient to win the firm a second Queen's Award for Exports in 1986.

Working abroad could have added excitement. In January 1986 seven staff returned from Aden after a five-day ordeal pinned down by rockets, tanks and machine guns. The seven men were working on a $25-million project to install 35 miles of water pipeline and became trapped on two sites when fighting broke out between government and rebel troops. Gerraint Parry recalled: 'The first we knew was that planes were zooming around dropping bombs. Shells were falling around us.'

He and quantity surveyor Tom Spilstead were under siege for five days and dug trenches with the terrified native workforce. In the meantime, Dave Clarke and Hugh Brown had taken shelter in the Aden Hotel where Bovis had an office, and were surrounded by government troops. They were all eventually rescued by the Royal Yacht *Britannia*. 'A tank destroyed a bedroom 15 feet from where we were standing,' said Dave Clarke, who was later awarded the OBE. 'On the way to *Britannia* we passed many dead bodies, the stench was terrible.'

Apart from such incidents, the London building boom was the main focus of interest for the British construction industry. William Fishlock's article in *Building* magazine at the start of January 1986 highlighted many reasons to be cheerful. Architects' commissions stood at £3.44 billion compared with £1.9 billion in 1980. New commercial building orders were up 52 per cent, and Jones Lang Wootton reported that 69 new developments had started in the year to September 1985, a 73 per cent rise on the previous twelve months. Fishlock noted the reasons for the boom, notably pressure from property owners for refurbishment, the growth of tourism, changes in the retail trade, plus the demand for high-quality office space in the City. He pointed out that projects on the horizon included the redevelopment of Fleet Street and White City, and the huge Canary Wharf office scheme in London Docklands.

For Bovis the flow of commercial building orders continued with a second major appointment on the Broadgate site. This was a joint venture with Schal to build the Bishopsgate office scheme enveloping Liverpool Street station, providing the large floor plates required for City dealing rooms as well as more retail space. Broadgate and Bishopsgate jointly comprised more than 400,000 square metres of office space, around half the floorspace of the massive scheme then on the drawing board for

139

139 *Assembling the magnificent steel arch for the Bishopsgate building that straddles Liverpool Street station.*

140 *In 1989 Bovis completed this building suspended from a steel arch above Liverpool Street station as part of Broadgate phase two, also known as Bishopsgate.*

140

141

141 *155 Bishopsgate completed the massive Broadgate office complex in the heart of the City of London.*

142 *Bovis worked alongside Lehrer McGovern on Victoria Plaza's trading floor above Victoria station in London. This Anglo-American relationship ended in marriage.*

143 *Liverpool Street station was extensively refurbished and modernised as a part of the Broadgate development scheme.*

142

Canary Wharf. Prime Minister Margaret Thatcher opened phase one of Broadgate in September 1986, and a large number of guests were gathered for a champagne reception around the skating rink. *Building* columnist and architect Owen Luder marvelled at the construction of 66,000 square metres of office space in 365 days: 'The implications are that attitudes and outdated procedures can no longer be tolerated. Where they form barriers to fast, efficient, quality buildings they must go. The excuses used for so long to justify late completion, poor construction and lack of proper management are no longer credible.'

A further article in the same magazine pointed to the importance of construction management as the contractual arrangement at Broadgate: 'Whereas management contracting can easily get bogged down in paper shuffling, the client in construction management can knock heads together by sitting down at the table with the project's construction managers, designers and trade contractors and mobilise the spectrum of experience at hand. The net effect is that the phenomenal speed of construction has been achieved through the rationalisation of construction techniques rather than by throwing thousands of men at the site. The Bovis team of 30 is fewer than would be required for management contracting.' The Broadgate developers' prime objective was to reduce the period the site is out of action and bring in revenues through rents as quickly as possible. So a lot of construction work was done away from the site. For example, pre-assembled toilet pods were skidded into place on mini-hovercraft skid pads at Broadgate, a fast-track construction technique earlier introduced into Britain by Bovis for St Catherine's College, Cambridge.

However, while Bovis rubbed shoulders with US construction managers on Broadgate, this was not the only Anglo-American encounter during this period. The successful fusion of Lehrer McGovern's American expertise and the skills of Bovis was underlined in a *Building* magazine article on the £100 million Chelsea Harbour development. 'Within a year 17 dissimilar buildings in reinforced concrete with a high quality finish will be about finished. It's a task that even a few years ago would have been considered impossible, particularly since there was no complete set of drawings available when the trade contractors began. The reinforced 20-storey apartment block was topped out in six months, a UK record for reinforced concrete construction, alongside an eight-storey crescent-shaped luxury apartment block which went up in eight weeks! To set a two-year construction period for building a village where over 4000 people will live and work, is a remarkable act of faith. That it was achieved by construction management will only underline that the likes of management contracting look decidedly sluggish by comparison. Chelsea Harbour is concrete's answer to steel frame in the quick build market.'

The Chelsea Harbour scheme included the rehabilitation of an old dock into a 75-berth marina. The developer was P&O and Globe Investments, and the client's representative was John Anderson of P&O, who was destined to become a managing director of Bovis Construction in 1993. It was hardly surprising that Bovis came to appreciate the special qualities of Lehrer McGovern on this job. Even the architect Ray Moxley commented: 'Lehrer McGovern have been really marvellous and opened up everybody's eyes to the problems. They are what I would call "facilitators" who really try to help and get things done.' As on Broadgate, American 'can-do' attitudes were important. Fritz Rehkopf of Lehrer McGovern, later managing director of Bovis Asia Pacific, gave one example: 'It took some convincing for the formwork trade contractor to put 65 men on a section of work where he would traditionally have put

143

144

35. But we showed him that there was plenty of work, and the continuity to keep all his men busy'.

In the autumn of 1986 Bovis took the first step towards the globalisation with the acquisition of a 50 per cent stake in Lehrer McGovern, the sixth largest American construction manager. Aside from the £100 million Chelsea Harbour, Lehrer McGovern had also worked alongside Bovis on the dealing room for the Victoria Plaza. But with 700 staff in five US cities, Lehrer McGovern represented an important east coast debut in the North American market for Bovis, adding to the presence already established by Bovis International in California (*see chapter eleven*).

Frank Lampl explained: 'Lehrer McGovern Bovis will operate exclusively in the United States and for American clients on overseas projects. American construction turnover is £370 billion annually, and if we can increase our share of this market fractionally we shall be pleased. But what we are really aiming at is large international projects financed by American multinational companies. Such clients are more likely to appoint American-based contractors. Lehrer McGovern earned some $30 million in fees from overseas work last year, and we hope to double this turnover within five years. Bovis can add punch to Lehrer McGovern by marketing ventures through the worldwide experience of Bovis International and the immense backing of P&O. We believe the two companies are complementary, as Bovis International's experience is in management contracting, whereas Lehrer McGovern's is in fast-track construction management. Bovis intends to second staff to the new company to learn the latest American management techniques.'

The newly combined Lehrer McGovern Bovis was quick to demonstrate that American clients arriving in Europe would favour a US construction manager. In the spring of 1987, LMB clinched the contract to manage construction of the £1 billion Magic Kingdom at the centre of the EuroDisney complex outside Paris, now Disneyland Paris, which would involve the letting of sixty main subcontracting packages. This giant project gave LMB a foothold in France, and the globalisation of Bovis took another big step forward.

At the same time Bovis bought a Hong Kong-based project manager, Gerry Long, and renamed the firm Bovis Far East Ltd. The eponymous Gerry Long remained as chief executive officer and Frank Lampl became chairman. The first project won was a £28 million, 380-room hotel in Beijing. A project co-ordination contract for the 100,000 square metre Bond Centre in Hong Kong soon followed. Hence in a matter of six months the foundation stones of Bovis's globalisation strategy were laid in the United States, continental Europe and the Far East.

Equally the deluge of new business in the United Kingdom showed no sign of abating. In the first half of 1987 Bovis won a £40 million management contract for the new 17,000-square-metre hall at Earl's Court and a £21 million management contract for Nicholas Grimshaw's *Financial Times* printing works in London Docklands. The restoration and extension of the famous Michelin building in Fulham was also completed, and the intriguing Museum of the Moving Image was handed over. P&O's financial statement reported that 55 projects were undertaken for Marks & Spencer in 1986, and that profits from construction, housing and property were up from £30 million to £50 million. But the best was yet to come for construction.

In the summer of 1987 the huge, Manhattan-style Canary Wharf office scheme in London Docklands was acquired from G. Ware Travelstead by the Reichmann brothers' development arm Olympia & York. The Reichmanns were incredibly

144 *At Chelsea Harbour, Bovis and Lehrer McGovern were partners in the construction team for a second time. Ironically it was Bovis Europe managing director John Anderson, then managing director of the client company P&O Developments, who insisted on the American appointment – much to the annoyance of Frank Lampl.*

145

145 *Chelsea Harbour client John Anderson later joined Bovis from P&O Developments and is now managing director of Bovis Europe.*

146

146 *Nicholas Grimshaw's printing works for the* Financial Times *in the London Docklands.*

147 *The Museum of the Moving Image provided an entertaining addition to London's South Bank cultural complex.*

147

successful property developers with an estimated net worth of $10 billion, placing them among the richest private citizens in the world. The sheer scale of Canary Wharf appealed to the Reichmanns, who saw the project as a new financial district to rival the City. And they immediately set about a radical redesign of G. Ware Travelstead's original proposals for the site.

For Lehrer McGovern Bovis this was exactly the sort of North American client moving into Europe that it wanted to attract. And in October came the sensational news that LMB had ousted Bechtel to be project manager on the £3 billion Canary Wharf project, the first time the company had worked for Olympia & York. Fritz Rehkopf explained the LMB role was 'to develop concepts of how to approach the construction process, help select management contractors and provide technical advice on major building elements such as structural steelwork and curtain walling'. LMB began to mobilise dozens of staff from the US and UK.

Once more the fast-track approach was to be employed, albeit on a project twice the size of Broadgate, and in an area of London that had long been derelict because its geography hindered the development of transport infrastructure. Canary Wharf is part of the Isle of Dogs, a peninsula formed by a loop in the Thames, and was abandoned along with most of London Docklands soon after the Second World War. Olympia & York intended to complete 700,00 square metres of top-quality office accommodation, including a 50-storey tower in just four years.

The Reichmanns were an extraordinary client. Escaping from Europe before the Second World War, the three brothers had reached Canada from Morocco and

148 *The Michelin building in Fulham was returned to its former glory and was extended to include a Conran shop.*

149 *Lord Joseph flew to Toronto with Peter Lehrer to see Albert Reichmann and clinch Canary Wharf. As Sir Keith Joseph he spent three periods on the Bovis board when out of government. His father Samuel Joseph became co-owner of Bovis in 1910.*

149

established a successful tile business in Toronto. From this unlikely base, Olympia & York grew to become the largest commercial property developer in the world, with huge holdings in New York. O&Y developed the 850,000 square metre World Financial Center at Battery Park City in New York, slightly bigger than the 700,000 square metres planned for Canary Wharf. For Bovis, Olympia & York was easily its most important client since Marks & Spencer, and Bovis non-executive director Lord Joseph made a secret business trip to New York to court the Reichmanns. 'Keith and I went to see Albert Reichmann on a Sunday,' recalls Peter Lehrer. 'It was through that meeting that we won the project and beat Bechtel. I suppose it was an example of how personal contact with clients became a differentiating factor. They knew they could reach us personally any time.'

Olympia & York vice-president Richard Griffiths was very clear about the reason for the appointment: 'We regard LMB as our staff arm in Britain. O&Y intends to keep its British contingent pretty lean with only about 15 staff, and most of these will be British. We chose LMB, even though O&Y hasn't worked with them before because they have the experience of building office developments in North America, and are at the same time already tied into the British scene through their ownership by Bovis. We plan to adopt the North American method of inviting lump-sum bids from trade contractors on the basis of drawings alone. LMB is already pioneering this approach in Britain on London Bridge City, and advises us that some British trade contractors are amenable to it.'

More than at Broadgate, Chelsea Harbour, or London Bridge City, the British

150

150 *Canary Wharf under construction in London Docklands. The 700,000 square metres of office space drew comparisons with Manhattan and was an ideal opportunity for Lehrer McGovern Bovis to provide Anglo-American construction management.*

construction industry would be exposed to American-style construction management on Canary Wharf. That this American expertise was owned by Bovis probably helped to sugar the pill, if indeed that was a problem. For after four years on site in the United Kingdom, Lehrer McGovern knew what they were up against. When Fritz Rehkopf was interviewed by *Building* magazine at the start of 1988, he said: 'If a US construction manager working here thinks a British worker is going to jump to it when they snap their fingers, they will generally be disappointed. The worker may be sent to a site without materials, without a proper set of tools, and perhaps without even a proper set of drawings to carry out the work. Frustrated, the worker goes for a cup of tea, and you lose efficiency.

'The key point to improving attitude and efficiency is to train managers to direct work at site level more than is normally done in the UK. What we have done is to bring the contractors, subcontractors and architects together to talk out the process and get full co-operation. They are there helping and encouraging people, saying "Do you need these pieces?" "I'll get that material for you" or "Come on Charlie, let's get this thing done before we go to lunch".' But Rehkopf was not a soft touch. When a young trainee interrupted this interview, he yelled 'don't bring me problems, bring me solutions'. The young chap disappeared quickly, and hopefully found a solution.

151

151 *Fritz Rehkopf led the Bovis team working on Canary Wharf, and later became the managing director of Bovis Asia Pacific.*

Meanwhile, Bovis was applying itself to matters slightly more domestic than the largest commercial office development in the world. In January 1988 Bovis bought the City of London contractor Ashby & Horner for £10 million. Founded in 1740, Ashby & Horner's 500 staff had made a profit of just £314,000 on a turnover of £31 million in 1985. It also offered a specialist masonry and joinery division, plus a City office in Earl Street which was actually its most attractive asset. With a burgeoning City order book, Bovis quickly merged Ashby & Horner into its Yeomans subsidiary to undertake smaller high-quality rebuilding and refurbishment projects. The new division was to have a £60 million annual turnover.

Looking back Sir Frank is the first to admit that the Ashby & Horner takeover was a 'complete disaster', in contrast with the many other acquisitions of this period. Eventually most of the company was closed and Bovis lost money. The reason? 'An alien culture', says Sir Frank. 'It was a throw-back to the old days of the clash between fee-based work and lump-sum contracting, and Bovis remains a fee-base firm par excellence. All our other acquisitions fitted in with the fee system.'

On the other hand, globalisation continued in the early months of 1988 with the formation of a joint venture with the Tourism Bank of Turkey, Turban Bovis, to capitalise on the hotel building boom. Nobody seems to have realised the amusing title of the new company, until *Building*'s Hansom column suggested other companies in the company should be named Beret Bovis (France), Stetson Bovis (USA), or even Sombrero Bovis (Mexico). 'Turban' was actually a contraction of the 'Tourism Bank of Turkey'.

Seemingly unruffled by the stockmarket crash in October 1987, Olympia & York pressed ahead with the awarding of contracts for Canary Wharf in the first half of 1988. Apart from the overall construction management role, Bovis subsidiaries won two further large contracts on the Canary Wharf development. First, was the £200 million management contract for the infrastructure of the development, including roads, car parks, utilities and landscaping for phase one. And secondly, FC-2, a £90

152

152 *Almost the whole of the Chelsea Harbour development could have been squeezed into the 83,000 square metre FC-2 building at Canary Wharf, now 10 Cabot Square. Yet this was one of the more modest structures at Canary Wharf.*

million, neo-classical office block designed by Skidmore Owings & Merrill.

In May 1988 Bovis bought the outstanding 50 per cent shareholding in Lehrer McGovern Bovis. This purchase meant full ownership when added to the 50 per cent stake acquired in 1986. It also added 700 to the Bovis headcount of 2600, and made Bovis the world's fifth largest contractor with a £2.5 billion order book. Frank Lampl explained the acquisition in *Building* magazine: 'We have been involved for two years with Lehrer McGovern. In the first year they grew 50 per cent in volume and profit. This year I expect 20 per cent growth, and I hope to achieve the same next year. What we are trying to do is attack the international market from both sides. From America we want to go into countries where the United States is offering aid, and where the US Defense Department has investment in bases. We will come in from the United States on the back of American multinational investors who are looking more towards Europe. Then when Europe starts on multi-million pound projects – which they haven't so far – it is probable they will use architects who are experienced at it. They could be American. EuroDisney was the first example of such a project', said the Bovis chairman.

The completion of the Single European Market in 1992, through the elimination of 300 non-tariff barriers to free trade in the European Community, generated a lot of interest in the construction industry at this time. One school of thought held that cross-border mergers were now more likely, and the Government badgered contractors to prepare for 1992. Bovis was one of the few to heed the call of Europe, and the only British builder to successfully implant itself on the continent over the next decade. European contractors fared little better in Britain. Hochtief, for example, bought a 29.9 per cent stake in Rush & Tompkins, only to lose its entire investment when R&T ended up in receivership soon afterwards.

At home the construction industry was overheating by the summer of 1988. Building material prices were surging and labour was in short supply. Bovis was fined £2450 plus £6000 in costs for noise pollution from the Beaufort House site, blaming 'uncontrollable subcontractors' for the incident. Yet the flood of new contracts continued, such as the £50 million reconstruction of the Langham Hotel in Portland Place for Hilton Hotels International.

Strangely, Canary Wharf remained immune to supply problems. Alan Crane, than a Bovis project director told *Building* magazine: 'We put a lot of time and effort into planning – about nine months' work before we even moved the first bucket of soil. The 80 staff involved with preplanning were inundated with tenders and spent a lot of money visiting every single company before awarding contracts. We may have lead times of 12 weeks on steel tubing and up to 24 on curtain walling, but from the start we built early purchase into the securement of materials. We are buying at very competitive levels, and have not bought one component over budget.' The magazine commented that the size of orders for Canary Wharf – 1000 piles, for example – was helping procurement, and the fact that suppliers wanted to be 'associated with the biggest job going on in the whole of Europe'. Nonetheless, overheating is often a harbinger of trouble ahead, and by August 1988 UK base rates hit 12 per cent, and tellingly new construction orders registered a 12 per cent fall. The construction boom was now a balloon with a hole in it.

Construction and property share prices had weakened and in September came the announcement that P&O had bought a 9.9 per cent stake in Taylor Woodrow. Was Sir Jeffrey Sterling planning a takeover bid? City analyst Leslie Kent of Morgan Grenfell

153

153 *Bovis took over construction management of the 245 metre high skyscraper at Canary Wharf, One Canada Square, briefly the tallest building in Europe.*

154 *Les Chatfield took responsibility for Broadgate phase two or Bishopsgate, and for Ludgate after Ian Macpherson's departure. Later appointed a divisional managing director, he has overseen many of the major Bovis Europe commercial projects of the 1990s.*

154

commented: 'P&O could actively manage and trade Taylor Woodrow's property through its subsidiary Town & City Properties. We don't believe Sir Jeffrey Sterling has friendly ambitions, although Sir Frank Gibb (then chief executive of Taylor Woodrow) may disagree'. In the event, Sir Jeffrey's intentions were never made public. The 83-year-old founder of Taylor Woodrow, Lord Taylor, and his formidable wife whipped up a furious rearguard action by shareholders. Sir Jeffrey later sold the P&O stake in Taylor Woodrow for a profit of £25 million, boosting the construction, housing and property division's contribution to P&O profits from £57 million to £82.4 million in the first half of 1989.

As Bovis raced into 1989, there was a sense of reality suspended with huge construction projects being undertaken at breakneck speed for a property market that was dropping away beneath the feet of developers. It was ever thus. In 1929 the Empire State Building was completed just after the Wall Street Crash, and for the next decade it was labelled the Empty State Building. Construction managers cannot escape the sad irony that their greatest triumphs often occur when their clients are in deep trouble.

So it was that Bovis carried on building some fantastically ambitious projects in 1989, just as the United Kingdom moved into what became its longest ever post-war recession. On Broadgate phase two, or Bishopsgate as it was known, Les Chatfield's team organised the jack-up of 4500 tonnes of steel frame by 50 millimetres for the removal of temporary formwork to allow completion of a magnificent steel arch building that straddles Liverpool Street station. At the same time, Lehrer McGovern Bovis executives were masterminding the construction of 700,000 square metres of office space at Canary Wharf in London Docklands, which included the construction of the 245 metre One Canada Square skyscraper.

It would have been easy to become swept away with the hyperbole of the day. Previously unpublished figures show that pre-tax profits at Bovis Construction Group soared to £38.4 million in 1989, compared with £17.1 million in 1987. But Frank Lampl had read the warning signs, and the more frenzied building activity became at home, the more vigorously he pursued his globalisation strategy. The Bovis order book stood at a record £4.5 billion in 1989. Yet Frank Lampl's concern was that this feast would be followed by a work famine, leaving Bovis starved of new work. It puzzled some UK clients why Frank Lampl travelled the world when all the work was at home. But he saw contra-cyclical thinking as an essential aspect of his role in managing the group.

In early 1989 Bovis announced a technology transfer agreement with Daiwa House, a 38,000 homes-a-year Japanese house builder. Frank Lampl explained: 'Building up business contacts this way offers important opportunities for both companies, and it adds a new dimension to our global business strategy.' The company also bought a 15 per cent stake in the French project manager Copra. Further foreign initiatives were in the pipeline.

Bovis entered the German market through a 50:50 joint venture with Düsseldorf-based Senator Project Management. With 60 staff and branch offices in Frankfurt, Stade and Stuttgart, Senator offered experience in construction and project management, process studios and design, and environmental protection. The firm was founded in 1979, and had originally approached Bovis for work on the EuroDisney site in France. Despite being a relatively young company, Senator had an impressive client list including BP Hamburg, Bayer, Dow Chemical and Proctor & Gamble, and the firm clearly hoped to improve its £4 million a year fee income through an association with Bovis.

But by the autumn of 1989 the British construction industry was in turmoil, and interest rates hit 15 per cent. The strain began to show in the Bovis board between those who wanted to pursue pure construction management and downgrade other areas of activity, and the traditionalists who thought a recession was not the moment to be abandoning any source of income. The reality was that Bovis had to do what the clients wanted, but without compromising the principle of identity of interest. This difference of opinion led to the departure of Ian Macpherson with four senior staff, Ian Wylie, Ian Jepps, Bob White and Harry Thomas, to form a rival construction management firm. 'I am sure we will cover the hole', remarked Chris Spackman, managing director of Bovis, who later admitted Macpherson was a big loss to the company. As an interim measure Ron Peggs took over both the 'B' and 'S' divisions of Bovis, which had only been divided a matter of months before and were easily reunited, and Les Chatfield took over Ludgate, another City development for client Rosehaugh Stanhope.

Bovis chairman Frank Lampl announced the creation of a five-man inner cabinet in November 1989, comprising himself, Peter Lehrer and Gene McGovern from the USA, Chris Spackman, managing director of Bovis Construction, and Bovis International managing director Roger Mabey. John Anderson of P&O Developments joined the board as a non-executive director. Frank Lampl commented: 'Our new structure will integrate Bovis more fully at the group level, and improve the co-ordination of our activities globally. It will enable us to optimise our resources, improve our strategy and upgrade Bovis's technical and management skills.' Prophetically he noted that the 1990s would be a 'more difficult environment' but pointed to the opportunities at Canary Wharf, EuroDisney and the Columbus Center in New York.

Yet the new decade began with a happy event. Frank Lampl was knighted. It was the first time anybody from Bovis had received such a high honour for services to the construction industry. Sir Samuel Joseph's earlier baronetcy was in recognition for his outstanding public service as Lord Mayor of London during the Second World War. Sir Frank was widely credited as the mastermind behind the group's success in the United Kingdom and export markets. Nevertheless, the full impact of his globalisation strategy was yet to be appreciated.

Sir Frank likes to tell the story of how on the morning his knighthood was announced a young secretary greeted him as 'Sir Lampl'. He corrected her and said 'It's Frank'. She then said: 'All right, good morning Frank'. But 1990 was not destined to be a great year for Bovis, or for that matter for British construction in general. Indeed, this was the industry's *annus horribilis* when many projects ended, and the shortage of new work became most acute. British contractors had little alternative but to shed members of thier labour force and retrench or face insolvency. Casualties soon began to emerge.

Bovis undertook a large redundancy programme in 1990. As far as possible Bovis applied the techniques of natural wastage and encouraged early retirement. The long history of a humane approach to staff relations was adhered to in this difficult process that nobody pretended to enjoy. But without a flow of new projects in the United Kingdom, a shrinking headcount was unavoidable and inevitable. 'I had seen the business quadruple since becoming managing director in 1985,' recalls Chris Spackman. 'And in two-and-a-half years I cut it in half, with staff levels down from 1800 to 900

155 *Completion of the £111 million Meadowhall shopping mall in Sheffield in 1990 left Bovis short of work in the north of England.*

155

156

156 *Manchester's Strangeways prison, a welcome public sector contract when boom turned to bust in the UK.*

in the UK. It was the most frustrating part of the recession, and it was very sad to lose so many quality staff that I had lived and worked with over the years.'

The situation overseas was more encouraging. The UK recession of the early 1990s was largely due to errors in domestic economic management, and was not mirrored by problems abroad. European markets were buoyant. Asia was excellent. And the United States merely weathered a short slowdown. Most British contractors were not in a position to profit from this clement international climate. Bovis just pressed on with its globalisation strategy while other UK contractors faced a massive fall-off in new orders.

In February 1990 Bovis formed Lehrer McGovern Bovis SA in France, and sold its stake in Copra at a small profit. New contracts were not long in coming. Marks & Spencer shortly unveiled a £109 million expansion plan to open 17 new stores in France. A Bovis International executive explained: 'Our year-long association with Copra has proved interesting and valuable, giving us an insight into the business methods adopted by the domestic construction industry in France. However, with the approach of the single European market, we feel that a wholly-owned Bovis subsidiary would serve both our clients and ourselves in France. Our relationship with Copra remains friendly, and further co-operation is envisaged.' It was announced that the new head of Bovis SA would be the general manager of Bovis-Copra, Thierry Pourchet. Sir Frank was 'unable to comment because he is in Czechoslovakia'. It was a hint of what was to come next.

Sir Frank had returned to his native land of Czechoslovakia for the first time since he left as a refugee in 1968. With the sudden fall of the Berlin Wall communist regimes had collapsed across Eastern Europe, opening up new business opportunities. For a Czechoslovakian *émigré* like Sir Frank the lure was irresistible. But his first concern was practical. A gaol sentence had been passed in his absence and Sir Frank wrote to William Waldegrave at the Foreign Office for an assurance that he would not face instant arrest on setting foot in Czechoslavakia. 'It did not feel like coming home', Sir Frank told *Building* magazine. 'Had I suffered 20 years' hardship perhaps I would have, but I have built up my home in Britain. Still it was emotional, Prague is a wonderful city, though I must say they are in a terrible mess.' Bovis signed an agreement to take 15 construction managers from Czechoslovakia. 'At £150 per month, the cost of labour is comparable with the Third World in a population with an education and outlook nearer to the West', noted Sir Frank.

He also paid a nostalgic visit to his old Moravian construction company, and commented: 'The most striking thing was that nothing much had changed in 22 years. The organisation had hardly changed, and the people who ran the system were still the same men I worked with before. Imagine what it would be like if Bovis were still the same as it was 22 years ago!' Sir Frank saw big opportunities, particularly in tourism where the potential was similar to Austria with revenues from tourism that were 150 times higher than in Czechoslovakia. Based in Prague, Bovis Czechoslovakia Ltd was formed to operate as a construction management and management contracting company.

From its continental debut in spring 1988 on EuroDisney in France, Bovis was now making enormous headway in the rest of Europe. And in May 1990 the company was named as the *Times*/DHL European Business of the Year for its continental commitment and language training. It was a rare example in the building industry. *The Economist* magazine noted in July 1990: 'Battered by high interest rates, British builders have decided to play it safe and stay at home. If they fail to take a longer-term view and develop concrete European strategies, British construction companies will see their own national market slowly demolished, and will miss out on the burgeoning European one too.' Bovis was not about to be left behind, and its rapid expansion abroad continued with the highly significant acquistion of Southern US contractor McDevitt and Street in the autumn of 1990 (*see chapter eleven*).

In the United Kingdom things turned from bad to worse, and a number of major jobs came to an end. Sir Norman Foster's ITN headquarters at 200 Gray's Inn Road was handed over, and the £111 million Meadowhall shopping mall opened in Sheffield. New projects were thin on the ground, although Bovis won the rebuilding of Strangeways prison in Manchester, and began work on the Ludgate office development for Rosehaugh Stanhope.

The economic outlook in Britain generally was not good. After hesitating for several years, Britain finally joined the European Exchange Rate Mechanism in October 1990, and interest rates fell by one per cent. But crucially the £/DM exchange rate was set too high on Britain's entry into the ERM. Professor Alan Budd warned 'it will be difficult and painful to remain within the ERM'. With Chancellor of the Exchequer John Major becoming Britain's Prime Minister in November, Britain's fate was cast. The British construction industry was doomed to its worst post-war recession.

157

157 & **158** *The Lanesborough Hotel, London's first new five-star hotel for many years, is now a favourite with visitors as diverse as Bill Gates and Madonna.*

158

CHAPTER II

Crossing the Atlantic

Almost half the 5000 staff working for Bovis is now based in the United States and the development of this Anglo-American axis has taken barely a decade. From a standing start, Bovis has made three major acquisitions – Lehrer McGovern in New York, Schal in Chicago and McDevitt & Street in Charlotte, North Carolina. These companies have been skilfully moulded into a single entity, now ranked as number one construction manager in the United States, and one of only two American firms able to operate globally for multinational clients. Bovis has a considerable reputation as a US construction company, to the extent that many people in the industry perceive Bovis solely as an American organisation. There can be no better test for the successful penetration of a foreign market.

Yet the links are older, and the original fee contract of the Bovis System was based on the US model. Another example of this link was Vincent Gluckstein's visit to the Architects' Samples Bureau in New York in 1929, which led to the creation of a similar institution in London known as the Building Centre. Over the years many senior Bovis directors have crossed the Atlantic looking at new construction management techniques, and marvelling at the greater efficiency of construction in the United States. Bovis one-time managing director Fred Cosford came back from America in 1968 fired with enthusiasm about management contracting, and its adoption has gradually revolutionised the Bovis approach to building in the United Kingdom. It was in the late 1970s that Bovis established a small presence in Oakland, California, from which US operations have now expanded to become the largest US construction management company. Today Bovis Americas, which includes Central and South America, has projects worth £7.7 billion under its management, and 2200 employees based in 28 offices.

In other chapters the importance of Lehrer McGovern and Schal in developing Bovis's construction management operations in Britain, Europe and the Far East is considered in detail. It is hard to overstate the importance of Lehrer McGovern Bovis in the globalisation of the company, as LMB's construction management skills have been instrumental in winning key contracts in foreign markets for American clients. The outstanding examples of projects won by Bovis and its New York construction management team are EuroDisney and Canary Wharf. Either project award would have made the takeover a huge success. Likewise Schal proved instrumental in opening up the Japanese market to Bovis. But this chapter confines its scope to the recent progress of Bovis in the United States.

159 *Restoration of the Statue of Liberty established Lehrer McGovern's reputation as a New York construction manager.*

'The United States will continue to be extremely important for us,' said Sir Frank in 1999.'The majority of our clients now come from the US, and it is the main source of global clients. As American companies invest around the world, they need a construction manager that will deliver the same standard of work in foreign markets as they are used to at home. There are really very few companies which can offer this service.'

Buildings are generally built faster and for lower cost in the United States than in the rest of the world. There are many reasons for this phenomenon, such as the sheer scale of projects, the avoidance of architectural indulgence and the use of standardised components. But the precise explanation is difficult to pin down, and has exercised a continuous fascination for the British construction industry. Perhaps it is the American 'can-do' attitude that often contrasts with the more negative and cautious 'cannot-do' approach of the British. But that cannot be the whole story.

In 1981 a young US construction management firm called Lehrer McGovern came to Britain to work on London Bridge City, the office complex which snakes along the South Bank of the Thames from London Bridge down towards Tower Bridge. The Manhattan market was then in a serious slump, and Lehrer McGovern was called in by British contractor John Laing to help on London Bridge City. Lehrer McGovern stayed and met Bovis while working together on the Victoria Plaza above the Victoria railway terminus, and later on the £100 million Chelsea Harbour mixed-use scheme. At Chelsea Harbour it was P&O Developments' managing director John Anderson who insisted on importing US construction expertise, much to Frank Lampl's annoyance. Bovis was initially sceptical about the value of US construction management, and this was doubly ironic in that John Anderson himself later became a managing director of Bovis. 'At the start it was a relationship with a few rough edges, but we learnt to love each other,' recalls Peter Lehrer.

Despite being a relatively new construction management firm, Lehrer McGovern already had a string of high-profile projects under its belt. Peter Lehrer had started his company 'in the kitchen' with Gene McGovern back in 1979 following their resignation as construction managers with Morse Diesel. Lehrer McGovern had made its reputation on the Statue of Liberty restoration project. This very high-profile contract was won against stiff competition in 1983 and completed in time for the Bicentennial celebrations in 1986. How had the young company managed to win what was probably the most sought after construction contract in America?

'They liked our approach,' recalls Pete Marchetto, Lehrer McGovern's first-ever recruit and now president of the North East Region of Bovis Inc. 'We employed the largest ever free-standing scaffold and included a viewing platform and exhibition centre so that visitors could watch the project in progress. We were a very small player then, and our success on the Statue of Liberty led directly to our appointment on the Ellis Island project.' Right from the start, Lehrer McGovern did things differently. Future president of Bovis Inc, Charlie Bacon recalls his interview in 1982: 'Peter Lehrer kept me waiting ten hours and then offered me a job on the spot. I accepted immediately. I saw the excitement and go-go-go entrepreneurial spirit and knew it was for me. And that is why I've stuck with Bovis. The excitement has never stopped.'

Apart from the headline-grabbing Statue of Liberty and Ellis Island projects, the young construction management company also completed the Vietnam War Memorial and work for the Museum of Natural History, the Metropolitan Museum of Art and Central Park Zoo. Later senior vice-president Steven Sommer remembers

160

161

160 *Peter Lehrer proved brilliant at marketing his young company's construction management services.*

161 *Gene McGovern made sure projects came in early and ahead of budget.*

164 *The Museum of Natural History in New York, one of a string of long-standing institutional clients signed up by Lehrer McGovern in the early days.*

finishing a polar bear enclosure at the Central Park Zoo and then waiting armed with a rifle, just in case the bear could get out!

Other notable projects included a new trading floor for the New York Stock Exchange, One Seaport Plaza, the Rockefeller Estate at Pocantico New York as well as the New Jersey State House. There was also the 36-storey One Reading Center in Philadelphia, where a youthful Charlie Bacon – now president of Bovis Inc – made his reputation, rising at 4.30 am every day to commute two hours to the office and finishing the project in a record 17 months.

In the mid-1980s the Big Bang financial reforms in the City of London produced an upsurge in demand for high-quality office space similar to that found in New York,

162

163

162 *Pete Marchetto, Lehrer McGovern's first employee, now runs the North East operation.*

163 *Charlie Bacon, President of Bovis Inc, joined Lehrer McGovern straight from college.*

164

165

165 *New York Vietnam Veterans'
Memorial was completed on a tight
schedule and carried enormous
prestige for Lehrer McGovern.*

166 *The polar bear enclosure at
New York City's Central Park Zoo.
Steven Sommer stood guard with a
rifle to test whether the bears could
get out!*

166

167 *In 1988 Lehrer McGovern
won the programme and project
management for a $340 million
assignment to improve traffic flow at
New York's La Guardia Airport,
its first big contract award as a
subsidiary of Bovis.*

and it was only logical that British contractors should look for American advice on
such projects. And while John Laing brought Lehrer McGovern to London for the
London Bridge City office complex, it was Frank Lampl and John Anderson who
jumped at the opportunity to create a more permanent Anglo-American relationship.
In the autumn of 1986 Bovis acquired a 50 per cent stake in Lehrer McGovern, and
eighteen months later took its holding to 100 per cent.

Peter Lehrer explains the logic behind the sale: 'The tremendous advantage of
Bovis is that it gives us a financial statement quite unlike any other US construction
company, and an ability to obtain performance bonds which are difficult to get. While
the relationship worked very well at the level of equity ownership, we believed the
commitment from P&O would be very different at 100 per cent. But we did not want
the staff to feel acquired, and viewed it more as an association. Most of the interface
with London was done by myself. It remained a family-type of environment, so that
people would feel part of something small.'

Charlie Bacon remembers how all the Lehrer McGovern staff were called together
for a meeting in the Metropolitan Museum of Art – a big client – and told about the
deal. 'That was where we met Frank Lampl, as he was then, for the first time. He told
us we were very profitable and running the business well, and that apart from a few
new reporting requirements, he would not be telling us what to do. Frank Lampl sent
out Barry Holmes and Bob Woodridge who proved incredible assets, and kept to his
word and did not interfere. Instead we kept learning from each other.'

In its early years with Bovis, Lehrer McGovern made substantial progress in
building up its New York business, as well as assisting Bovis on projects in Europe such
as Canary Wharf and EuroDisney. This overseas activity was the source of some
internal friction, but the company continued to pick up contracts in New York,
despite the downturn after the stockmarket crash in October 1987. One big win in

167

1988 was programme and construction management on a $340 million, five-year project to improve traffic flow at New York's La Guardia Airport. The complex scheme included reconstructing the central terminal by expanding the lower level by 50,000 square feet, and a new 250,000 square foot terminal with nine gates. It had to be finished without disturbing day-to-day operations.

Another important move for Lehrer McGovern, or LMB as it had become known, was its entry into program management services in the late 1980s. After winning Rutgers University's $480 million capital improvement programme in New Jersey, the company started to be noticed as a leader in the provision of programme management, especially in the higher education sector. This expertise took LMB into the lower education sector as well, the so-called K–12 (kindergarten to twelfth grade) public schools. As the K–12 market exploded in the early nineties, LMB was well positioned to capture a large share of this market across the north-eastern states. But in due course, the company secured K–12 programmes throughout the nation, including programmes in Los Angeles, Chicago and Charlotte.

Bovis was delighted with progress at LMB; in 1990 LMB started the year with a record 21 new projects worth $427 million, and a further 11 projects worth $423,000 in consultancy fees around the United States. Projects ranged from pre-construction work on Disney's 44-acre Boardwalk Entertainments Centre in Florida to the construction management of new JAL facilities at JFK Airport near New York, and renovation of 41 schools in Texas.

The second phase of Bovis's push into the United States was a more local affair, and was linked to the pursuit of a major contract – the programme management of the 1996 Olympic Games in Atlanta. In 1990 Sir Frank, as he had then become, heard that the family owners of North Carolina contractor McDevitt & Street were looking to sell out to a company with a commitment to looking after their employees. 'We seemed to share the same philosophy right from the start,' says Sir Frank. 'They had a lot of long-established, repeat business from clients, just like Bovis, and a similar attitude to their staff. The Deep South was a world away from the cut-and-thrust of New York, where we were also doing well, but we were able to convince the family that Bovis was the right company to sell to.'

Bovis bought McDevitt & Street for £27.5 million plus a three-year profit-sharing agreement in the autumn of 1990. Its £480 million turnover was 70 per cent construction management, and the addition of 1600 staff substantially boosted the number of American citizens on the Bovis payroll. The acquisition also decisively established Bovis as an Anglo-American construction company, albeit increasingly as a global player. McDevitt & Street's chairman and chief executive officer, Luther Cochrane – the man now named as Sir Frank's successor – joined Bovis as a part of the takeover.

Luther Cochrane explains the background to the deal: 'In 1982 I was a construction lawyer in general practice in the South East, and Bob Street of McDevitt & Street was a client and friend. For his will and for bonding purposes Bob had to name a successor. He named his father and me. I never thought it would be needed. Bob was a very healthy, dynamic guy. I became a developer in 1983 but kept my relationship with McDevitt & Street. Then in 1985 Bob asked me to become a more frequent participant in the company's executive management.

'Late in 1989 Bob was taken ill and died four months later. It was a big shock. He was only 51 and had run a marathon five months earlier. I assumed control of the

168

168 *Luther Cochrane, now chief executive of Bovis and successor to Sir Frank Lampl, came to Bovis with the McDevitt & Street acquisition in 1990.*

company in December 1989 and he died on 5 April 1990. Bob had wanted to reduce his family's dependency on construction and as an executor and trustee of his will I tried to find a good long-term owner. The North Carolina National Bank were our advisers. We told them the money was not important. What we wanted was cultural compatibility and a commitment to the long term.

'One Friday Peter Lehrer called from New York, and asked if he could come down. I knew him from the reputation of Lehrer McGovern Bovis as a construction manager, and agreed to a meeting. After that he said I should meet Sir Frank. We were highly sought after as a general contractor, and had a lot of cash in the bank. So we were not short of suitors. But I went to New York on 2 June 1990 and had four hours' of talks with Sir Frank. It was all about culture, compatibility and sensitivity to clients. We did not even discuss money.'

'I called my co-executor and told him we would be interested in working for Bovis. Two weeks later I went to London and met Sir Frank for lunch at the RAC Club. After lunch we went into a little room and Sir Frank sketched out a deal for the purchase on the back of a napkin. That was the first time a purchase price was mentioned. We had bigger offers from German and Canadian companies and Balfour Beatty. But we felt happier with Bovis. I asked Sir Frank to come to Charlotte and meet our people, and we shook hands on the deal.'

The McDevitt & Street business culture was unusually compatible with Bovis. An obituary of Bob Street published in the company newsletter of July 1990 highlights 'three management tenets Bob held dear: take care of your people, give them an environment in which they can grow and excel, and be client-driven in everything you do'. There was also a decentralised organisational structure to promote entrepreneurial attitudes and a commitment to applying total quality principles to construction. Like Bovis, McDevitt & Street was also an old family firm. In 1922 J. J. McDevitt and his wife Elma were already part-owners of a construction firm in Chatanooga, Tennessee, when they met C. P. 'Gabby' Street. He was recruited by the firm straight from Vanderbilt University. Then in 1925 the McDevitts formed their own construction firm in Charlotte, North Carolina, and took Gabby Street with them. J. J. McDevitt's health began to fail and Gabby Street took over day-to-day operations in 1929. After the McDevitts' divorce in 1940, which left Elma with the company's shares, she appointed Gabby Street as general manager. Twenty years later Gabby Street became sole owner of the company which his son Bob had inherited in 1972.

However, the sale to Bovis in 1990 was not an entirely smooth affair, and due diligence dragged on for sometime. Luther Cochrane recalls setting his alarm clock to put in a 2.30am call to catch Sir Frank as he arrived for work at 7.30am. 'He laughed and said, "you must have set your watch",' says Luther. 'I said I had been up all night worrying about the deal, which was almost true. There was a problem with the bonding company and we worked out a compromise for completion on 14 September 1990.'

In fact this was not an easy time for the US construction industry. Lehrer McGovern Bovis received a setback when the $1 billion Columbus Center was put on ice. The controversial skyscraper was a casualty of the US downturn at the end of the 1980s, and even the American Institute of Architecture had criticised its immense size. Peter Lehrer said: 'Investment banking firms have run into trouble, and are cutting back on lending; the government's problems with the federal deficit have a general impact; and the uncertainty over the situation in Iraq adds to the general malaise'.

The acquisition of McDevitt & Street also posed a different sort of challenge. There is a deep cultural divide between the north-east and southern states in the USA, in both personal style and business relationships. 'It was important to us to be a part of Bovis and not Lehrer McGovern,' recalls Luther Cochrane. 'It was New York really. It was not an easy relationship for us. It took a long time to work it out. At one stage we convened a meeting of executives from both firms at the Arrowhead Conference Center near New York, and tensions ran very high. LMB was very secretive and McDevitt & Street was much more open. It took a long time for us to like each other.'

At this time Bovis concluded its third acquisition Stateside, the construction manager Schal Northeast in New York and Washington-based Schal Mid-Atlantic. Like LMB, Schal was almost immediately important in winning large overseas construction contracts for Bovis, especially in Japan. Here Schal Bovis, as it was now called, benefited from the preferential treatment on public sector contracts secured for US contractors by the US Government as a part of a trade deal.

The Schal Bovis division was completed by the $40 million takeover of Chicago-based construction manager Schal Associates, and its 250 staff joined the Bovis payroll. This firm was founded in 1976, and its portfolio of projects included the redevelopment of O'Hare International Airport, but high-rise buildings were its speciality. In the previous 17 years Schal had built 18 major skyscrapers in Chicago, and provided pre-construction services on 50 others. Three recent examples for famous architects were: Murphy Jahn's 41-storey Savings of America Tower, Cesar Pelli's 47-storey Paine Webber Tower and the 36-storey Morton International Building designed by Perkins & Will. Schal Associates founder Richard Halpern remained chief executive officer and commented: 'This agreement increases our financial strengths to match our technical skills and will enable us to compete for the largest and most challenging construction projects in the world.' On the other hand, as Sir Frank later noted: 'It was unfortunate that the takeover coincided with a downturn in Chicago. But then again we would never have broken into Japan and Taiwan without Schal, which got political help from the United States.'

Thus by the end of 1991 Bovis had its four US divisions: Lehrer McGovern Bovis, McDevitt Street Bovis, Schal Bovis and Bovis Management Services in California. Fortunately for Bovis Inc the slowdown in orders in the USA was nothing like as severe as in the UK in 1989–90, and redundancies were largely avoided. All the same, it was at this juncture that Luther Cochrane and Peter Lehrer changed tack. 'By the time the recession was over in the USA in 1992, we had downsized and old attitudes had gone,' says Luther Cochrane. 'From 1992 to 1995 we worked at finding common ground for a co-ordinated presence in the USA. We began to find a happy medium.'

One exception to this new calm was Chicago, where an ambitious project called the Navy Pier turned out to be a serious setback. It started in late 1992. The scheme involved acting as general contractor on the $190 million redevelopment of the 76-year-old Navy Pier on the shores of Lake Michigan. The pier had been used by the US Navy in the Second World War, and since fallen into disrepair. In an imaginative scheme the Navy Pier was redeveloped into a cultural and leisure attraction featuring 170,000 square feet of exhibition facilities, a Children's Museum, a 32,000 square foot Crystal Garden for tropical plants, park, restaurants and retail areas.

Disaster also struck in New York at this time. The project itself was not the

169

169 *No. 77 West Wacker Drive is the latest of 18 Chicago skyscrapers built by Schal since 1976. By the end of 1991 Schal had become Schal Bovis.*

170 *Navy Pier on the shores of Lake Michigan proved a problem contract in the early 1990s, though this scheme is now a popular cultural and leisure attraction.*

171 *Barney's department store at 660 Madison Avenue involved the lavish transformation of a former 1950s office tower. The client sought Chapter 11 protection from its creditors and Bovis was not paid in full until 1999.*

170

171

problem; instead it was a client who filed for Chapter 11 protection from bankruptcy, leaving bills unpaid. The job in question was the New York clothing store Barney's at 660 Madison Avenue, the largest new speciality shop in Manhattan since the 1930s. It involved the very lavish transformation of a 23-storey 1950s steel-framed office tower, once owned by the oil billionaire John Paul Getty. It was completely gutted and the façade replaced with Luget French limestone. There were 30 new elevators and an atrium, and its first eight floors now comprise a 250,000 square foot fashion store. Technically and logistically Barney's was as difficult as anything LMB had ever done, and was a complete success. However, payment in full was not made until the end of the decade.

More typical of successful projects executed in the early 1990s was the programme management of the $200 million maintenance facility at Houston International Airport for Continental Airlines. This is a vast 2 million square foot maintenance facility able to accommodate ten narrow and two wide-bodied aircraft at the same time. A further big aviation job for LMB was construction management of a new maintenance operations centre for United Airlines on a 300-acre site at Indianapolis Airport. The $1 billion project included the fit-out of hangars, airframe repair shops and other support facilities. For Schal Bovis its biggest job was a $250 million

172 *NationsBank's headquarters in Charlotte, North Carolina. This 63-storey skyscraper is the tallest building in the south-eastern states and was finished one month ahead of its 34-month schedule.*

173 *The $240 million Foley Square Courthouse in New York City is the largest in the USA with 43 courtrooms on 27 storeys.*

174 *Lincoln Square, a $240 million mixed-use development in New York City, comprises 38 storeys of apartments above eight storeys for commercial use.*

175 *(Overleaf)Winning the 1996 Atlanta Olympic Games $500 million programme management contract united the US operations into 'One Bovis'. Before the Olympic success north-south tensions prevented a true synergy from emerging.*

2 million square foot headquarters complex for the Sears Merchandise Group in the suburbs of Chicago.

By contrast most of the projects undertaken by McDevitt Street Bovis were on a more modest scale, albeit often as part of vast general building agreements for health-care and educational facilities. A notable exception was the 63-storey corporate headquarters of NationsBank (then the fourth largest US bank), which is the tallest building in the south-east US at 875 feet. This 1.4 million square foot, $121 million project was finished in 33 months, one month ahead of schedule. But MSB's achievements were very impressive when projects were grouped together. The firm was named as most active builder of retail space by *Shopping Center World* in mid-1992, having built 12 million square feet in five years to March 1992, particularly out-of-town complexes. MSB was also carving out a niche in the nationwide healthcare boom with 50 projects underway nationwide – from an $80 million medical tower in Nashville, Tennessee to a $1 million extension in Plantation, Florida. In total, health-care projects provided $150 million a year, or a third of the MSB workload.

Meanwhile, in Manhattan LMB was building a new 921,000 square foot federal courthouse at Foley Square, the largest in the USA, with 43 courtrooms on 27 storeys. The $240 million complex included separate elevators for prisoners, the public and judges. And then LMB won a $240 million construction contract for a mixed-use project in Lincoln Square. It comprised 38 floors of apartments above an eight-storey commercial base. After the slowdown at the beginning of the decade, business was looking up. On 11 August 1993 Lehrer McGovern Bovis executives appeared live on coast-to-coast television to plead their case for winning the $100 million Los Angeles City Hall refurbishment and earthquake protection project. At the heart of the matter was a contention by rival contractor Turner that LMB had links with South Africa via its P&O parentage, which under state law precluded a company from bidding for public sector contracts.

LMB emerged as the preferred contractor from an exhaustive study by the council's technical staff, but it was in the council chamber that the more difficult charge of the South African connection had to be resolved. Here LMB played its three trump cards. First the celebrated lawyer Johnnie Cochran, who successfully defended the American football star O. J. Simpson, led the appeal. The LA Council President limited his statement to ten minutes, quipping 'I know how high your fees are, and want to save your clients some money'.

Then Sir Frank Lampl gave a short presentation of the Bovis company history, and alluded to his time in Auschwitz and Dachau to rebuff any inference of racism. And finally Bovis produced a letter from the African National Congress, then in opposition, signed by Thabo Mbeki, today Nelson Mandela's successor. It argued that times were changing in South Africa and declaring that the ANC had no objection to the LMB bid.

From the other side, Turner's lawyer twisted LMB's ability to obtain a letter from the ANC in 'just one day' as evidence of its impressive connections with South Africa, and clear contravention of the LA state law. And the rival contractor also tried to claim a greater commitment to local employment, which quickly collapsed under questioning, as both LMB and Turner have headquarters in New York and have substantial LA subsidiaries. The vote went 11:2 in favour of LMB. Only in the USA could the award of a construction contract turn into a televised public debate, although it was a unique event, even for LA.

176

The critical factor in bringing the Bovis companies together into 'One Bovis' proved to be the Atlanta Olympic Games – an appropriate forum for teamwork and multicultural co-operation. In September 1991 Bovis began chasing the highly prestigious programme management contract, and executives from LMB and MSB began to appreciate the quality of their opposite numbers. Winning this $500 million contract in June 1994 was a turning point. Before then, the north-south tensions lingered and prevented a true synergy emerging. But both sides realised that they would not have won the Olympic Games bid without each other. LMB offered construction management expertise to co-ordinate work on 26 sites in a 100-mile radius of Atlanta, while MSB provided the skills of a southern general contractor and its renowned quality control.

As the decade progressed the Bovis subsidiaries in the US were successfully building up their order book across the country. Big projects like the $500 million Olympic Games, or $550 million hangars for United Airlines, hit the headlines. But

176 *Luther Cochrane (right) led the Bovis team that won the Atlanta Olympics programme management contract. Lehrer McGovern Bovis provided the construction management expertise for work on 26 sites, while McDevitt Street Bovis offered quality control and southern contracting skills.*

177 *Mega projects returned in the 1990s, like this Metro-Tech business park in Brooklyn with a $750 million construction budget.*

178

178 *Concrete is poured on the first phase of Donald Trump's Riverside South mixed-use development on the Upper West side of Manhattan.*

177

179

179 *Jim D'Agostino, head of the West Coast operation.*

the backbone of the operation remained hundreds and hundreds of smaller schemes scattered around the nation. Examples for MSB ranged from a $50 million neuroscience facility for the Brain Institute of the University of Florida to the $100 million Grand Bay condominiums on Longboat Key. And, for LMB, from the $35 million terminal building for Westchester County Airport to the $33 million laboratory facilities complex for Stanford University in San Francisco.

Mega projects also gradually returned in the USA in the 1990s. An early example was the Metro-Tech business park in Brooklyn, built by LMB between 1992 and 1998. Its seven buildings totalled 7.5 million square feet, and the construction budget of $750 million was on the scale of Canary Wharf in London. The blue chip tenants were to be Chase Manhattan Bank, Brooklyn Union Gas, Syac, Morgan Stanley and the Fire Department of the City of New York's doomsday headquarters in case of a disaster on Manhattan Island.

One big new client was Donald Trump, a larger-than-life-character, even by New York standards. Emerging triumphant from his well-documented financial difficulties at the start of the 1990s, the Trump New World Organisation appointed LMB to manage the $350 million first phase of its Riverside South mixed-use development on the Upper West Side of Manhattan. This is a vast mixed-use scheme covering 74.6 acres of the former Penn Central railway yards. When completed, the development will have 16 buildings of 15–49 storeys containing 5700 apartments, 1.8 million square feet of commercial space and a huge public park will fill the western approach to the property. For Bovis this was the beginning of a profitable relationship with Donald Trump, who soon came to appreciate the company's many qualities.

There is an old British saying that 'some achieve greatness, some are born to greatness, and others have it thrust upon them'. Unbeknown to Luther Cochrane in mid-1995, he was about to have greatness thrust upon him for the second time. For quite out of the blue Peter Lehrer flew down to see him in Charlotte and announced his intention to retire. He wanted Luther to replace him, and told him to fly to London to see Sir Frank. 'I really thought Peter would change his mind,' recalls Luther Cochrane. 'He certainly needed a break and was giving 120 per cent to the business. Perhaps it was too much.' Sir Frank says he told Peter Lehrer to take a six-month break. But he only took two weeks and was still resolved to step down. 'Working seven days a week and with young children, I just felt it was time to do something else', explains Peter Lehrer, who has since been a successful developer and tireless supporter of Jewish charities. 'I never had enough time to savour our achievement, and hope what I left behind about integrity, doing the right thing and never giving up will carry on.'

So circumstances beyond his control had once more led Luther Cochrane to replace a big figure in the construction industry. With the encouragement of Sir Frank, he decided to immediately accelerate the creation of 'One Bovis'. This was probably an easier job with all the three founding entrepreneurs out of the way, for Richard Halpern had also bowed out by this point. 'I loved creating one construction company,' says Luther Cochrane. 'We had a very good balance between international experience and youthful energy, and share the same attitudes to people and clients. There were two big initiatives: first to create a common culture for the group, and second to forge a better, more efficient business with less duplication of functions.'

The company centralised accounts and information technology in Charlotte, and legal services and human resources in New York. And it divided into six regions,

180 *New York Giants' $37 million Meadowlands stadium features two 50 metre high towers, enclosed seating and 28 luxury suites.*

181 *In the fall of 1996 work started on the 51-storey Santa Maria condominium in Miami, the tallest residential building south of New York City.*

formed more to suit the talents of the six brightest executives than for geographic reasons. Jim D'Agostino was sent from New York to run the West Coast operation, while Pete Marchetto headed up New York. LMB's Charlie Bacon was dispatched to Princeton and the old Schal territory became the Midwest under Jeff Arfsten. Meantime, the South East was split up between Larry Atkins in Charlotte and Larry Beasley in Atlanta. 'One Bovis' made another stride forward.

These corporate changes came against the background of an accelerating workload for Bovis. In July 1996 the Nashville office won its biggest contract in 15 years, the $292 million Tennessee Stadium in Nashville. In the same month LMB was selected for a $37 million construction management assignment for New York Giants' Meadowlands Stadium which featured two 50 metre high towers, enclosed seating and 28 luxury suites. Indeed, there was something of a post-Olympics sports facility boom for Bovis. Other contracts included the new 21,600-seat Centennial Coliseum adjacent to the North Carolina State University's Carter Finley Stadium.

In the second half of 1996, LMB finished work on the $280 million colour printing plant for the *New York Times* and topped out the $64 million six-storey Central Life Science Library for the University of Kentucky. Down in Miami, MSB started building the tallest residential building south of New York City, the 51-storey Santa Maria condominium overlooking Biscayne Bay.

One later key appointment to the management team was Bill Moss. He was Bovis' client on the Atlanta Olympics, and by the end of 1996 was in the market for another job. Luther Cochrane recruited him to come to New York as the head of general projects and sports. 'There was still some north versus south feeling in the management, and I came from the outside,' recalls Bill Moss. 'It was a question of marrying the different skills of the companies, though Luther was the key to getting the three companies together.'

At the end of 1996 Luther Cochrane became president of Bovis Inc, taking over from Peter Lehrer. He also won the 1996 Golden Hammer award for service to the community and North Carolina construction industry. The nomination praised his work with the National Development Council of the University of North Carolina, Board of Advisors to the Blumenthal Centre for the Performing Arts and the Board of the Chapter of the Associated General Contractors of America.

Luther Cochrane greatly accelerated the 'One Bovis' policy on his appointment to the top job, commuting regularly between Charlotte and New York. The Bovis identity was strengthened with new letterheads and business cards. In New York the hummingbird and the name 'Bovis' appeared on site, with 'Lehrer McGovern Bovis Inc.' in much smaller lettering underneath. Only the existence of long-term legal contracts under the Lehrer McGovern name prevented it disappearing altogether.

United under the Bovis banner, the old divisions between north and south were gradually fading out, and Bovis Inc was increasingly viewed by observers as 'One Bovis'. In July 1997 the journal *Building Design & Construction* listed Bovis Inc as the number one construction manager in the USA. The ranking highlighted 263 active projects nationwide under Bovis' management, with a total value of $1.94 billion, and split 45 per cent commercial, 40 per cent institutional and 12 per cent industrial.

The good news continued to flow. In November 1997 the New York office commenced work on Two Columbus Towers, a development of 42-storey condominiums for the Brodsky Organisation and Peter Lehrer, who was now carving himself a second career as a New York property developer. The first two months of

182

182 New York Times*'s $280 million colour printing plant was completed in the second half of 1996.*

183

183 *Bill Moss was Bovis' client on the Atlanta Olympics and joined Bovis as head of general projects and sports in late 1996. He became chief executive officer at Bovis Inc on Luther Cochrane's promotion to group chief executive in September 1998.*

184 *Thirteen sections for a $400 million extension to the New York Hospital were craned from barges and positioned over the highway in late 1998.*

1998 gave a flavour of how contracts were now spread fairly evenly across the United States. The Chicago office won the $49 million Liberty High School programme. The Atlanta office won the $49 million renovation and expansion of the McGhee Tyson Airport in Knoxville. Orlando won the $40 million, nine-storey Crowne Plaza Suites Hotel in Charlotte. New York won the $91 million Queen's Hospital Center and a 300-room JW Marriott Hotel in Miami. And finally, Seattle won the $30 million Seatac International Airport Hotel.

Bovis Inc appeared at the head of another ranking in March 1998. Modern Healthcare placed Bovis first for healthcare projects. Bovis had projects worth $672 million under its management, against runner-up Turner at $639 million and Centex at $503 million. This triumph represented a doubling of Bovis healthcare projects in two years. In New York alone Bovis was overseeing the $100 million five-year plan for Beth Israel Medical Center, a $93 million seven-year program for Memorial-Sloan and the multi-million dollar redevelopment of New York Hospital. The summer of 1998 saw yet more major project wins. There was pre-construction work for JW Marriott's $250-million Grande Lakes Resort in Orlando, Florida, a $450 million 7-year program for terminal expansion at Metropolitan Oakland International Airport in San Francisco, and a $330 million mixed-use residential and hotel scheme for Millennium Partners, again in San Francisco.

In September 1998 Sir Frank appointed Luther Cochrane as chief executive officer of the Bovis Group, and his designated successor. Even now Sir Frank continues as life president and Luther's mentor. 'It's Frank's company, he loves his job and I would not like to see him go,' says Luther Cochrane, whose rivals for the top position were the other joint global managing directors John Anderson and Fritz Rehkopf. 'I think he

184

185 *In April 1999 Bovis began construction of the world's tallest residential tower for Donald Trump. This 70-storey skyscraper is situated close to the United Nations building in New York City.*

picked me because of our common view on the corporate culture of Bovis, but our relationship just continues as it has always done.'

Luther Cochrane's elevation meant a further realignment of roles within Bovis Inc. Bill Moss stepped up to chief executive officer responsible for operations at Bovis New York Construction Corp, and 38-year-old Charlie Bacon became president in charge of marketing, support services and expansion into South America. That in turn created a vacuum in the regions and the six divisions were merged into four, bringing operations closer together. Charlie Bacon reminisced on how the company had changed in his 17 years: 'In the early days I don't know how many doors I had to knock on and hear "Who are you?" Now we are the largest construction manager in the United States, taking on 60 or 70 new projects a year, with a presence in virtually every building sector. Clients now call and want Bovis on their projects. We have established a great reputation.'

As the new century begins Bovis is also construction manager for a $1 billion portfolio of US commercial properties being developed for Millennium Properties in New York, Washington, Boston, Miami and San Francisco. Even healthcare projects have stepped up a notch. A $400 million extension to New York Hospital spanning a major highway was recently completed, with 13 sections craned into position from a river barge at night. And Bovis is engaged on four major hotel projects in New York City. In April 1999 Bovis started work on the world's tallest residential tower for Donald Trump, a 70-storey, $180 million skyscraper near to the United Nations building. The famous New York property tycoon has been a happy client since LMB

186 *Grand Central Station was the most prestigious New York restoration project since the Statue of Liberty and included restoration of the constellation ceiling whose astrological signs had vanished under layers of dirt.*

187 *The $2 billion Venetian hotel, casino and resort complex in Las Vegas was the largest single project ever undertaken by Bovis in North America and was handed over on time and to budget in April 1999.*

successfully completed part of his huge Riverside South development on the West Side of Manhattan, and recently came into the New York office to personally sign a hundred copies of his book *The Art of the Comeback* as a thank you.

Mid-1999 also saw LMB finish its most significant New York restoration since the Statue of Liberty – the $200million refurbishment of the famous Art Deco Grand Central Station. Returning the grace and grandeur to this 1913 landmark included restoring the constellation ceiling 150 feet above the main concourse – with 60 blinking stars and astrological signs. It also entailed refurbishment of a network of passages connecting the terminal to buildings in Midtown Manhattan, and the creation of 80,000 square feet of new retail space.

A further pre-Millennial handover was the biggest single project ever undertaken by Bovis in North America, the Venetian. This $2 billion hotel, casino and resort complex in Las Vegas has 6000 suites in twin towers. The size of a small town, the Venetian features architecture modelled on Venice's St Mark's Square, Campanile Tower and Grand Canal. The scheme also has 750,000 square feet of retail and restaurant space and a 1.6 million square foot convention centre. Such a huge project drew heavily on the project management resources of the group, but was still delivered on time and within the budget. The first phase of 3200 rooms was handed over in April 1999.

For Bovis Americas this was a fantastic way to close a decade of achievement. To have assembled the largest construction management company in North America in such a short space of time was a remarkable achievement in itself. For a British company to put such an entity together was almost unprecedented, and for a construction company was without parallel. And whatever his initial misgivings may have been about the value of US construction management, Sir Frank Lampl has turned his vision of a US construction arm for Bovis into a world-beating reality, almost as big as its parent company. But Sir Frank readily concedes that the real credit should go to Luther Cochrane whose ceaseless travelling, energy and determination have made the creation of One Bovis possible.

CHAPTER 12

Global triumph, British recession

I n the good times everybody does well. It is only in the bad times that the best companies come out on top, or at least manage to reinvent themselves in a form that will triumph in a later recovery. By 1991 Bovis was firmly set on a globalisation strategy with its American acquisitions, solid expansion into Europe and a foothold in the Far East. Bovis was fortunate. The company had seen the recession coming, unlike most of the British construction industry which found itself teetering on the edge of the abyss. Our narrative now returns from the United States to Britain to examine how the group coped with the worst post-war recession, and continued to implement its ambitious globalisation strategy in the face of domestic disaster.

If anything captured the spirit of the age in the early 1990s, it was the international mood of optimism about globalisation, propelled forward by the almighty US dollar, cheap money and the arrival of market economics in formerly communist countries. Britain's flirtation with the European Exchange Rate Mechanism meant that the UK languished in deep recession for the first few years of the decade. Indeed, even the most perceptive UK business leaders did not anticipate such a long domestic recession, nor one that would cut so deeply into the British construction industry. Yet it was largely a British phenomenon. When you stepped off a plane in many other parts of the world, recession suddenly lifted as though you had landed on another planet.

But anchored in the ERM at a disadvantageous exchange rate, and therefore forced to follow a policy of high interest rates during a cyclical downturn, the British construction industry faced the deepening recession. Orders were evaporating, clients going bust and empty offices littered the capital. Former Bovis boss Frank Sanderson's construction and property company Egerton Trust went into receivership three weeks after his retirement. And famous names such as Elliott and Rush & Tompkins were also early casualties of the recession. This was hardly going to be an easy time for Bovis in Britain, and the company found itself under fire from many different quarters.

Bovis Construction's managing director Chris Spackman had the unenviable task of steering the UK company through this long nightmare. High points were now on the lower end of the Richter scale. In early 1991 Bovis finished the new £40 million exhibition hall at Earl's Court that straddled underground railway tracks with a clear 85-metre span. Another modest tremor followed the completion of Sir Norman Foster's award-winning Sackler Galleries at Burlington House for the Royal Academy of Art, comprising simple barrel-vaulted rooms installed above existing premises.

188

188 *Managing director Chris Spackman had the difficult job of steering the company through the UK's worst recession since the war in the early 1990s, and cut staff levels from 1800 to 900 in the UK. He became group managing director in 1985.*

189 *Earl's Court 2 represented a major addition to a famous London landmark.*

190 *Sackler Galleries for the Royal Academy of Art. Prestige projects in the UK were on a smaller scale in the early 1990s.*

Building magazine also paid tribute to Bovis's part in constructing the £14 million White Cliffs Experience heritage centre at Dover, which chronicled the history of the Channel port from earliest settlement to the present day. The centre was intended to pull tourists into Dover, whose traders were worried that the Channel Tunnel would cause visitors to bypass their town. More accolades followed the completion of the £14.5 million *Western Morning News* building outside Plymouth, a post-modernist design by Nicholas Grimshaw & Partners in the form of a ship. And in late 1991 the new Jewel House in the Tower of London was warmly received. However, for the builder of Broadgate and Canary Wharf, these were hardly heart-stoppingly exciting projects.

191 *Diana, Princess of Wales, opens the exhibition centre, Earl's Court 2, and is pictured with Bovis Europe divisional managing director John Spanswick (left) and Bovis chairman Sir Frank Lampl (right).*

192 Western Morning News' *post-modernist building outside Plymouth, which echoes the nautical traditions of the city.*

The £400 million Ludgate office development for Rosehaugh Stanhope was the exception to this rule. This 76,250 square metre air-rights office development arranged in four low-rise buildings spanning the new Thameslink railway line was dubbed 'the son of Broadgate' by commentators. It was a sign of the times that cost, and *not* speed, became the prime construction target. Stanhope construction director Peter Rogers commented: 'We moved from Broadgate with fairly specific ideas and set about looking at how we could bring costs down. I reckoned that Broadgate could have been built for 20–30 per cent less if we had done things differently.' Virtually all the Broadgate subcontractors transferred to Ludgate, and some of the saving came from recession-hit tender prices. The rest of the 30 per cent cost reduction was down to value management.

Small savings on cost and wasted floor space were made across the board, such as the selective use of high-grade finishes, four elevators instead of five, a reduction in external wall thickness from 300mm to 250mm, and a standardisation of cladding design. The whole emphasis was switched from saving on time to saving on cost, and by doubling up on job functions Bovis staffing was cut by 40 per cent, with four to seven working managers on each of the buildings.

Even tea breaks were managed more effectively, with tea-and-bun-points located

192

193

193 *The £400 million Ludgate office development in the shadow of St Paul's Cathedral. Value management helped cut costs by 30 per cent compared with Broadgate.*

194 *Ludgate office specifications were no less demanding than earlier projects. It filled the City of London's last remaining bomb site from the Second World War.*

194

on alternate floors of the building and total flexibility in break times contributing to a five per cent improvement in actual useful work time. Chris Spackman could justly claim to have 'the most efficient construction site in Britain'. The project also involved mainline railway work, which Bovis had not undertaken before and which would prove useful in the future to secure contracts from Railtrack.

More often Chris Spackman found himself on the defensive. Management contracting came under fire in a report from Reading University, which promoted the idea that construction management was cheaper and less adversarial. Its arguments were promoted in a vitriolic campaign by the *New Builder* magazine, then trying to make its mark as a controversial journal, and later itself a casualty of the recession. In response Chris Spackman warned, 'there is a risk that clients may now be deterred from using management contracting'. And he reminded clients that in construction management *they* are in a contract with the trade contractors, which is hardly suitable for every project.

It was a theme he returned to in a letter to *Building* magazine. 'Comparing the performance of management contracting with other forms of procurement in terms of the achievements and objectives like time and cost can be very misleading. Such comparisons should be resisted, and are not useful because of the difficulty of measuring goal attainment across multiple goals, effects of external factors and uncertainty about the appropriateness of goals set.' Chris Spackman was fighting to keep the very *modus operandi* of Bovis alive in an extremely tough market.

By the close of 1991, he succeeded in turning the debate on its head by launching an initiative to cut the cost of UK projects by 30 per cent to match US levels. Chris Spackman was clearly aided by a recessionary 15 per cent fall in subcontractors' prices, but the additional 15 per cent had to be squeezed from elsewhere. He wrote to 42 subcontractors with a raft of proposals, reorganised graduate training and asked architects to consider greater standardisation in their designs. Clients obviously warmed to the idea and Bovis was back on the offensive.

In the depths of the recession, some directors wanted to look at non-fee work. Except for some McDevitt & Street contracts, the company was still exclusively fee-based, and the board rejected the idea of returning to lump-sum tendering. The argument against bidding for lump-sum contracts was that in a recession tender prices are at rock bottom, and that contractors face the risk of rising materials and labour costs in a subsequent recovery which will cut into profits.

The extent of the downturn began to be reflected in figures from P&O. Operating profits from homes, construction and property fell from £155.6 million in 1989 to just £15.8 million in 1990, after a £22.5 million write-off against falling asset values. It was not until late August that Prime Minister John Major met representatives from the construction industry to discuss the crisis. By then P&O had published its results for the first half, showing that housing, construction and property had slipped £3.5 million into the red. However, the construction division's pre-tax profit remained in the black, as it has since the nadir of 1974.

Recessions are also full of false starts and frustrations, which must have been all the harder for a company used to big successes. In September 1991 Bovis seemed to have hit the jackpot with an appointment for the early planning of the £1 billion Heathrow Terminal Five. But as travellers will know, even today the site for Terminal Five remains a vast sewage works, and not a pile has been driven. Similarly Olympia & York applied to the London Docklands Development Committee for a 30 per cent

195 *The 'grotesque Gothic'*
architecture of Minster Court
invited controversy. Bovis returned
to the complex when it was
seriously damaged by fire after it
had been handed over.

increase in the final phase of the Canary Wharf site, holding out the prospect of £150 million in new work. Nobody knew then that the mighty O&Y was set to tumble.

Meanwhile, the Government's privatisation of public sector building activity took a step forward with Bovis winning a contract to oversee the splitting up of the Property Services Agency's Building Management Division for sale to the private sector. Future Bovis managing director John Anderson spent two years working on this highly significant project. It set the ball rolling for a whole series of moves to privatise public sector construction activity, and gave Bovis a headstart on other companies. Nonetheless, Bovis felt it unwise to bid for any constituent parts of the PSA, because of its supervisory role, which would have caused a conflict of interest. Lord Joseph's advice to the board was *not* to bid for what would have been a marvellous acquisition.

196 **197**

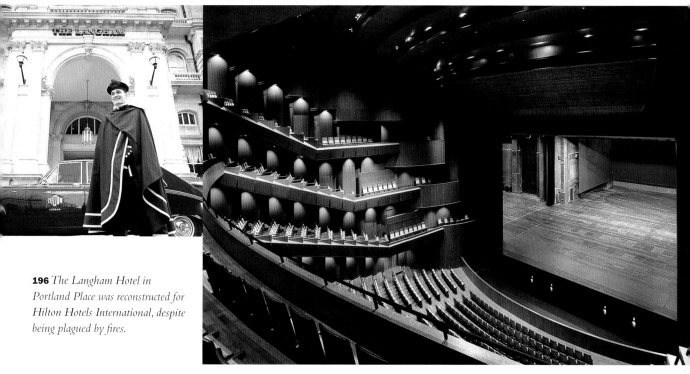

196 *The Langham Hotel in Portland Place was reconstructed for Hilton Hotels International, despite being plagued by fires.*

197 *The National Theatre in Tokyo, Japan. It was unprecedented for a British-owned construction company to secure Japanese public-sector projects.*

There were problems overseas as well. When the Kuwait Investment Office liquidated its Spanish subsidiary Bovis did not get paid for its unusual 'leaning' twin office towers in Barcelona. Elsewhere, things were far brighter with yet more ground-breaking initiatives in new markets. Early in 1991 Bovis announced the acquisition of the Chicago-based contractor Schal Northeast, and certain interests of Schal Mid-Atlantic – a purchase that opened the massive Japanese construction market to the group via preferential treatment secured by the US Government for American contractors. 'Our entry into Japan was entirely down to Schal and the US Government's insistence on opening the Japanese market to US contractors,' recalls Sir Frank. 'But while the others have now left, we are still there and have twice as much work as the US Government programme brought us. The major contractors still feel we have something to offer, particularly in disciplines such as programming and scheduling.'

In Poland, Bovis International won its first project, to refurbish an existing building in Warsaw into offices for a consortium of American corporate and Polish clients. And Sir Frank and Gene McGovern flew to Kuwait to inspect damage to the National Assembly, a former Bovis project that had been looted and set on fire by the retreating Iraqi army in the Gulf War. But in the event British firms won very little work from Kuwait, which favoured US contractors in its reconstruction programme.

Back in London for the European Construction Symposium, Sir Frank shared the platform with Jacques Attali, controversial president of the European Bank for Reconstruction and Development, and European Commissioner Martin Bangeman. Several delegations from eastern Europe excited the interest of delegates, yet few British

198

companies attended. They were all far too busy with their own domestic business crises. It would be fair to say that UK contractors had dug their own graves by over-expansion in the late 1980s, and were generally far too overstretched to tackle new markets in the early 1990s. Bovis was one of a small number of firms that successfully exported its product and established a presence in many markets around the world.

Indeed, the Bovis policy of globalisation was starting to impress industry commentators. In March 1992 *Building* magazine marvelled at the phenomenal £4 billion of projects won in three years, worth over £60 million in fees, 'enough to keep a few site managers going'. The occasion for its comment was the award of the contract to manage construction of the £500 million Olympic stadiums in Atlanta, Georgia to McDevitt & Street Bovis and Lehrer McGovern Bovis. But the magazine also reminded its readers of the £700 million Oberhausen shopping mall and city centre project in Germany, orders worth £1.1 billion in Malaysia and the Middle East and the anticipated management contract for the £430 million second phase of EuroDisney.

Sir Frank said at the time: 'The orders are a part of a very deliberate strategy of geographical expansion and the best possible testimony to the efforts of all those people who have dedicated themselves to this global strategy.' It was also firm evidence that Bovis had a premium skill which clients were prepared to employ anywhere in the world. For instance, the huge Oberhausen retail project in Germany was conceived by Eddie Healey, the same developer responsible for Sheffield's £111 million Meadowhall shopping centre in August 1990, and Bovis completed both projects.

In March 1992 P&O's financial results revealed that 73 per cent of Bovis' £5 billion order book was now outside the UK. Without globalisation Bovis would have been savaged by the UK recession, which now entered its fourth year with no end in sight. Not surprisingly, the next major project announcement was abroad, the £290 million Tokyo Telecom Centre, with Schal Bovis named as the sole foreign member of the Kajima-led team. In penetrating markets like Japan, Bovis was going where no British-owned contractor had gone before.

In spring 1992 *Building* published an article celebrating the completion 'on time and to budget' of the EuroDisney site outside Paris. EuroDisney phase one comprised five theme parks, six hotels and associated infrastructure. Around 400 staff from Lehrer McGovern Bovis worked on the massive 600-hectare project at its peak. LMB liaised closely with Disney Imaginering staff managing the entire project, and also built the £100 million Disneyland hotel at the park entrance. 'It was a very complicated operation,' says project director Barry Holmes. 'Interwoven activities were going on all the time. You have hundreds of people with 14 different nationalities and languages all working next to each other, and you have to co-ordinate work so that one group of workers does not get in the way of another. EuroDisney always demanded that it would open on time. We just broke down the work by facility, or by themeland, and produced a very strict schedule that everyone had to stick to.'

Holmes was being rather modest in his assessment of the achievement. EuroDisney was the second largest building project in Europe after the Channel Tunnel, and an enormously complex undertaking for the most challenging of clients. There was 11 kilometres of pipework for compressed air alone, and more than 90 kilometres of irrigation and drainage pipework. After Canary Wharf, EuroDisney was

199 *Disneyland, Paris was the second largest construction project in Europe and, after Canary Wharf, the biggest scheme handled by Bovis in the twentieth century. It was completed on time and to budget in spring 1992.*

the biggest project handled by Bovis this century. The only disappointment was that EuroDisney put the second phase of the project on hold when initial visitor figures failed to match expectations, as the impact of the poor weather of northern Europe seems to have been underestimated.

The by now rather familiar picture of Bovis's successful progress abroad, and setbacks at home, was even more sharply drawn in 1992. British construction firms were heavily in debt and the business climate became increasingly litigious as companies struggled to stay afloat. Bovis was sued by clients and subcontractors, and executives spent more and more time sorting out legal problems. The biggest blow came in June, however, when Canary Wharf was placed in receivership owing unsecured creditors £54 million. Bovis lost £1 million in unpaid fees, and several subcontractors decided to sue Bovis to try to recover money from Canary Wharf. With new construction orders experiencing their biggest fall since 1974, this was a bad time for Bovis in the UK. Fortunately the group had nothing like the exposure to secondary banking that pulled it under in 1974, and was doing well overseas.

In the second half of 1992 Bovis scored a series of global breakthroughs. The first

200

200 *American Express offices in Frankfurt.*
201 *The acquisition of Tillyard (Deutschland) brought Bovis several major projects in Germany.*

201

was an appointment in Russia for the redevelopment of three buildings controlled by the Moscow Philharmonic Orchestra. Then the Frankfurt office was awarded pre-construction work on Foster Associates' 54-storey Commerzbank Tower in Frankfurt in joint venture with Lahmeyer International. And Bovis was appointed development manager for the Brno Technology and Business Park in Czechoslavakia.

More followed. In October Schal Bovis won the £260 million contract to manage the building of a performing arts centre from the Japanese Ministry of Construction. Then Bovis made an acquisition in Germany, buying Tillyard (Deutschland), a project and construction manager with 34 staff at offices in Frankfurt, Munich and Berlin, and a ten-strong Swiss subsidiary. Sir Frank said: 'The acquisition represents a significant expansion for Bovis in Germany and the German-speaking market place. Tillyard's long experience in project management and construction management will offer German clients a service that is very much in demand.' Boris Feigl, who founded Tillyard in 1969, later admitted that he initiated the sale after Bovis had beaten them on the Commerzbank project: 'It was pointless being in competition and I was amazed how quickly and smoothly the sale arrangements were made. Before we were not large enough to cover the whole of the German market. Now we will be able to compete with anyone.'

Two more announcements capped another exciting year for international expansion. Schal Bovis scored again in Japan as part of a consortium for a £285 million skyscraper in Osaka, and reported that it had just started work on the 52-storey twin towers of the Rinku Gate development, also in Osaka. Finally came the news that Lehrer McGovern (Malaysia) was to project manage the 85-storey twin towers being built by the state oil company Petronas in Kuala Lumpur – at 450 metres high it would be the tallest building in the world. The Malaysians had been impressed by a presentation of Bovis' involvement with Canary Wharf, and included up to 35 staff from Bovis in the Twin Towers project team.

Three metres higher than Chicago's Sears Tower, which was co-built by Schal founder Richard Halpern, the Petronas Towers were scheduled for completion in 1996. The inclusion of Bovis must be seen as all the more remarkable in view of a

202 *The 52-storey, twin tower, Rinku Gate office development in Osaka. Japanese clients have warmed to Schal Bovis' expertise.*

202

203

20

203 *President of the Board of Trade Michael Heseltine visits the site of the Petronas Towers in Kuala Lumpur. Soaring 450 metres into the sky, these are presently the tallest buildings in the world.*

204 *The 85-storey Petronas Towers in Kuala Lumpur, with longstanding client Marks & Spencer in the foreground. Wholly-owned Bovis subsidiary Lehrer McGovern (Malaysia) circumnavigated a trade ban against British companies.*

trade ban that prevented other British contractors from working in Malaysia. Lehrer McGovern (Malaysia) was not covered by this ban, as a US-registered company. The Petronas Towers symbolised Malaysia's emergence as a modern industrialised nation. For Bovis the project represented a showcase for international expansion. In a matter of five years the group had successfully globalised its activities to the extent that even building the tallest-ever skyscraper on the other side of the world, was well within operational capability.

How could it be that the successors of C. W. Bovis, a modest London builder, were now showing the world how to build the most complex structures? In a sense this is the question this book tries to answer. What does emerge as a common thread in the history of Bovis is a commitment by its management and staff to professionalism, new ideas and latterly, internationalism. The professional approach is seen in pride in the job, a willingness to serve clients and a fee-based construction system. New ideas embraced by the company included the fee system leading to management contracting and construction management, with many innovations imported from abroad, especially the United States. And an international outlook meant that when the UK construction market fell into recession, the group globalised its activities and created an international construction company.

The key to understanding why Bovis succeeded overseas is in its 'local and global' philosophy allied to a very selective acquisition strategy. In each case Bovis looked for a local partner, preferably one pursuing a major contract. The relationship with Bovis therefore strengthened the local firm – with additional expertise and financial muscle. It was a welcome bolt-on international dimension for any national construction company wanting to pursue big projects.

This approach was somewhat more subtle than that used by most British contractors. They expected to arrive in a foreign city, open an office and begin looking for work. Quite apart from the cultural differences encountered, they were immediately seen as rivals to local construction firms that generally had a considerable hold over their own markets. To be fair, in the 1970s oil boom, for example, UK contractors won work in the Middle East on this basis, and so had Bovis for that matter. But by the late 1980s construction markets around the world had achieved a level of sophistication which prevented the land-with-your-trowel variety of construction exports.

Bovis offered smaller local contractors the chance to make the big time with an infusion of international management expertise and the financial strength of the P&O balance sheet. Developing and mature countries welcomed this transfer of technology, and saw Bovis as an aide to improving the efficiency of their construction sectors, rather than another name to add to a tender list. It was a different approach to winning contracts in new markets overseas.

Sir Frank says Bovis offered clients two major advantages overseas: 'First, we offered quality, and would build to the same standard everywhere, though not necessarily for the same price. We would not expect to do a shabby job just because we were in a developing country, it would always be the same standard. And secondly, we are totally free of corruption. It is the Anglo-American approach and in the whole world there is a huge movement against corruption in construction.'

A lot of attention was also given to finding the right personal chemistry between Bovis and its overseas acquisitions. While cultural differences were unavoidable, there was a considerable benefit to be derived from finding people who could get on with

205 *National Auditorium and Hotel Pacifico, Yokohama. Japanese public-sector projects mushroomed as the Government tried to stimulate its moribund economy.*

each other. It sounds an obvious point. But many mergers, acquisitions and takeovers have foundered because people find it impossible to work together, and Bovis did not always get it right either.

At the start of 1993 the UK recession was beginning to lift. The pound was by now out of the ERM, and interest rates were beginning to fall. However, construction is a late-cycle industry, and it would be some time before construction orders began to pick up. That meant 1993 was likely to be another year of modest achievement in Britain. Chris Spackman kept the Bovis flag flying and took up the chairmanship of a Department of Trade and Industry committee to cut the red tape burdening the construction industry. Under Michael Heseltine as President of the Board of Trade, the DTI produced a number of initiatives to help the construction industry. Perhaps the most memorable innovation was the introduction of export promoters, who were seconded from industry to help boost exports.

Unfortunately, the outstanding success of Bovis in export markets was concealed by its inclusion in the P&O accounts as a part of 'homes, construction and property'. This division posted an operating loss of £39.8 million for 1992, with Lord Sterling blaming 'very competitive fee levels', though a year-end Bovis order book of £3.4 billion was healthy enough. The P&O board accepted that Bovis was being done a disservice by this presentation of the accounts, and in 1993 separate figures were released for 1992. These showed Bovis Construction Group posting a pre-tax profit of £9.55 million, a considerable feat in the worst post-war recession. All the same, the fall in UK staff numbers from 1302 to 1048, and the decline in the total wage bill from £32.55 million to £24.9 million, were more indicative of the times.

Famous construction companies continued to sink under the weight of bad debts and over ill-judged expansion into property. In April 1993 the respected Central London firm John Lelliott Construction was placed in receivership with debts of over £60 million, mainly due to the liquidation of one big client, Land & Property Trust. On the day the axe fell the company's founder, John Lelliott, phoned Sir Frank to tell him that the receivers were arriving at 2pm. Sir Frank agreed to meet John Lelliott at 1.30pm, and when the receivers arrived they were delighted to find that Bovis was interested in buying certain assets. Within a week Bovis announced an agreement with Coopers & Lybrand to take on 40 contracts worth £23 million and 70 staff. John Lelliott himself joined Bovis to smooth the process. 'Ironically Lelliott was very profitable for us,' says Sir Frank. 'We needed a firm with smaller projects to train our graduates. On a Lelliott job they can experience the whole construction process in a year, whereas on a mega-project they would only see a small part of it. Lelliott also took us back into the tendering market, but within very specific limits. Usually inside the M25 and for contracts of less than £10 million.'

In July 1993 Chris Spackman was nearing retirement, and handed over as managing director to John Anderson. Anderson had been managing director of P&O subsidiary Town & City Properties (later known as P&O Developments) from 1984 to 1992, and a non-executive director of Bovis since 1989, as well as leader of the team advising the Government on the privatisation of the Property Services Agency. His arrival coincided with a change in the geographical spread. 'We are following the clients, and many, especially in the public sector, are moving outside London,' Anderson said. 'It does not take a rocket scientist to deduce that this is where the work will be.' An increasingly European bias to the workload was also recognised, and by the end of 1993 Anderson was heading a seven-strong

management board for European operations within Bovis.

Indeed, one of the highlights of 1993 was the completion of the £21 million construction management contract for the 192-bed Hyatt International hotel at the La Manga Club in Spain. And probably the most significant contract in a pretty thin year was the project management of a 100,000 square metre, £167 million retail and office development in Barcelona. The establishment of offices in Mumbai and Bangalore in India was another notable event, and contracts eventually followed from clients such as BAT, Volvo Trucks and SmithKline Beecham. On the other hand, there were some prestigious completions in Britain during 1993, such as the Savoy Theatre restoration, the £22.6 million Glyndebourne opera house on the Sussex Downs, and £130 million Waterloo International terminal for Channel Tunnel trains. Work was also underway on the futuristic new headquarters for Channel Four in London, although it was not finished until 1994.

Architect Michael Hopkins & Partners' opera house at Glyndebourne revived construction techniques not used since the First World War, and was finely built in traditional materials with load-bearing brick walls and a leaded roof. On 24 July 1992 the curtain fell on the last performance at the old opera house, and Bovis had 16 months to complete the new building. 'Although it's a handmade building, we got together with the architect to prefabricate as much off-site as possible,' said project manager Alan Lansdell, whose team was widely praised for a 'virtuoso performance'.

Nicholas Grimshaw & Partners' distinctive Waterloo International terminal was also handed over on schedule, although delays to the Channel Tunnel project meant it was over a year before the Eurostar trains pulled into the 400 metre long platforms. This sinuous 59,000 square metre tubular steel and glass terminal was described as 'a viaduct with a building underneath'. And finally, the £35 million Channel Four headquarters designed by Richard Rogers created quite a stir in 1993. The architect of the Lloyd's building again courted controversy with sharp geometric forms, external lifts and 'advanced technological expressionism' in marked contrast to the traditional architecture of Victoria. Prestige British building projects may have been on a smaller scale in 1993, but they were not boring, and most of them were still being built by Bovis.

In an October 1993 interview Sir Frank outlined plans to increase the overseas workload over the following two years to the point where the UK would be less than 50 per cent of a worldwide total of £3.5 billion. His aim was to dramatically increase activity in Russia and the Far East. UK orders alone were worth £3.5 billion in 1988, such was the dramatic downscaling of domestic operations. Why the massive transfer of activity overseas? 'Profit margins in the Far East are about twice what we make in the UK, so the Far East will be a far more important market for us,' said Sir Frank, who had just been awarded the CIOB President's medal for lifetime achievement. 'We can be choosy about what we take on in the Far East. At the moment it is expensive for us to win work in the UK, in terms of presentations and processing a large number of enquiries.'

Sir Frank explained: 'As a niche construction manager with a potential market of £5–6 billion out of a £30 billion UK market, we do not have the possibility of tapping many new markets at home, so perhaps that has made us look abroad.' He was especially interested in the growth potential of Russia, where twenty-five Bovis staff members were engaged on seven commercial refurbishment contracts worth £200 million. 'I am delighted with Russia. All our contracts are for Western joint ventures,

206

206 *Michael Hopkins & Partners' Glyndebourne opera house revived old-fashioned construction methods and featured load-bearing brick walls and a leaded roof.*

207 *Nicholas Grimshaw & Partners' sinuous Waterloo International terminal for Eurostar trains was completed a year before the Channel Tunnel.*

209

208 *Lord Rogers' £35 million Channel Four headquarters caused a stir in 1993. Its advanced technological expressionism contrasted with the traditional architecture of the Victoria district of London.*

209 *Pilkington's Sandoglass factory, Poland. This old British client commissioned a £55 million glass plant located 200km outside of Warsaw.*

210 *Both one-time political prisoners, Sir Frank Lampl and Nelson Mandela met after Bovis won contracts worth £40 million in South Africa. This success contrasted with the disastrous South African ventures of the early 1950s.*

210

but we do have a World Bank training scheme for construction managers. There is considerable potential for infrastructure development in Russia with the mortgaging of enormous energy resources, and for further joint ventures with Western oil companies.'

Against this background, it is hardly surprising that news columns in the trade press for the next year were dominated by foreign projects, as Bovis redoubled its efforts to capture more foreign projects. In Poland, Bovis won its first big contract, an appointment to build a £55 million float glass plant in Poland for a Pilkington joint venture with Sandoglass 200 kilometres outside of Warsaw. In the second half of 1994, work pressed ahead on the 450 metre high Petronas Towers in Kuala Lumpur, and the first phase of Peter Foggo Associates' Czech Technology Park was topped out in Brno. At the same time the £70 million National Auditorium was completed by Schal Bovis in Yokohama as part of a management joint venture, an Indonesian client was in dispute with Bovis, and in Moscow a letter leaked to the press showed that capitalist attitudes were taking root. Bovis International director Erwin Stern commented: 'Yes we had that letter. The client wants the contractor to work 24 hours a day, seven days a week.' Later in the year Bovis won its first two jobs in South Africa, and Sir Frank Lampl travelled to meet President Nelson Mandela at his home in Johannesburg, a great honour.

Building magazine featured a review of the £700 million Oberhausen town centre and CentrO shopping mall development, then under construction. 'This is the largest project in Germany in terms of rate of spend,' said Bovis International director Barry Holmes. 'It compares with EuroDisney where we were spending £3 million a day at the peak and is not technically difficult; it is a logistical nightmare'. Globalisation was beginning to pay dividends. Bovis Construction's pre-tax profit was up from £9.55 million to £12.9 million in 1993, and for the first half of 1994 profits were marginally improved at £5.4 million.

In 1994 the biggest UK event was the handover of the Civil Aviation Authority's £105 million Air Traffic Control Centre in Swanwick, near Portsmouth. The 42,000 square metre complex was due to become operational in late 1996, but subsequent computer installation problems have delayed its inauguration. There was also the

211

211 *CentrO shopping mall in Oberhausen, part of a £700 million urban regeneration scheme. In terms of rate of spend, it represented the largest construction project in Germany in the early 1990s.*

212

212 *The Civil Aviation Authority's £105 million Air Traffic Control Centre in Swanwick near Southampton was handed over in 1994.*

opening of the second phase of Lloyd's Bank's 20,000 square metre headquarters in Bristol, and a newly revamped £10 million home for the Crown Jewels in the Tower of London. Otherwise 1994 was a quiet year in Britain, although the Latham Report on the construction industry made a few waves with its proposals to reform the industry. Bovis promised to 'cascade down' the Latham principles to its building sites, which included the payment of money into holding accounts to safeguard subcontractors and measures to make the industry less adversarial, a cause long championed by Bovis.

At the close of 1994 came the sad news of the death of Lord Joseph at the age of 76. It was his father, Samuel Joseph, who had become joint owner Bovis in 1910 and served as a wartime Lord Mayor of London. Sir Keith Joseph was chairman of Bovis Ltd in 1958–9, deputy chairman of Bovis Holdings from 1964 to 1970 and a non-executive director in the late 1980s. But of course Sir Keith is best remembered for his political career. He served in the last Macmillan Government of the early 1960s, and became Mrs Thatcher's philosophical mentor in the late 1970s. Sir Keith held three cabinet portfolios – education, health, and trade and industry – in three Thatcher administrations. Yet he remained keenly interested in Bovis and was helpful in the earlier research for this book.

Lord Joseph was the last link between Bovis and the Joseph family, a connection that spanned the whole of the twentieth century. Sir Frank fondly remembers Lord Joseph's period as a non-executive director and the parade of cabinet ministers who visited the Bovis headquarters for lunch. Mrs Thatcher was also a guest and dedicated the second volume of her memoirs to Keith Joseph. 'It used to embarrass me the way he would wait outside my office until I was free', says Sir Frank. 'He was always such a shy and modest man, and an enormous help with his clear views on economic issues. He used to say he went into politics to improve the lot of the people, but didn't seem to have achieved it. I certainly found his help very valuable.'

213

213 *Her Majesty the Queen opens the new £10 million home for the Crown Jewels in the Tower of London.*

214

215

214 *The fabulous Art Deco theatre at London's Savoy Hotel was devastated by fire in 1990, and completely restored by 1993. Meticulous research of historic records allowed the re-creation of specialist finishes.*

215 *Exquisite Art Deco detailing at the Savoy Theatre.*

CHAPTER 13

Towards the millennium

The final years of the twentieth century saw Bovis complete its metamorphosis into a global contracting giant, with 75 per cent of its multi-billion dollar order book outside the United Kingdom. It was a big turnaround for a company whose workload had been 90 per cent sourced from the UK just a decade earlier. But as the British economy finally shook off the recession of the early 1990s, Bovis was also very successful in winning contracts to manage the construction of the huge out-of-town shopping malls which marked a revival in the fortunes of the construction industry.

These massive retail palaces were built on the fringes of the major urban areas to serve car-owning consumers. After the £111 million Meadowhall project in Sheffield, for which Dennis Bate was made the 1991 Building Manager of the Year, Bovis won similar projects in Manchester, Glasgow, Bristol, London, Oberhausen and even Barcelona. At one stage shopping malls comprised more than half the workload of Bovis Europe. In some senses Bovis was returning to its roots as a retail contractor. But the historical precedent can be overdone. There was a world of difference between building stores for Marks & Spencer and Safeway around Britain and an out-of-town shopping centre costing hundreds of millions of pounds. The latter had more in common with a major City office development like Broadgate than small-scale shop construction, and drew heavily on Bovis' expertise in managing the very largest building projects.

A second important theme of the late 1990s was the provision of private finance for infrastructure projects, both through the Private Finance Initiative in the United Kingdom and Build-Operate-and-Transfer schemes overseas. In Britain private finance was slow to lift off, but has now gathered momentum at home and abroad, and promises to be a major source of work for the Bovis group in the next millennium.

This was a period of rationalisation and downsizing for most British contractors, as the longest post-war recession had decimated balance sheets and profits. While smaller contractors went to the wall, all the bigger groups managed to stagger on, albeit with massive redundancies and support from their banks and shareholders. The obvious answer was a spate of takeovers and mergers to consolidate the sector. But this was difficult to achieve in practice. Pure contractors have few assets, other than their workforces, and it was difficult to accurately assess their liabilities, particularly after a deep recession. For those with property and housing divisions it was even

216

216 *Dennis Bate became the 1991 Building Manager of the Year for the Meadowhall shopping mall. He was made a CBE in 1999 for his services to the Government's New Deal work experience programme.*

217 *Manchester's new Trafford Centre. In the mid-1990s Bovis Europe was simultaneously managing construction of half a dozen major retail developments across Europe.*

21

harder to put a value on the company. Then there was a very real human problem. What happened to the management team made redundant by a takeover, merger or acquisition?

Some deals emerged. Trafalgar House was acquired by the Norwegian conglomerate Kvaerner, which had failed in its bid to buy Amec. Tarmac swapped its housing division for Wimpey's construction and aggregates operation. Bovis and Costain talked about a merger at one stage, but it was impossible to reach a deal after Costain's sale of its US coal business fell through. In March 1995 Sir Frank said: 'I would like to see more merging of companies. The saving from putting two large firms together is £6–9 million per annum. UK construction has become competitive beyond what is reasonable. And now we seem to be taking the same competitiveness to the Far East, where tendering is now costing firms £100,000 for each project. It is very silly.'

He was speaking shortly after an Aoki-led consortium, including Bovis as construction manager, was placed second in the competition to build the £800 million Hong Kong airport terminal. The Bovis bid for Foster Associates' magnificent 490,000 square metre terminal building was favoured on technical grounds, but was apparently lost on a board vote at the Provisional Airport Authority. One press report rather melodramatically commented that 'a Bovis man was in tears'. Whether the story is true or not, it certainly caught the enormous disappointment accurately enough.

Such setbacks did not deter the continuing globalisation of Bovis, and less than a month later a £12 million deal to acquire two Australian construction companies was announced – a Sydney-based cost consultant McLachlan, and a construction manager Total Project Control. Their combined workforce of 140 raised the Bovis Asia head-count to more than 250, and added contracts as far flung as Malaysia, Thailand and the Philippines. 'Bringing these companies into Bovis means we can now give a more effective and extensive service to a continent which offers real potential for the group,' said Sir Frank. He also pointed to their success in securing prestige contracts in Australia, most notably the multi-million pound Tangara commuter rail link into Sydney and consultancy work on the 2000 Sydney Olympics Stadium.

On the other side of the world, Bovis International secured £40 million of work in South Africa, including its first-ever management contract for a £25 million high-

218

218 *Cribbs Causeway in Bristol, one of the five enormous out-of-town shopping malls Bovis completed in the United Kingdom during the 1990s.*

219 *The Ultimo/Pyrmont Light Rail System started running in August 1997, the first road-rail system in Sydney since the trams stopped in 1962. It was a Build-Own-Operate-Transfer contract.*

219

220 *400 George Street, Sydney, a £65 million landmark office tower and retail complex completed in late 1998 for BT Funds Management.*

221 *The £40 million first phase of the refurbishment of Warringah Mall in Sydney for AMP Asset Management, handed over in August 1998.*

222

222 *Nestlé's headquarters outside Paris where a beautiful 123-year-old chocolate factory was transformed into executive offices. British construction techniques were adapted to the French model.*

rise development in Johannesburg for Old Mutual Properties. The group also formed a joint venture with Thebe Investments to provide construction management and training for the reconstruction and development programme to provide five million new homes by the year 2000. And Bovis won a £3.5 million management contract to refurbish Woolworth's flagship store in Cape Town, and a further £10 million contract for six more stores. It was a welcome contrast to Bovis' loss-making foray into South African contracting after the Second World War.

Across the Channel, Bovis International's work on the £83 million Nestlé headquarters outside Paris was profiled by *Building* magazine. Here Bovis was assisting an in-house team and using the French construction system, on a 14-hectare campus-style site to include 60,000 square metres of office accommodation in 11 buildings. The focal point of the scheme was a 123-year-old chocolate factory which was refurbished as executive offices. 'It's a very complicated job because of its nature, being two-thirds restoration', said Peter Gould, then director of Bovis International in France. 'However much planning you do, something is always likely to pop out of the

woodwork and surprise you. We have had to adapt the traditional Bovis service quite significantly to match the way that the French work. It is better to do that than to come and preach a new religion which, apart from being tactless, is ineffective.' A further important French project completion was the £30 million Lille International Airport. Here Bovis combined the responsibilities of project and construction manager on a 18,800 square metre building designed by Denis Sloan.

In order to pursue privately financed infrastructure projects more effectively, Bovis International promoted US lawyer Patricia Aluisi from company secretary to be head of its eight-strong Build-Operate-Transfer (BOT) unit in July 1995. Her brief was to seek contracts to design, build and finance infrastructure projects around the world. In fact Aluisi had already spent more than a year working on private finance, and was close to securing a major appointment. In September came the news that a joint venture between Bovis and Thames Water had been awarded a £70 million BOT concession in Shanghai for a water treatment plant. This was a far larger project than an earlier BOT water treatment scheme in Malaysia, and also marked a significant breakthrough for Bovis into one of the world's biggest future construction markets, China. 'It was a springboard for expansion into China' noted Fritz Rehkopf, head of Bovis Asia.

Two further major appointments followed in China in the closing years of the century, although the Asian crisis of 1997–8 later caused them to be put on hold. In May 1996 the group won the construction management contract for the £250 million Bund Centre in the Pudong financial district of Shanghai for the Sinar Mas Group. It features a 50-storey office tower, two 22-storey residential blocks and 14,000 square metres of residential space. Just a year later, and Bovis was appointed construction manager on what may one day succeed the Petronas Towers as the tallest building in the world, the 462 metre high Shanghai Daewoo Centre in the Xuhui district. Not for the first time Bovis was applying the experience of projects like Canary Wharf to a scheme on the other side of the planet. 'Multinational clients get the same level of service from us, anywhere on the globe', said Fritz Rehkopf. 'Bovis is the first global service provider, and that makes us unique.'

The future potential of the Chinese market is clear for everyone to see. In China

223 *Pat Aluisi headed the BOT unit and was the first woman on the Bovis board since 1975*

224 *The £30 million Lille International Airport. Bovis provided project and construction management services on this unusual design by Denis Sloan.*

225 *Bovis and Thames Water won a £70 million BOT concession in Shanghai for a water treatment plant, a significant breakthrough into the Chinese market.*

224

225

226 & 227 (overleaf) Bluewater near Dartford in Kent is the largest retail and leisure development in Europe. Bovis won the £350 million construction management project in October 1995. It opened in spring 1999 to great acclaim.

the gradual introduction of capitalism is proceeding far more effectively than Russia's sudden conversion, and the development of Shanghai from a low-rise slum into a Manhattan-style financial capital in the past few years is a stunning achievement. Now the challenge is to use Western expertise and capital to improve infrastructure to Western standards. And as Western multinationals expand in Shanghai and the Asian financial crisis lifts, Bovis will expand with them. 'When we arrived we spent a lot of time with ex-communist staff without much experience,' recalled Rehkopf. 'We have established a strategic relationship with the largest state contractor. But now many Chinese Americans have returned, and lots of people speak English and are well trained. They are very supportive of people who show a commitment to the development of their city.'

If 1995 represented a turning point for Bovis in the Far East, it was also the year when life began to improve for British construction. Bovis's UK staff rose by 400, and there was a recruitment drive in the UK. 'We wrote to those who were made redundant when the chips were down, and some have come back to us', said Sir Frank, who was able to report a 15 per cent rise in UK work-in-hand which now totalled 30 per cent of the £4 billion worldwide order book. Jobs in progress included the Vector 2000 Arena, originally conceived for Manchester's bid for the Olympics, and the £35 million refurbishment of Terminal One at London Heathrow Airport. Bovis also secured the £45 million second phase of the Waltham Forest Action Trust programme to rehouse 6500 council tenants and the £40 million redevelopment of Sadler's Wells Theatre, the first theatre to be reconstructed with funding from Britain's National Lottery.

But the biggest triumph came in late October 1995 when Bovis was appointed construction manager for the £350 million Bluewater shopping centre near Dartford in Kent. The client was an Australian developer, Lend Lease, which was beginning its expansion into Europe and had identified a 100 hectare former chalk quarry as the ideal location for its 150,000 square metre shopping mall, the largest retail and leisure development in Europe. Twenty Bovis staff under John Spanswick and five staff from Lend Lease Global formed the core construction team, in a fashion reminiscent of previous relationships with major clients. When asked by a journalist why Bovis was selected, a spokesman for Lend Lease said 'an ability to procure internationally, IT and accounting systems, attitudes to site welfare and a cultural fit with Lend Lease'. These were all the hallmarks of a classic Bovis–client relationship.

The Bluewater project also represented a further strengthening of the Bovis reputation for building mega retail projects. Over the next three years Bovis won more huge shopping mall contracts, and at one point was building no less than six of these retail palaces simultaneously. In May 1996 Bovis won the £250 million Braehead Park scheme in Glasgow for Capital Shopping Centres – a 109,000 square metre

227

shopping, leisure and maritime heritage complex. The £120 million Trafford shopping centre in Manchester followed, and in January 1997 Bovis became involved in preconstruction work on the £250 million White City shopping centre in West London for Chelsfield, with 64,000 square metres of retail space. Another massive retail scheme was built in an underground complex at Manezhnaya Square in Moscow adjacent to Red Square.

Even long-standing clients such as Safeway increased their construction programmes, and Bovis was awarded an £18 million package of projects, including new stores at High Wycombe and Thamesmead. As the 1997 General Election approached in the United Kingdom, a consumer boom was evident and developers and retailers were keen to cash in. So did Bovis. Profits for 1996 showed a 16.5 per cent rise to £14.8 million, mainly down to increased margins on retail work which accounted for half its order book in Europe.

The IRA bomb attack on Manchester city centre in April 1997 provided the final pre-millennial retail order. It devastated the Marks & Spencer store, happily without any loss of life, and Bovis was quickly engaged to build a 32,515 square metre replacement, the world's largest branch of Marks & Spencer, each of its five floors covering an area the size of the Old Trafford football pitch. This store was to be 25 per cent larger than the Marble Arch M&S flagship, and half the size of some of the massive shopping centres Bovis was building. To minimise lost revenue, Marks & Spencer wanted the £80 million project finished in two years. Naturally M&S turned to its contractor of sixty years' standing for its biggest-ever project and Les Chatfield mobilised the Bovis team for this prestigious appointment.

Aside from a spate of retail mega-projects, business began to pick up in other core markets. In the United States Bovis won the £110 million refurbishment of Grand Central Station in New York and a £190 million football stadium in Nashville. The sound of pile hammers also returned to Canary Wharf for the first time in five years, and Bovis won two large contracts: a £70 million hotel and leisure development for a joint venture between Hotel Properties of Singapore and Canary Wharf Ltd; and a £90 million headquarters building for Citibank. In the same months Bovis picked up the £52 million Kuwait Petroleum Corporation headquarters in Kuwait City in a joint venture with a local company, and minor projects in Budapest and Bratislava for the first time.

Yet the UK Government's private finance initiative was slow to produce work. Projects were complicated and expensive to put together and difficult to evaluate in tender competitions. It was very frustrating to spend a great deal of time arranging a PFI scheme, only to find it beaten by a competitor, or worse, overtaken by events. One example was Bovis's £200 million PFI redevelopment of the Treasury building in Whitehall, which was axed by the new Labour Government in July 1997, much to the chagrin of those involved in generating this innovative project. Fortunately this particular decision has now been reversed and Bovis is back on the job which has been revised.

But early 1997 was a good time for Bovis with new orders flowing from every quarter of its global empire. It was also the year that *Engineering News Record* ranked Bovis as the world's largest international contractor in the general building sector for the first time. Yet the odd lacuna still existed in this seamless web. In March Sir Frank returned from a ten-day trip to South America to announce his intention to create a £300–400 million a year business in the region. 'Brazil is undoubtedly a growth

228

228 *Long-standing client Safeway accelerated its building programme as the decade closed. Bovis won an £18 million bundle of contracts, including new stores at High Wycombe and Thamesmead.*

229

229 *Even traditional clients like Tesco wanted high-tech styling by the close of the millennium. This new store in Warwick Road, West London, is typical.*

230

230 *The Citibank building under construction at Canary Wharf. Bovis has now resumed work on this massive office development which entered receivership in the early nineties.*

231 *First client for the new Brazilian office was British Gypsum which has a global partnering agreement with Bovis.*

231

market', he said. 'The list of companies investing there is enormous.' Bovis immediately opened a São Paolo office, and began a search for possible acquisitions. Towards the end of the year a joint venture was formed with Servlease, a leading Brazilian property and services manager, and its first client was British Gypsum which has a global partnering agreement with Bovis. Other contracts soon followed for £90 million trade centres in Rio de Janeiro and the Amazon state capital of Manaus.

The development of multinational client relationships also took a lucrative turn. British Petroleum advertised in the *Official Journal of the European Commission* for a contractor to undertake a £1.3 billion, five-year construction programme across Europe. For Bovis this was the sort of long-term client relationship that was its bread-and-butter. A deal was struck to 'raze and rebuild' hundreds of service stations in 16 countries by 2001, and to cover the maintenance of 9500 stations.

Group board director Roger Mabey recalls that at first there was little enthusiasm or understanding as to why Bovis should become involved with the construction and maintenance of petrol filling stations. But he and group commercial director Tony Ring soon persuaded fellow directors to pursue a contract that made full use of Bovis' carefully nurtured network of construction operations around the world. The challenge from this extraordinary 'partnering' agreement is that Bovis' profits have to be generated by savings on current building costs. The original target was a 30 per cent saving over three years, and John McCloy was given the tough job of realising this objective. For contractors such long-term projects offer better margins, and provide a steady flow of work, to some extent avoiding the traditional building cycle. But partnership arrangements are nothing new for Bovis. Its special relationship with Marks & Spencer began in 1926 and will continue into the next century. The old Bovis business principle of 'identity of interest with the client' has served the company well, and will be the guiding light in winning new global clients in the same way that it originally brought the group to national prominence in Britain.

The global structure of Bovis was encapsulated in the three-way split of the managing director's role in spring 1997, with John Anderson, Luther Cochrane and Fritz Rehkopf becoming joint managing directors for Europe, the Americas and Asia Pacific. Sir Frank remained executive chairman and a main board director of P&O, and the question of who would succeed him was settled in September 1998 with the appointment of Luther Cochrane as chief executive. News of the changes reached staff through the pilot Intranet scheme, an inter-company computer network using the Internet. Sir Frank said: 'The Intranet can make people feel more part of an organisation and know what is going on. It will make a big difference to organisational cohesion and skills'. For a company with offices spread all over the world, the Intranet offers a valuable means of instant communication, and in the final years of the twentieth century Bovis has invested heavily in the World Wide Web.

The Intranet is excellent for email, disseminating best practice and the collection of bid data in standard format; and was christened *WingSPAN* in 1998. The group has also developed a self-development programme on CD-Rom to teach staff about the company and its operations. Allied to *WingSPAN*, Bovis has created a series of teams offering centres of expertise for different market sectors. Thus if the Bovis office in Shanghai is looking for advice on high-rise residential construction it can quickly find the right person via email anywhere in the world.

232 *Group commercial director Tony Ring played a key role in negotiating PFI contracts to construct and run new hospitals in Halifax and Worcester.*

232

233

233 *Global senior directors in 1997 (left to right): John Anderson (Europe), Luther Cochrane (Americas), Sir Frank Lampl (chairman) and Fritz Rehkopf (Asia Pacific).*

234

234 *Roger Mabey received the Companion of the Order of St Michael and St George in June 1997 for services to exports. It is the highest honour short of a knighthood.*

235 *British Foreign Secretary Robin Cook talks to Sir Frank Lampl at the opening of Bovis Polska's new Warsaw office in late 1997. Bovis Polska is building Central Europe's tallest building in Warsaw for Daewoo.*

236 *Another project in Moscow, the upgrading of an existing office building in Belinskaya Street. Prior to the Russian financial collapse in 1998, the Bovis order book was growing rapidly in Russia.*

237 *(Overleaf) Mayor of Moscow Yuri Luzhkov called in Bovis to complete a £200 million underground shopping centre near Red Square. British Prime Minister Tony Blair later came to view the development.*

In June 1997 Bovis board director Roger Mabey was made a Companion of the Order of St Michael and St George for his services to exports, the highest honour short of a knighthood. Indeed, orders continued to flow from overseas, particularly the Far East. Bovis Asia Pacific signed a joint venture for construction of the Bonifacio Global City on the site of a former US military base in Manila. Bovis also clinched the project management of the world's first 'moveable turf' sports stadium, the £180 million Sapporo Dome in Japan for the 2002 World Cup. Schal Bovis general manager John Dickison commented: 'It's our first success in a Japanese design-build competition, and we shall be the first non-Japanese firm to complete a public works project in Hokkaido.'

At the end of 1997 Bovis received two VIP guests. British Foreign Secretary Robin Cook formally opened Bovis Polska's new offices in Warsaw, while Prime Minister Tony Blair paid a visit to the giant £200 million underground shopping complex Bovis had completed on four levels near to Red Square in Moscow. However, the devaluation of the Thai Baht in August 1997 triggered what quickly became known as the Asian financial crisis, a series of currency devaluations and stockmarket crashes across the Far East. Clearly Bovis Asia Pacific was exposed to this economic storm, which also plunged Korea, Hong Kong, the Philippines and Indonesia into recession, and sent Japan into further decline. China, Taiwan and Singapore avoided the worst of the crisis, but saw growth rates clipped.

Bovis Asia Pacific was to some extent insulated by its reliance on very large contracts in Japan. But some important projects were shelved, such as the Shanghai Daewoo Centre and Bund Centre in Shanghai. The sudden recession and the acute problems faced by clients in certain countries, could hardly be good for business. On the other hand, the general policy was to stick with these troubled markets and gain credit for tenacity, rather than beat a hasty retreat. 'We will not pull out of the Far East. That would be a very unsound thing to do', Sir Frank told the press in March 1998.

235

236

238

238 *Siam Discovery Centre, Bangkok. The Asian financial crisis, which began in Thailand in August 1997, put similar orders on hold.*

239

240

239 *Fubon Banking Centre, Taipei. Taiwan proved more resilient than most Asian economies to the financial problems which dogged the region in the late 1990s.*

240 *Hansol Corporation headquarters in South Korea. The Asian financial crisis has depressed this market but, by the end of the decade, the Korean economy was already picking up.*

'We have project management work in Japan worth £80 million out of joint ventures worth £536 million, and can repatriate some staff from the Far East to cope with skill shortages elsewhere.'

He was speaking after releasing financial results showing a ten per cent rise in operating profits to £16.3 million in 1997 – and £6.3 million in interest income should be added to this figure for a true comparison with other construction companies, a total of £22.6 million. And in a cost-cutting exercise in the UK, Bovis and Tarmac agreed to merge their plant hire operations. Wyseplant and Castle Plant Services were combined into Maxxiom, with joint assets of £56 million, 30 depots and 800 staff.

Construction costs were also falling. In 1998 Bovis completed the 217,000 square foot Garrard House office development for Stanhope, and delivered the cheapest building with an atrium in the Square Mile at £96 per square foot. That figure compared with £95 per square foot achieved on Broadgate a decade earlier. Allowing for inflation this represented an impressive improvement in productivity, and showed that Bovis continued to offer clients better value for money. But the autumn of 1998 was dominated by takeover rumours, and in November Sir Frank confirmed that Bovis was in talks with W. S. Atkins, the stockmarket-quoted building services group. It was a logical marriage to create a giant global construction and facilities management group, offering international clients an even more comprehensive service. But the two parties were unable to agree a new structure for the group, and Bovis pulled out of negotiations. Thirty seconds after the breakdown of talks had been confirmed, an Intranet message to staff worldwide ensured that everybody heard the news at the same time.

Speaking to *Building* magazine, after the negotations were over, Lord Sterling commented: 'For five years Sir Frank and his colleagues have felt that if they could widen the services that could be rendered by Bovis, it would help Bovis in the next century. The most important thing about Bovis is its clients. Expanding the service for them is important, too. W. S. Atkins had a lot of experience in these areas. Now you can acquire that experience by buying people, bolt-ons or through a major deal. In this case, Bovis was looking at a major deal.' Lord Sterling stressed that the price of Bovis 'was not a problem' and added: 'As far as we were concerned it was to be a merger from day one, with the top management being integrated fully. In that sense, it proved to be too early for there to be a complete get-together.' Indeed, P&O's concern about the fate of Bovis staff in a merged entity was the principal stumbling block to the Atkins merger.

Clients now had the millennium in sight and 1998 was another exceptionally good year for orders. Bovis beat all the other British contractors in winning new work in 1998, and came top of the *Contract Journal*'s annual league table. It was the third year in a row that UK orders had topped £1 billion, and a long way from the gloom and doom of the early years of the decade. 'Clients are working towards the concepts that Sir Michael Latham pointed to four years ago,' John Anderson told *Contract Journal*, 'Fewer clients award work on the basis of the lowest margin; instead they choose the people they wish to work with in a more convivial, less-adversarial way than in the past. This is benefiting the industry as a whole.'

In 1998 the group was also relieved to secure its long-awaited first project under the British Government's Private Finance Initiative, as part of a consortium to build, maintain and service Halifax's new £76 million Calderdale Hospital. Bovis Europe was chosen as project manager for the £50 million reconstruction and extension of the Prague Congress Centre, clinched the £107 million Toyota factory in northern France and started work on a £220 million cigarette factory in St Petersburg for Philip Morris.

The changing balance of work in the UK is shown by *Contract Journal*'s list of the top ten Bovis contract awards in 1998. There are five London office projects listed, ranging from £25 million to £90 million, two £55 million retail schemes, the Calderdale Hospital, a £30 million local authority project, and the biggest award is the £101 million upgrade of Leeds station. In total, Bovis was awarded UK projects worth £1.2 billion which will keep the group gainfully occupied well into the twenty-first century.

As the last year of the millennium dawned press speculation about a recession left Sir Frank looking blank. 'There is no recession', he said. 'We have a record order book, and the commercial market is strong. There is practically no speculative construction. All the schemes are either pre-let or pre-sold. It is totally unlike the late 1980s. I am very confident about this market for us. We have not made a pre-tax loss in twenty-five years, and have no intention of starting now.' Indeed, 1999 began well. Bovis won a tough competition to become construction manager on the prestigious £50 million Scottish Parliament building in Edinburgh, another triumph for Bovis Scotland which had just completed the extremely complex £32 million new Museum of Scotland. And on the other side of the Atlantic, Bovis was appointed to head a construction management team on a £400 million airport expansion programme at Oakland International Airport in California.

In February 1999 the sixty-ninth Anniversary Dinner of the Guvnors' Club took place in the Royal Lancaster Hotel in London. It was remarkable how many of the

241

241 *Garrard House in the City of London. This 217,000 sq ft office project for Stanhope cost £96 per sq ft compared with £95 per sq ft achieved on the Broadgate development ten years earlier.*

242

242 *The National Maritime Museum in Greenwich, London, has been extended ready for an influx of guests for the millennium.*

243

243 *The £32 million Museum of Scotland was an extremely complex building set in the heart of historic Edinburgh. Bovis will also be constructing the new seat for the Scottish Parliament.*

old traditions had survived from 1929. Beer was served in tin tea cans, once a familiar utensil on building sites, by waiters dressed as tea boys in flat caps. The silver concrete mixer presented at the first Guvnors' Club Dinner still graced the top table and the tradition of a 'physical' menu survived. For 1999, tool manufacturer Stanley sponsored a retractable tape measure attached to a belt on which the menu was printed. The main course was the usual massive steak and kidney pie, paraded into the room by the chefs. Legend has it that the club abandoned the Grosvenor House after the chef provided individual steak and kidney pies.

On the top table sat club president Sir Frank Lampl and chief executive Luther Cochrane. Sir Frank had been up early that day to attend the opening of the new £80 million Marks & Spencer store in Manchester by the Deputy Prime Minister John Prescott, and had dashed back for the Guvnors' Club. Vice-president Philip Warner of Bovis Homes and former managing director and war hero John Gillham MC, were also on the top table with club chairman Dennis Bate. The principal guest was Felicity Goodey of the BBC, who is a Bovis client as chair of the Lowry Centre, an art gallery and theatre complex now under construction in Salford. She was the first ever woman to address the Guvnors' Club in its 69-year history.

However, Felicity Goodey was still presented with the traditional club cartoon by Sir Frank as a souvenir of her visit, and received a rapturous reception from the audience of 800 guvnors, life-guvnors and guests. The after-dinner speaker was also a departure from tradition. Instead of hiring a famous comedian, club chairman Dennis Bate had secured an unknown general practitioner from Wigan, Dr Kevin Jones. He proved far more successful than some of the professionals to address the Guvnors' Club in recent years whose blue humour is no longer *de rigueur*.

Yet the last Guvnors' Club Dinner of the century did not just look to a glorious past and relive former Bovis triumphs. Responding to a warm welcome, newly appointed chief executive Luther Cochrane promised to create 'something similar' to the Guvnors' Club in the US. It was a reminder that Bovis is now a global company with a worldwide presence, although its roots as a fee-based British builder are as strong as ever, and Bovis still retains the paternalistic spirit of its founders.

244 *Deputy Prime Minister John Prescott visits the Lowry Centre site with Sir Frank Lampl and Carillion chief executive Sir Neville Simms, all donning Bovis hard hats and fluorescent jackets.*

245 *The Lowry Centre, an art gallery and theatre complex under construction in the north of England as the twentieth century came to a close.*

244

245

CHAPTER 14

The Future

The last year of the century has proved to be one of the most dramatic and exciting in the history of the company. The aborted merger talks with W. S. Atkins were a clear indicator that Bovis's parent of 25 years, P&O, was ultimately intending to divest itself of its construction business. In a move designed to counter this uncertainty, Bovis proposed the idea of a public flotation to the P&O board. In March 1999, announcing a year of record profits for Bovis, P&O confirmed that course of action. Its chairman, Lord Sterling, declared his intention to float Bovis in the course of the next 12 months. In reality the plan was to accelerate the process to six months, with a flotation in the autumn. As an intensive due diligence exercise got underway in readiness for Bovis' return to public ownership, careful consideration was given to the merits of seeking a listing in London, in New York or possibly both markets.

But, as the Bovis-led campaign to woo analysts and fund managers gathered pace, so too did interest from another quarter. Lend Lease Corporation, the entrepreneurial Australian developer of Bluewater, had established a strong rapport with Bovis during the course of the complex three-year project. The culture and values of the two businesses had proved to be remarkably similar, helping Bovis to win other major retail projects for Lend Lease in Dundee, Solihull, Madrid and Warsaw.

The international network that Bovis had built up over the past decade was another major attraction for Lend Lease, which had global ambitions for its own project management business, already well established in Australia and Asia and now looking to Europe and the USA as new markets.

As P&O's financial advisers, Merrill Lynch, were finalising the Bovis prospectus, Lend Lease launched a bold and decisive bid for the business, an unexpected move that caught the City and the media completely off-guard. The first they or the public knew of this latest twist in the Bovis tale was an early morning announcement from P&O on Monday 4 October, 1999 following a weekend of intense and secret negotiations. The announcement confirmed that P&O had accepted an offer from Lend Lease of £285 million for Bovis. 'As a trade buyer, the clear synergies with Lend Lease's existing business meant they were able to offer a good price,' Lord Sterling told the press. 'It also provides an excellent opportunity for Bovis to strengthen its position as a global project management company.'

Sir Frank was emphatic in his endorsement for the deal. 'Although flotation would have offered Bovis an exciting future, I have no doubt that becoming part of Lend

246 Sir Frank Lampl and Luther Cochrane lead Bovis Lend Lease into the next millennium, confident in the knowledge that the combined company now has the capacity to build any project anywhere in the world for any client.

247

247 *Dr Rolf Stromberg, former chief executive of BP Oil and Sir Frank Lampl sign the Bovis-BP Alliance. This long-term, non-adversarial, contractural relationship is the modern equivalent of the special relationship established with Marks & Spencer in the 1920s.*

248

248 *A BP service station in Moscow. Bovis shares in the cost savings on the construction of BP petrol stations around the world.*

Lease will be better for us. Bovis' skills complement those of Lend Lease while their strong balance sheet and leading position as a global property company will provide a firm foundation for our future growth.'

Later, talking to construction journalists, Sir Frank spoke candidly of his concerns for the future of Bovis as a public company. 'Had we floated, our market capitalisation would have been quite modest, making us easy prey for any rival wanting to buy into the business. Next they would demand a seat on the board and that begins to threaten the character and culture of the company. It is those values, together with our global reach and quality of clients, that makes us so appealing to Lend Lease. They regard us as a core business, enabling them to offer a fully integrated service to clients all over the world.'

In Australia, news of the acquisition added 70 cents to the Lend Lease share price, with analysts quick to acknowledge the merits of the purchase and the long-term benefits to the group's income stream.

David Higgins, Lend Lease Corporation chief executive, commented: 'We have a clear strategy to aggressively grow our existing business and balance our investment management skills with the entrepreneurial and technical skills of development and project management. Acquiring a successful multi-country, multi-industry project management, design and construction operation such as Bovis will significantly accelerate our growth and extend our capabilities globally, into new market sectors. We have a high regard for Bovis' senior management, who are world class and many of whom will occupy senior positions within Lend Lease's real estate business, and for its employees. With Lend Lease's expertise in risk management, together with the synergies Bovis brings in terms of skills, geography, technology and people, we shall be able to offer a more integrated service, both to Bovis and Lend Lease clients.'

It was not just the Australian stockmarket that responded positively to the news. Within Bovis, initial surprise at the turn of events quickly turned to enthusiasm for the new parent. Lend Lease's reputation with Bovis and with the British construction industry had been fostered by its forward-looking attitude at Bluewater, earning it an important accolade as *Contract Journal*'s Client of the Year for 1999. The actual award to Lend Lease was presented just three days after the announcement of the sale.

For Bovis, the merger with Lend Lease Projects significantly strengthens its operations in Australia and Asia, bringing the combined staffing in the region up to 2000 and putting it on a par with Europe and the Americas. Lend Lease Projects brings with it a long and successful track record in the region, borne out of the group's earliest days in Australia.

The origins of Lend Lease date back to the 1950s, when the Dutch construction company Bredero established a new subsidiary in Australia named Civil & Civic, a name derived from its two key areas of activity, civil engineering and urban development. Like Bovis, Civil & Civic had its own distinctive approach to managing projects. Founder Gerald Dusseldorp regarded traditional contracting methods as outmoded and unproductive. In Australia he sought to recruit like-minded staff and to deliver projects based on collective endeavour rather than individual achievement. In 1958 Civil & Civic established a finance and investment company, Lend Lease Corporation, to help fund its own development activities. Both businesses prospered and Lend Lease continued to diversify, setting in place the foundations for the present enterprise, which ranks among Australia's top twenty listed companies.

Today the group comprises two key areas of business, financial services and real estate development, which embraces the newly created Bovis Lend Lease, with a staff of 7000 and a presence in almost forty countries. Bovis chief executive Luther Cochrane retains that role, heading the new company, with Sir Frank as its chairman.

One emotive issue that has had to be swiftly reconciled is the branding of the combined business. Earlier in 1999 Civil & Civic had been rebranded Lend Lease Projects and within months it was facing another potential change of identity. 'Both companies had visually strong but graphically different identities, and marrying the two was not a practical option so we sought a mutually agreeable solution,' explained Sir Frank. 'Lend Lease acknowledged the commercial value of the Bovis name around the world and we recognised the benefits of being under the Lend Lease canopy, which does, quite literally, cover the whole project lifecycle.'

Lend Lease also acknowledged the importance and quality of the many brand name businesses with which Bovis works. A latter-day equivalent of its special relationship with Marks & Spencer in the 1920s and Safeway in the 1970s, is the Bovis

249 *Women construction managers are likely to become a more common sight in the next century as recent Bovis trainees move up the company hierarchy.*

249

250

250 *David Higgins, chief executive of Lend Lease Corporation.*

BP Alliance. Established in 1997 to cover sixteen European countries, it has now spread to Japan, Venezuela and, most recently, the USA.

The long term contractual relationship, based, as ever, on a non-adversarial attitude and a genuine commitment to its clients' goals, has reached new heights with BP, where profits are derived exclusively from the savings achieved. Now running at nearly 30 per cent on 1997 out-turn costs, those savings enable BP to further expand its retail network and that in turn generates more work for the alliance team.

The challenge for the twenty-first century will be to win many more multinational clients like BP, and to create alliance-style contracts that will deliver profits unlike anything seen in the construction industry in recent times. 'There are at least 150 accounts like the BP deal we could win,' says Luther Cochrane. 'They range from banks with multiple branches to almost any kind of commercial building.'

Of course, other companies will copy Bovis, just as they copied management contracting and construction management. Yet global alliance relationships demand very special skills, and a capacity to deliver such skills locally, which few companies possess. If profits are linked to cost cutting, there is no scope for overcharging the client, or putting in claims for extra payment. That is not to say that alliance contracts will necessarily replace lump-sum and fee-based contracting in the twenty-first century; there will always be clients for these services. But look at the way the world is moving. A low inflation regime controlled by central bankers means that cost reduction is critical to achieving greater corporate profitability. And companies are increasingly operating on a global scale, developing world brands. They need construction professionals who can offer the same service in Shanghai or Buenos Aires. The business world is becoming a smaller and smaller place, dominated by bigger and bigger multinational corporations. Construction companies have to adapt their services to meet these new conditions, and Bovis has already done just that.

For the last two decades of the twentieth century the construction industry in general has been bedevilled by low profit margins. Not since the oil-boom years of the 1970s have margins been good. By contrast almost every other major industry has enjoyed sustained profit growth. Could it be that the new century will see the profitability of the construction industry catch them up?

While the millennium might be followed by a short downturn in activity, the omens are favourable. Certainly if global growth rates increase significantly, and ex-communist economies are turned around, the outlook should be encouraging in terms of demand for construction services. Asian countries such as Korea and the Philippines are already showing signs of recovering from their recent financial crises. Granted the finite nature of construction expertise available in the world, demand alone could be enough to boost profitability. Over-capacity could swiftly move to under supply, and the sort of expertise offered by Bovis Lend Lease would be in particularly short supply.

'This is a demand-driven rather than speculative economic climate, funded by equity rather than debt,' says Luther Cochrane. 'Equity used to be 10–11 per cent of funding. Now it is 20 per cent. This is a far sounder situation for economic fundamentals, and in the US and UK the former oversupply of property has been eaten up. There is tremendous scope for growth, particularly in the European Union as it becomes one economic entity. South America could also take off dramatically.'

Capitalism works its own magic. World savings will chase higher returns, and these will be found in the emerging markets. Provided these countries can establish stable political and financial systems to handle such investment, and they have an enormous incentive to do so, then Asia, Latin America, Russia and Central Europe will boom. Growth in emerging markets will always be patchy and prone to boom-slump business cycles. Nonetheless, the greater openness to foreign capital that has followed the recent financial crisis should promote the creation of more stable financial institutions, with more banks under Western ownership.

For a company with acknowledged leadership in its industry and the ability to form long-term, cost-driven contracts with multinationals to deliver construction services anywhere in the world, the future could be very profitable indeed. For multinationals to grow around the world they need a construction management company that can deliver on time, to budget and to the same standard, wherever they operate. That is where the modern Bovis Lend Lease is heading and where Sir Frank has positioned the company.

He is confident of achieving further globalisation and broadening the company's range of specialist skills in niche markets such as pharmaceuticals and semi-conductors. Mastering the opportunities of e-commerce will add further scope for future growth. 'But the bigger the business, the greater the danger of complacency. If we are to match our future targets, we must constantly challenge everything we do and, in this respect, continuous improvement of techniques will be a powerful tool. Most importantly, we have to foster a true spirit of openness, working together with our clients and our colleagues, learning from each other and developing a mutual trust.'

In the middle of 1999 Bovis had worldwide projects with a construction value of £13.6 billion under its management, the largest order book in the history of Bovis. However, if world economic growth continues on an upward path and Bovis gains a greater market share of the construction services required by multinational companies around the globe, this figure is set to grow over the coming decades.

'I am delighted that Luther Cochrane is now taking the reins,' said Sir Frank in the summer of 1999. 'Over the past ten years I have worked closely with him in many situations, and have witnessed the clarity of vision and integrity which are his particular qualities. He combines a great understanding of the technical and commercial aspects of our business with a caring attitude towards staff and clients alike. Within Bovis there is a tremendous will for the business to succeed, and I know that Luther will get the support he needs to continue our success far into the next century.'

Reflecting on the creation of Bovis Lend Lease, Sir Frank is unequivocal, both on the reason for the merger and the merits of it. 'It's the calibre and quality of our staff and management which made Bovis a sought after business. It is they who helped make Bovis a brand leader and Lend Lease was quick to recognise that fact. So too was our former parent P&O, and, in appreciation of their efforts, P&O rewarded Bovis staff with a loyalty bonus. As Bovis Lend Lease, we are able to build on the values we have always held dear. We can now offer a complete spectrum of project services and will be looking to further expand our presence, both globally and in new markets such as build-operate-transfer, private finance initiative and other turnkey types of contract. Our ultimate goal is to be the first choice for our clients and for staff as well.'

Charles William Bovis would doubtless be proud of his successors' achievements. But the company's founder would certainly be staggered by the scale of their success. There is a great legacy from the first 115 years of the company, and now, as Bovis Lend Lease, an even greater opportunity in the next century.

251

251 *A new logo for a new millennium; how Bovis Lend Lease will be branded across the globe.*

APPENDIX

Index

Acknowledgements

Particular thanks are due to former Bovis Construction commercial director Bernard Hodgson for his extensive and illuminating research into the early history of the company. Commissioned by Bovis, this work also included interviews with former directors and valuable advice and assistance on the photographic content of this book.

The author is also indebted to Andrew Bond, Gerry Gillespie and Helen Lodge at Bovis Corporate Communications in London, and to freelance architectural photographer Tony Weller. In New York, Mary Costello and Jennie Morgan from Corporate Communications were most helpful, as were Michael Dover and Marilyn Inglis from Cassell & Co.

Many Bovis executives, past and present, were interviewed in the nine months spent on this project. I am particularly grateful to Philip Warner for his substantial contribution to the chapter on Bovis Homes, and for useful anecdotes and comments from: Luther Cochrane,

John Gillham, Malcolm Paris, Chris Spackman, John Anderson, Roger Mabey, Barry Holmes, Jim Kane, Richard Dawborn, Dennis Bate, Henry Liszka, Jan Koci, Sergio Casari, Jacques Demol, Ken France, Eduardo Sposito, Lou Reid, Brian Adams, Masanobu Oka, Malcolm Harris, Ken Parsons, John Grant, Fritz Rehkopf, Peter Lehrer, Charlie Bacon, Ron Deffenbaugh, Jim D'Agostino, Pete Marchetto and Colin Parkes.

I would also pay tribute to my ex-colleagues at *Building Magazine*, whose Bovis chronicles were invaluable: Graham Rimmer, Peter Bill, Penny Guest, Graham Ridout, Alastair Stewart, Denise Chevin, Adrian Barrick, Giles Barrie and Martin Spring. Finally, my thanks go to Bovis executive chairman Sir Frank Lampl for his unfailing enthusiasm and encouragement, and for inviting me to write this book.

PETER COOPER
LONDON, 1999

Picture credits

CHAPTER 1
All photographs and artworks from Bovis archives except page 14 by Anthony Weller.
CHAPTER 2
All black and white photographs from RCHM. All colour photographs by Anthony Weller.
CHAPTER 3
All colour photographs by Anthony Weller. All black and white photographs and artworks from Bovis archives except page 37 which belongs to Shropshire Records and Research.
CHAPTER 4
All colour photographs by Anthony Weller. All black and white photographs and artworks from Bovis archives.
CHAPTER 5
All colour photographs by Anthony Weller. All black and white photographs and artworks from Bovis archives except photographs pages 64, 65, 66, 67, 69, 70, 71, 72, 76, 77 which

belong to the Imperial War Museum.
CHAPTER 6
All colour and black and white photographs and artworks from Bovis archives except photographs on pages 92 and 93 by Anthony Weller.
CHAPTER 7
All colour and black and white photographs and artworks from Bovis archives except photographs on pages 96, 100, 103, 105 and 92 by Anthony Weller.
CHAPTER 8
All colour and black and white photographs and artworks from Bovis archive.s
CHAPTER 9
All colour and black and white photographs and artworks from Bovis archives except photograph on page 132 by Anthony Weller.
CHAPTER 10
All colour and black and white photographs and artworks from

Bovis archives except photographs on pages 147, 149 by Morley von Sternberg;165 by David Williams; page 155 (Lord Joseph photo) by John Farren; page 156 by Anthony Weller; page 157, 158 by *Building* magazine; page 148 by Grant Smith.
CHAPTER 11
All colour and black and white photographs and artworks from Bovis archives except photographs on pages 178–9 by Tommy Hindley; page 174 (West Wacker Drive) by Peter Fish; page 177 (Lincoln Square) by Nava Benjamini.
CHAPTER 12
All photographs and artworks from Bovis archives except pages 191(*Western Morning News*), 194 by Anthony Weller; 207 (Pilkington Glass) by Morley von Sternberg; 206 by John Edward Linden; 209 (Savoy) by Matthew Weunreb; page 207 (Mandela) by Jimmy

Limberis; page 201by Lawrence Hill; page 209 (the Queen) by Press Association; page 204 by Martin Charles.
CHAPTER 13
All photographs and artworks from Bovis archives except pages 218, 215, 227 (Garrard House) by Anthony Weller; page 227 (National Maritime Museum) Morley von Sternberg; page 219 by Ian Kerr; 229 by Paul Tyagi.
CHAPTER 14
All photographs and artworks from Bovis archives except page 232 (BP service station) by BP. Endpapers and preliminary pages
All photographs from Bovis archives.

Every effort has been made to contact all copyright holders. The Publishers will be pleased to hear from any copyright holders not here acknowledged.

Metreon San Francisco

Gallery of Modern Art Prague

Bluewater Dartford

BP Hanger Lane Ealing

Grand Central Terminal New York

National Theatre Tokyo

Heathrow Terminal 1 London

Canary Wharf London

Nottingham Trent University Nottingham

Nestle Headquarters Paris

Olympic Stadium Atlanta

Garrard House London